Britain was totally unprepared for war with France in 1793 and relied on German auxiliaries to supplement her own meagre resources to pursue her strategy in the Low Countries and beyond. The contingents were drawn from the smaller German states, whose armies still followed the rigid linear tactics of Frederick the Great. They therefore had to adapt to deal with the new threat posed by the mass French armies, with a greater emphasis on light troops and more flexible tactics.

Although the German troops formed a major part of the Allied army in the Low Countries, there has been no detailed English-language account of their role. Their story is told here for the first time, based on extensive research in British and German archives, together with contemporary accounts and 19th century German sources.

Previously unpublished information is given on the process of negotiating the treaties with the German princes, the organisation of the troops taken into British pay, and their experience on campaign, focussing on the key events for the various contingents. Their varied and colourful uniforms are also described and illustrated from contemporary sources.

The German auxiliaries fought bravely, often against overwhelming odds, and the failure of the campaigns owes more to disunity among the allies and the muddled and unrealistic policies of the British government than to any shortcomings of the troops on the ground.

Paul Demet was born and brought up in Manchester and now lives in Northamptonshire with his wife, chickens, and cats. He is a retired company director with a life-long interest in military history, particularly the French Revolutionary and Napoleonic Wars and the armies of the small German states. For many years he has spent as much time as possible visiting archives, museums, and historic sites in Britain and on the Continent and is an enthusiastic collector of old books and prints. He is a long-standing member of numerous British, French, and German historical societies. Although this is his first book, he is a regular contributor to Napoleonic era discussion forums.

'We Are Accustomed to do Our Duty'

German Auxiliaries with the British Army 1793-95

Paul Demet

Helion & Company

Helion & Company Limited
Unit 8 Amherst Business Centre
Budbrooke Road
Warwick
CV34 5WE
England
Tel. 0121 705 3393
Fax 0121 711 4075
Email: info@helion.co.uk
Website: www.helion.co.uk
Twitter: @helionbooks
Visit our blog at http://blog.helion.co.uk/

Published by Helion & Company 2018
Designed and typeset by Mach 3 Solutions Ltd (www.mach3solutions.co.uk)
Cover designed by Paul Hewitt, Battlefield Design (www.battlefield-design.co.uk)
Printed by Short Run Press, Exeter, Devon

Text © Paul Demet 2018
Illustrations © as given in the Notes on the Colour Plates
Maps © Paul and Jane Demet 2018
Cover: Hochfürstlich Hessisches Jägercorps: (Brabant 1793), coloured lithograph by and after
Oeynhausen. (Anne S.K. Brown Military Collection, Brown University Library)

ISBN 978-1-912174-96-6

British Library Cataloguing-in-Publication Data.
A catalogue record for this book is available from the British Library.

For details of other military history titles published by Helion & Company Limited, contact the
above address, or visit our website: http://www.helion.co.uk

We always welcome receiving book proposals from prospective authors.

Contents

List of Plates

List of Maps

Preface

If they are remembered at all, the campaigns in the Low Countries are mainly regarded as a miserable backdrop to the later successes in the Peninsula and Waterloo. This attitude is summed up by the Duke of Wellington, when asked many years later about his first experience of war during those campaigns, 'Why – I learnt what one ought not to do, and that is always something'.[1] There were certainly lessons that had to be learned the hard way as the allies had to find a way to defeat the new mass armies of the Republic, against which the established ways of waging war were to prove inadequate. For too long, reliance continued to be placed on cautious advances, taking each fortress before moving forward, dispersal of forces in the cordon system, and rigid linear tactics. The failure of the allied efforts in the War of the First Coalition also demonstrated the difficulty of creating an effective coalition from the competing powers in the face of a determined and energetic enemy. Another lesson which the British government should have learned was the futility of pursuing too many objectives at once with insufficient resources.

The last comprehensive English language accounts of the campaigns were in Volume IV of Fortescue's *History of the British Army*, first published in 1906, and Burne's *The Noble Duke of York* from 1949, which attempted to restore the Duke's reputation after Fortescue's harsh criticism. Since then, aspects of the campaigns have been covered in biographies of British generals and monographs on specific actions or the development of the British Army. The role of the German auxiliaries, who provided the bulk of the troops in British pay until the summer of 1794, has been largely ignored. There is certainly no shortage of information to draw upon, with extensive correspondence files and reports in the British and German archives, and the works of German and French military historians of the 19th and early 20th Centuries.

Although British contemporaries were often dismissive of the fighting abilities of the German troops and criticised their fondness for looting, their record of service includes cases of great courage and steadfastness in the face of the mass armies mobilised by the French Republic. It also includes examples of the unnecessary suffering and losses caused by the actions or neglect of their British masters. This book does not set out to give a detailed account of the campaigns, but to explain how the contingents were engaged and organised and to describe important events during their service, linked by a brief connecting narrative to provide context. The title, *We Are Accustomed to do Our Duty,* is part of Hanoverian *General-Major* von Hammerstein's response when summoned to surrender at Menin, and sums up their spirit and determination.

---

1   P.H. 5th Earl of Stanhope, *Notes of Conversations with the Duke of Wellington 1831-1851* (New York: Longmans, Green, and Co., 1888), p. 182.

Acknowledgements

This books draws heavily on the records preserved in British and German archives, and I would like to thank the staff of the various institutions listed at the start of the Bibliography for their courtesy and assistance. I would also like to thank those institutions which gave permission to reproduce images.

I have also received considerable support and encouragement from friends and correspondents too numerous to mention, who have been generous in sharing information on 18th century uniforms and the campaigns in the Low Countries. I would like to record my gratitude to Michael Wenzel, who provided invaluable help in deciphering 18th century German handwriting.

I could not have kept up the effort to research and produce this book without the constant support of my wife Jane, who also prepared the drawings of uniform coats and the maps, and of my children, John and Sarah, who encouraged me to complete it and made helpful suggestions on how to improve the text.

Finally, my thanks go to Andrew Bamford, the series editor, whose, patience, guidance and support made it possible for me to complete my first book.

Note on Form

The spelling of place names in contemporary sources varies considerably, particularly for those located in what are now the Netherlands and Belgium where there is often a French and a Dutch or Flemish version, as in Bois-le-Duc or 's-Hertogenbosch. I have picked one version, generally that most commonly used by the British at that time, and tried to apply it consistently. Where there is an alternative, I have put it in parenthesis the first time the name appears. As for the names of the German states which provided the contingents, I have used the English name and in the case of Hesse Cassel I have stuck with the 'C' in Cassel rather than the later 'K', as this was the form in use throughout the Landgraviate's existence.

The spelling of personal names also varies considerably and I have generally followed the form used in the relevant *Staats-Kalender*. The prefix 'von' is used the first time an individual is introduced and thereafter generally omitted. As it was common for several members of the same family to be serving in these contingents, I have identified individuals by their forenames or initials to avoid confusion in such cases.

I have used the English form for titles, such as Landgrave rather than the German *Landgraf*, although personal names have been left in German, such as Wilhelm rather than William. Titles of regiments, such as Leibgarde, Erb-Prinz, and Landgraf, have been left in their German form, although terms such as dragoons, light infantry, and artillery have been translated into English, with the exception of 'Jägers' to describe light companies. The English for military units, such as battalions and companies, has been used throughout. Contemporary sources show variations in the spelling of German military ranks and French forms are sometimes used, particularly in the *Tableaux* attached to the treaties. Ranks have been translated into English as set out in Table 1, except for a few cases where there is no appropriate translation or when referring to a named individual, for example *Oberst* von Wurmb.

The hierarchy of ranks of Austrian general officers was quite different. At the top was *Feldmarschall* (army commander), then *Feldzeugmeister* and *General der Cavallerie* (wing commander), then *Feldmarschall-Lieutenant* (division commander), and finally *General-Major* or *General-Feldwachtmeister* (brigade commander).

I have retained the German names for some weapons, as follows:

Degen: A light sword with a narrow straight blade, as used by infantry officers, generals, etc.
Hirschfänger: Literally 'deer catcher', a long knife or short sword used in hunting, typically carried by Jägers
Kurzgewehr: A type of pole arm used by infantry NCOs, while officers carried a spontoon or half pike

Pallasch: A sword with a wide straight blade used by heavy cavalry

Translations from the original French and German have been made by me and any inconsistences and errors are solely my responsibility.

Table 1: English Equivalents of German Military Ranks

English	German	Comments
Generals		
Field Marshal	*Generalfeldmarschall* or *Feldmarschall*	
General	*General der Cavallerie* or *Infanterie*	
Lieutenant General	*General-Lieutenant*	
Major General	*General-Major*	
Officers of the Staff		
Adjutant General	*General-Adjudant*	
Quartermaster General	*General-Quartiermeister*	
Quartermaster	*Quartiermeisterlieutenant*	Quartermaster to a contingent
Flügel-Adjudant	*Flügel-Adjudant*	Senior ADC to the ruler or commanding general
Aide-de-camp	*Ober-Adjudant*	
Major of Brigade	*Brigade-Major*	
Brigade Adjutant	*Brigade-Adjudant*	Assistant to major of brigade
Regimental Officers		
Colonel	*Oberst* or *Obrist*	
Lieutenant Colonel	*Oberst-* or *Obrist-Lieutenant*	
Major	*Major*	
Captain	*Capitain* or *Hauptmann* *Rittmeister*	Infantry, dragoons, artillery Cavalry
Captain-Lieutenant[a]	*Stabs/Staabs-Capitain* etc.	
First Lieutenant	*Premier-Lieutenant*	
Second Lieutenant	*Second Lieutenant*	
Ensign	*Fähndrich* or *Fähnrich*	Infantry, dragoons, artillery
Cornet	*Cornet*	Cavalry
Regimental Staff	*Mittel- und Unterstab*	
Regimental Quartermaster Adjutant	*Regiments-Quartiermeister Adjudant*	Also paymaster
Regimental Riding Master	*Regiments-Bereuter/Bereiter*	
Chaplain	*Feldprediger*	
Judge Advocate or Auditor	*Auditeur*	
Regimental Surgeon	*Regiments-Chirurgus/ Feldscherer/ Feldscheer*	

English	German	Comments
Regimental Farrier	*Regiments-Pferdearzt*	
Drum Major	*Regiments-Tambour*	Infantry and artillery
Staff Trumpeter	*Stabs-Trompeter*	Cavalry
Waggon Master	*Wagenmeister*	
Armourer	*Rustmeister/Buchsenmacher*	
Saddler	*Sattler*	
Smith	*Kurschmied*	
Provost	*Profoss/Stöckenknecht*	
NCOs and Other Ranks		
Sergeant major	*Feldwebel*	Infantry
	Wachtmeister	Cavalry
Master Fireworker	*Oberfeuerwerker*	Artillery
Sergeant	*Sergeant*	
Sergeant/Quartermaster	*Quartiermeister*	Cavalry
Fireworker	*Feuerwerker*	Artillery
Gefreite-Corporal[b]	*Gefreite-Corporal*	
Quartermaster	*Fourier*	
Corporal	*Corporal*	
Company/Squadron Surgeon	*Compagnie-/ Eskadron- Feldscherer/Chirurgus*	Described as surgeons mate in the British returns
Smith	*Kurschmied*	
Drummer	*Trommler or Tambour*	
Fifer	*Querfeifer or Pfeifer*	
Horn Player	*Halbmondbläser*	Jägers
Trumpeter	*Trompeter*	
Lance Corporal	*Gefreiter*	
Bombardier	*Bombardier*	Artillery
Schütze	*Schütze*	Marksmen, sometimes armed with rifles
Private	*Gemeiner*	
Gunner	*Canonier*	Artillery
Miscellaneous		
Colonel-in-Chief	*Chef*	Proprietor of the regiment
Titulair	*Titulair*[c]	
NCO	*Unterofficier*	
Musicians	*Spielleute or Hautboisten*	
Driver or servant	*Knecht*	

Notes:
a   A senior subaltern who commanded a company or squadron nominally commanded by a more senior officer.
b   An NCO who was training to become an officer and carried the regimental colours.
c   An officer who carried out the duties of the rank shown but only received the pay of the rank below. This is often abbreviated to tit. before the rank.

Introduction

On 20 April 1792, the French Legislative Assembly declared war against Franz II, King of Bohemia and Hungary. His father, Leopold II, had died on 1 March and Franz had not yet been elected as Holy Roman Emperor to succeed him. France hoped to be able to isolate Austria and that the other states of the Empire would remain neutral. However, contrary to French expectations, Prussia honoured its treaty of alliance with Austria and joined the war, followed by several of the smaller German states. After the unexpected failure of the allied invasion of France and the retreat following the check at Valmy, the French marched into Germany, capturing Mainz and Frankfurt, and swept through the Austrian Netherlands.[1]

At first Britain had remained neutral towards the French Revolution and, as late as November 1792, the Government hoped and expected to be able to stay out of the war. Lord Grenville, the Foreign Secretary, wrote to his brother the Duke of Buckingham that he blessed God that 'we had the wit to keep ourselves out of the glorious enterprize of the combined armies' and, after speculating about what the various powers would do next, he concluded that 'We shall do nothing'.[2] However, tensions were rising in the wake of what appeared to the British to be extreme French provocation: the conquest of the Austrian Netherlands; the declaration reopening the navigation of the Scheldt; the perceived threat to the United Provinces (the Dutch Republic), with which Britain and Prussia had entered into a defensive alliance in April 1788; and the French offer of fraternity and assistance to all peoples wishing to regain their liberty. In particular, the threat that the United Provinces would fall under French control could not be tolerated and it was hoped that tough talk, backed up by the despatch of a naval squadron, would be sufficient to shore up Dutch resistance and persuade the French to back down.

As it became increasingly clear that this strategy was unlikely to succeed, the Government started to sound out the other major powers about the possibility of concerted action, including the use of force if necessary, to compel France to give up its conquests and to pledge to no longer 'foment troubles, or to excite disturbances against other Governments'.[3] It also began to take steps to augment its naval and

---

1   The Austrian Netherlands encompassed the southern part of the Low Countries, roughly comprising modern Luxembourg and Belgium, excluding the Prince-Bishopric of Liège.

2   Grenville to Buckingham 7 November 1792, in Duke of Buckingham and Chandos *Memoirs of the Court and Cabinets of George the Third* (London: Hurst and Blackett, 1853), Vol.II, pp.221-5.

3   Grenville to Charles Whitworth, the British ambassador at St. Petersburg, 29 December 1792, TNA: FO 65/23, ff. 262-71.

military forces, although it was expected that Britain's involvement if it came to war would be primarily naval, supporting operations against the Coast of France and in the West Indies.

Protracted political discussions failed to resolve the differences between Britain and France and war seemed inevitable when the French Ambassador, Chauvelin, was expelled following the execution of King Louis XVI on 21 January 1793. Finally, the Convention declared war on the King of England and the Stadtholder of the United Provinces on 1 February 1793.

The state of Britain's armed forces at the outbreak of war is aptly summed up in Bunbury's remark that 'never was a kingdom less prepared for a stern and arduous conflict'.[4] The problem arose from Parliament's suspicion of the Army and unwillingness to pay for more than was absolutely necessary in peacetime. The administration of the Army was divided and kept under civilian control, with numerous checks and balances, and always the overriding requirement to account for every penny spent. This left the Army unready for war, with inadequate command structures in place and large numbers of additional troops having to be raised and trained at short notice.

The total theoretical strength of the British and Irish establishments for 1793 was around 97,000 men, including the artillery, invalids, embodied militia, and fencibles.[5] However, many of these troops were stationed overseas in the Plantations (North America and the West Indies), Gibraltar, New South Wales, and the East Indies. The only regular troops in the British Isles were 16 regiments of cavalry, the Foot Guards, and 14 regiments of foot on the British establishment, and 12 regiments of cavalry and 24 of foot on the Irish establishment; the latter figure excluding the five Irish regiments of foot which were serving in Gibraltar and the West Indies. The effective number of privates in Great Britain on the outbreak of war was 2,769 cavalry, 2,933 foot guards and 3,990 line infantry and in Ireland 1,510 cavalry and 8,134 infantry, fewer than 20,000 in total.[6] These totals do not include the Life Guards or the little over 600 men in the two regiments of foot stationed on Guernsey and Jersey.

These troops were required to perform a variety of duties in maintaining the peace, coastal patrols, guarding the Royal family, defending against possible invasion, and serving as marines on board the fleet, before any could be spared for service abroad. The Army also suffered from the effects of prolonged service overseas and, even for the regiments at home, from the regular movements and dispersal in carrying out its role in support of the civil power. Units were understrength and had few opportunities to practice more than the basics of arms drill, which precluded developing expertise in advanced manoeuvres and tactics. Thus, the country was bound

---

4   Sir H. Bunbury, *Narratives of Some Passages in the Great War with France (1799-1810)* (London, Peter Davies, 1927), p.xv.

5   The Hon. J.W. Fortescue, *A History of the British Army* (London: Macmillan and Co., 1915), Vol. IV Part II, p. 938.

6   Returns for Great Britain 1 February 1793, TNA: WO 17/835 and Ireland December 1792, TNA: WO 17/1071.

to be unprepared for 'a stern and arduous conflict' as the peacetime arrangements ensured that this would be so.

As tensions rose in early 1793, the King issued a number of warrants to increase Britain's forces and estimates for an additional 25,000 men were presented to Parliament on 11 February, including 10,900 to come from 100 independent companies of foot to be raised during 1793.[7] In addition to these regular troops, 12 independent companies of invalids were to be raised for garrison duties and measures were taken to increase the militia and to raise fencible regiments for the duration of the war. These latter troops were only available for home service.

The situation became critical when the French under Dumouriez launched an invasion of the United Provinces on 16 February. Dutch collapse seemed imminent and the British government was forced to act quickly to stem the French flood. It responded reluctantly on 20 February by ordering the Duke of York to be sent to the United Provinces with a force of a little over 2,000 men, made up of the first battalions of the three regiments of foot guards and detachments of artillery and engineers. The Duke, at 29, was by far the youngest of the generals on the Army List and had no practical experience as a field commander. However, he had spent much of the 1780s in Germany, attending manoeuvres and reviews and learning from the Duke of Brunswick, who was considered one of the foremost commanders of the age. He was also given experienced officers to support him in his new role, most importantly Sir James Murray, who was appointed Adjutant General to the forces serving under the Duke of York and effectively chief of staff, with responsibility for the Duke's official correspondence. In any event, York's role was expected to be largely a symbolic one, to steady the resolve of the Dutch, and the government did not anticipate a lengthy military campaign.

The limited scope of the operation was made clear in the instructions given to the Duke. He was to assemble the troops in British pay in the way he thought best for the defence of the United Provinces and for acting against the enemy but, as far as possible, he was to avoid dividing his forces or placing them in frontier garrisons. He was also to conform to the separate instructions given to Major General Lake, who was appointed to command the Brigade of Guards, in relation to operations involving the Guards.[8] Lake's instructions contained the additional secret stipulation that he was not to move his forces more than 24 hours distant from Helvoetsluys without further instructions, in case they needed to be recalled to England.[9]

This force was reinforced by a brigade made up of the 14th, 37th and 53rd Regiments of Foot under Major General Abercromby which sailed on 21 and 22 March. It had only been possible to bring the brigade up to a total strength of just over 1,700 of all ranks by drafts from the new independent companies and Lieutenant General Fawcett, the Adjutant General to the Forces, warned the Duke that it was not fit for

7   Anon., *Journals of the House of Commons* (London: Re-printed by Order of the House of Commons, 1803). Vol. 48, pp.152-4.
8   Commission dated 23 February 1793, TNA: WO 25/41, pp.17-19 and Instructions of the same date, TNA: WO 6/7, pp.1-3.
9   Instructions and secret letter dated 23 February 1793, TNA: WO 6/7, pp.3-5.

active service.[10] As no more infantry could be spared from England, it was decided to send a body of cavalry to join the Duke's army, but the cavalry regiments were also understrength and this force of fewer than 3,000 men had to be drawn from 11 regiments. The first of these troops reached the Duke's army at the beginning of May and the rest were sent over the next two months.

At first, things had seemed desperate as the Dutch border fortresses of Breda, Klundert, and Gertruydenberg fell and Willemstad was besieged, but the strategic situation was changed completely by the defeat of Dumouriez by the Austrians at Neerwinden on 18 March and the defection of Dumouriez shortly afterwards. Following this decisive defeat, the French were driven from the Austrian Netherlands in disarray.

A 'triumvirate' of Prime Minister William Pitt, Home Secretary Henry Dundas, and Foreign Secretary Lord Grenville was responsible for the British Government's conduct of the war, with Dundas having the prime responsibility for the direction of operations and communicating with the commanders in the field. Following the change in circumstances in the Low Countries, the Government's plans became much more ambitious. Dundas wrote to Sir James Murray that the former requirement to stay within 24 hours march of Helvoetsluys was removed and that the Duke was now free to deploy his troops as he felt best to cooperate with the Allied armies.[11] This letter also referred to the possibility of taking possession of Dunkirk if it could be accomplished easily. Then Grenville wrote to the King that he was sending instructions to Lord Auckland, the British ambassador at The Hague, and to Murray, authorising the Duke of York and Auckland to proceed to Antwerp for a conference of the allied leaders, and also empowering the Duke to move the British troops towards the frontier of French Flanders.[12]

The allied commanders and political representatives met at Antwerp at the beginning of April to review the forces available and agree their plans for the future campaign. From now on, the troops in British pay would cooperate with the main Austrian army in launching an offensive against the French. However, the British Government was already considering the withdrawal of its troops from the Low Countries for other operations, as Pitt wrote to Grenville 'to strike a blow in some other part of France'.[13] Additional troops would be required to meet the demands in the Low Countries and for the other expeditions that were planned as opportunities arose. Inevitably this would mean looking for other sources of men to make up for the shortage of Britain's own forces.

10 Fawcett to York 27 March, TNA: WO 3/11, pp.77-8.
11 Dundas to Murray 19 March 1793, TNA: WO 6/7, pp.8-10.
12 Grenville to the King 3 April 1793, in Historical Manuscripts Commission, *The Manuscripts of J.B. Fortescue, Esq., Preserved at Dropmore* (London: Printed for her Majesty's Stationery Office by Eyre and Spottiswoode, 1894), Vol. II, p.389.
13 Pitt to Grenville 1 April 1793, in Historical Manuscripts Commission, *Manuscripts of J.B. Fortescue*, Vol. II, pp.388-9.

Part I

The Campaigns in the Low Countries

1

Making up the Numbers

Parliament's reluctance to maintain substantial armed forces in peacetime meant that the British government generally faced the need to supplement its own forces quickly when emergencies arose and the long-established solution was to engage German auxiliaries. German troops had played a major part in the wars with France during the eighteenth century and had served in Britain against the Jacobites, in the American colonies against the rebels, at the siege of Gibraltar, and in India. Since the personal union of the thrones of Great Britain and the Electorate of Hanover, the first call was on the King's electoral troops, followed by subsidy treaties with various medium sized and small German states who offered troops for hire. The most important of these were Hesse Cassel and Brunswick, with which the British royal family had dynastic connections.

The possibility of engaging German troops was being considered even before the outbreak of war. The Landgrave of Hesse Cassel had written in December 1792 to offer 6,000 of his troops, which could be augmented to 10,000 if required, to serve 'in whatever part of the world or expedition His Britannic Majesty thinks proper to employ them'.[1] The King had also been in discussions in early 1793 to engage 13,000 of his Hanoverian troops to be sent to defend the United Provinces, proposing that his second son the Duke of York be appointed to command this force.[2] The Landgrave of Hesse Darmstadt had also sent an agent to London in February to offer Britain a corps of troops, but this was not pursued as the British government was reluctant to enter into negotiations with the King of Prussia to release these troops and some of the Landgrave's proposals were considered 'rather extravagant'.[3]

In early 1793, the Dutch were becoming increasingly nervous about French intentions and Grenville wrote to Lord Auckland in The Hague to reassure him of British support for the United Provinces. He informed Auckland that the King had ordered the assembling of around 13,000 of his electoral troops for their defence, but the first detachment would not be ready to march in less than two months. He also referred to the offer by the Landgrave of Hesse Cassel and suggested that the

---

1   Copy of a letter from the Landgrave dated 21 December, TNA: FO 31/5.
2   York to George III 19 January 1793 and George III to Pitt 22 and 24 January 1793, in A. Aspinall (ed.), *The Later Correspondence of George III* (London: Cambridge University Press, 1962 and 1968), Vol. 1, pp.645-9.
3   Letters from Graife to Grenville 1, 19 and 26 February 1793, TNA: FO 31/5 and George III to Pitt and reply 17 February 1793, in Aspinall (ed.), *Later Correspondence.*, Vol. 2, pp.7-8.

Dutch government might wish to take advantage of this proposal.[4] Auckland passed on this information to the Dutch government but noted that, although they were grateful for these proposals, in the current emergency they would prefer one or two battalions immediately, rather than the prospect of 10 or 20 battalions in April.[5]

Lieutenant General Fawcett was instructed to finalise the negotiations for the Hanoverian troops with *Oberst-Lieutenant* von Spörken and the Hanoverian Chancery.[6] The composition of the corps and the arrangements for them to 'serve upon the Continent, on such Service as the Exigency of Affairs may require' were set out in 'Preliminary Articles between Great Britain and Hanover', which were signed on 4 March by Baron Alvensleben, Hanover's minister in London.[7] Orders had already been given on 22 February for the corps to be assembled and to march to the Low Countries.

Major William Gunn of the 6th Dragoons received a commission from the King dated 2 March 1793, appointing him 'Commissary for Mustering a Body of Our Hanoverian Forces taken into the Pay of Great Britain'. His instructions of the same date required him to proceed without delay to the most convenient place to muster the troops and administer to them the usual oath of fidelity to the King of Great Britain. He was to send 'an Exact and accurate State of the Condition, numbers and completeness of each Batalion [sic]' to one of the Secretaries of State.[8] Gunn's future correspondence in relation to his duties was conducted with Henry Dundas.

Once the arrangements for the Hanoverian troops had been concluded, the British government's attention turned to Hesse Cassel. Grenville sent instructions to the Earl of Elgin, appointing him as His Majesty's Plenipotentiary to conclude a treaty for a body of Hessian troops to be taken into British pay, together with his credential letter and 'Full Power under the Great Seal'. The number of troops to be engaged was to be no more than 8,000, preferably including one third cavalry, but none of the troops currently serving with the Austrians or Prussians were to be used to complete the corps. Elgin was to base the negotiations on the treaty concluded with the Landgrave at the time of the Dutch crisis in 1787 and he received very detailed instructions on the key issues to be agreed:

- The term of the treaty was to be limited to two or three years and under no circumstances to exceed four years;
- The subsidy was to be reduced after the return of the troops;
- The destination of the troops could be limited to Europe, but the stipulations in the previous treaty that they would not serve beyond sea except in England

---

4   Grenville to Auckland 24 January 1793, BL Add MS 34447, ff. 237-8.
5   Auckland to Grenville 8 February 1793, BL Add MS 34448, ff. 36-7.
6   George III to Pitt and reply 17 February 1793, in Aspinall (ed.), *Later Correspondence*, Vol. 2, pp.7-8.
7   J. Debrett (ed.), *A Collection of State Papers, Relative to the War against France now carrying on by Great-Britain and the several other European Powers*, (London: J. Debrett, 1794 and 1795), Vol.I, pp.31-41. The text of the articles is in Appendix I.
8   Commission signed by Henry Dundas 'By His Majesty's Command', TNA: HO 51/147, pp.40-1 and Instructions dated 2 March 1793, TNA: HO 51/147 pp.43-53.

or Ireland should be omitted 'as being inconsistent with the Plans of Operation which may probably be adopted';

- The former provision for the troops to be returned if the Landgrave's dominions were attacked was not to be included;
- Any suggestion of putting the troops on English pay should be 'absolutely discouraged' as contrary to the practice with other German troops;
- He should prevent the insertion of any provision for the Landgrave to command his troops in person;
- He was to proceed with the negotiations without loss of time and keep Grenville informed of progress.[9]

Elgin was delayed in his passage to the continent and then visited the Prussian and Austrian headquarters to get an update on the current situation, so that he only arrived in Cassel on 5 April. The negotiations were concluded rapidly and he was able to send a copy of the signed treaty to Grenville on the 10th, together with an account of the negotiations.[10] On his arrival, he had met the Landgrave, who was happy to meet the British requirements, and the only point he had proposed at this stage was that the troops provided to Britain be allowed to join those serving with the Prussians, making a total of 14,000 which he would command in person. Elgin made it clear that this was impossible and was not raised again in the subsequent negotiations.

The negotiations began in earnest the following day with two of the Landgrave's ministers, Baron von Münchausen and Mr Kunckel. They held frequent meetings, at which the main sticking points were the term and the amount of the subsidy. Elgin rejected attempts to increase the levy money, the proposal to have the troops put on the footing of British troops and a request for an advance of £10-20,000. He also obtained positive assurances that the corps would not be completed by taking troops from those serving with the Prussians. After much discussion, the Hessian ministers reluctantly accepted the terms put forward by Elgin. However, just as the treaty was about to be signed, news arrived that Dumouriez had declared against the Convention and it was believed that he was marching on Paris, so Britain might not need the Hessian troops after all. Elgin informed the Hessian ministers that he would have to seek fresh instructions from London, unless they agreed to accept the payment of the levy money and a double subsidy of 300,000 crowns as sufficient compensation for the Landgrave's expenses if the corps was not required. Although this provoked 'the utmost consternation' and the 'strongest entreaties' for it to be dropped, Elgin stood firm and they finally agreed the insertion of the additional Article 15.

The main points of the treaty were that the Landgrave agreed to provide 8,000 men for a period of three years in return for an annual subsidy. The contingent was available for service anywhere in Europe, but not on board the fleet, and was to serve as a combined force under its Hessian commander, but under the overall command of the British general commanding the whole army. The Treaty specified that 'this

---

9   Grenville to Elgin 10 March 1793 and enclosures, TNA: FO 26/20.
10   Elgin to Grenville 10 March 1793 and enclosures, TNA: FO 26/20.

Corps shall be completely equipped, furnished with tents, and all necessary equipage, in a word, shall be put upon the best possible footing', with each battalion to be provided with two field pieces, along with the necessary men and equipment. The sick and wounded were to be treated by Hesse Cassel's own medical services. In return, Britain agreed to pay levy money for each cavalry or infantryman, an annual subsidy, the costs of transporting the corps, pay and allowances and the cost of making good any losses. A British commissary would be appointed to ensure that the corps only included men who were fit for service.[11] This was to form the template for the subsidy treaties later agreed with the other German states.

Elgin wrote again to Grenville enclosing a letter from the Landgrave, who had asked for the unfairness of Article 15 to be brought to the King's attention. Elgin stated that he had been treated very well during his time at the Landgrave's court and that 'the gentlemen with whom I had to negotiate the Treaty, have entered into the discussions & transacted the Business, in the most fair & candid manner possible'. In a separate private letter of the same date, Elgin asked for a commissary to be sent to muster the troops.[12]

Grenville's reply passed on the King's 'entire Approbation' of the manner in which he had conducted the negotiations and noted that Article 15 was 'much to be commended' in the circumstances then prevailing. However, as the King wished to have the immediate use of these troops, Elgin was to inform the Landgrave that the article would not be invoked and that a commissary would be sent to muster the troops previous to the date fixed in the treaty for the march of the first division.[13]

Although already committed to the campaign in the Low Countries, the British government was now also planning to launch operations in the West Indies, which would require the use of the British troops who were available for foreign service, so its attention turned again to sources of additional German troops. Grenville wrote to Lord Beauchamp, who later became Lord Yarmouth, instructing him to go to Stuttgart at the earliest opportunity to see if reports that the Duke of Württemberg might be willing to provide some troops to Britain were true. If so, he was to propose a treaty based on that negotiated with the Landgrave of Hesse Cassel for as many men as were available.[14]

Yarmouth's mission made slow progress. He had to inform Grenville that no Württemberg troops were available, but he believed that some might be obtained from the Margrave of Baden.[15] Grenville also wrote to him that the Landgrave of Hesse Darmstadt had offered to provide troops in the spring, but the discussions had not proceeded as the terms proposed by the Landgrave were 'so extravagant that they could not be listened to for a moment'. However, Yarmouth was authorised to negotiate with the Landgrave on the basis of the treaty with Hesse Cassel, and it was

---

11 Debrett (ed.), *A Collection of State Papers*, Vol. 1, pp.5-10. The full text of the treaty is in Appendix II.
12 Elgin to Grenville 11 April 1793 and enclosures, TNA: FO 26/20.
13 Grenville to Elgin 26 April 1793, TNA: FO 26/20.
14 Grenville to Beauchamp 27 June 1793, TNA: FO 29/1. Beauchamp was created Marquess of Hertford and Earl of Yarmouth in July 1793 and from then on he signed his dispatches as Yarmouth.
15 Yarmouth to Grenville 22 July 1793, TNA: FO 29/1.

hoped that the successful end to the long drawn-out siege of Mainz might mean that German troops would become available.[16] This was indeed the case, as the German princes were keen to find alternative employment for their troops, and saw Britain as a good potential source of income.

The Landgrave of Hesse Cassel wrote to inform his ambassador in London, Baron von Kutzleben, that he was now recalling his troops who had been engaged in the siege of Mainz and that the King of Prussia wished for them to be used elsewhere against the French. Therefore, he was able to offer Britain 4,000 men, made up of a 'well mounted' regiment of dragoons, a regiment of grenadiers and two regiments of infantry, on the same terms as previously agreed, 'to be employ'd with His Royal Highness the Duke of York, or where else the King of Great Britain thinks proper to employ them'.[17]

Yarmouth wrote to Grenville, asking for authority to conclude a treaty with the Landgrave of Hesse Cassel, who had offered 5,152 additional troops, although this total was later reduced to 4,000 when the Landgrave decided not to include the Regiment Garde in the contingent. At the same time, Dundas notified Yarmouth that the King had approved the Landgrave's offer of additional troops. Yarmouth was to ask the Landgrave to order their march and he was informed that Major Gunn would be instructed to take his directions for the muster and inspection of the corps.[18]

The British government was keen to have the ability to use at least 4,000 Hesse Cassel troops for operations outside Europe and Grenville instructed Yarmouth to propose this to the Landgrave and also informed Kutzleben.[19] The government was prepared to exclude any particular corps the Landgrave wished, and to confirm that the troops would not be required to serve in Africa or the East Indies, so the clear implication was that they would be sent to the West Indies.

While these negotiations were underway, the army in the Low Countries, with the first of its German auxiliaries, was moving forward against the French.

16 Grenville to Yarmouth 26 July 1793, TNA: FO 29/1.
17 Landgrave to Kutzleben 1 August 1793, TNA FO 31/5.
18 Yarmouth to Grenville 12 August 1793 and enclosures and Dundas to Yarmouth 12 August 1793, TNA: FO 29/1.
19 Grenville to Yarmouth 16 August 1793, TNA: FO 29/1, and Grenville to Kutzleben 23 August 1793, TNA: FO 31/5.

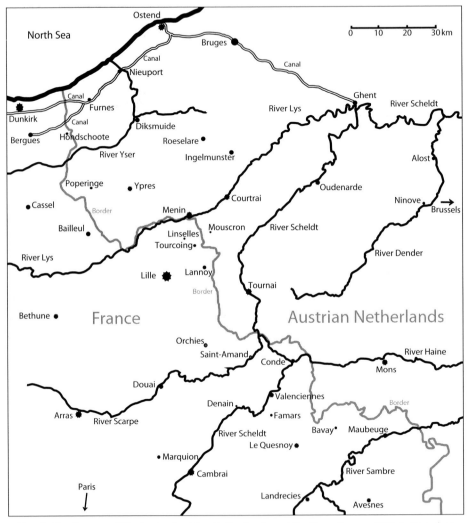

Map 1 The Theatre of War in the Austrian Netherlands and Northern France, 1793-4. (Based on map 1 in the atlas to A. von Witzleben, *Prinz Friedrich Josias von Coburg-Saalfeld, Herzog zu Sachsen*)

2

Early Successes

Following the conference of the allied commanders and political representatives at Antwerp at the beginning of April, Prince Friedrich Josias von Sachsen-Coburg-Saalfeld, the commander of the Austrian forces in the Low Countries, issued a plan for the forthcoming campaign. The total allied forces were estimated at 90,000 men, with further reinforcements of 5,000 Austrians and 8,000 Hessians expected at the beginning of June. This was not considered sufficient to besiege Lille immediately, so it was decided to proceed with the siege of Valenciennes and then to move on to Dunkirk, which it was hoped could be taken towards the end of August. The major part of the army would then move on to Lille, which would be blockaded through the winter, if it could not be taken more quickly.[1] Dundas wrote to Murray, authorising the Duke to act in conjunction with Coburg in carrying out the plan and noting with satisfaction that Coburg had specified the attack on Dunkirk as 'the next immediate object of the Campaign.'[2]

The Hanoverian Auxiliary Corps had marched to join the Duke of York's army in two divisions. The first set off between 20 and 26 March and consisted of the 1st, 4th, 9th, and 10th Cavalry Regiments, the 4th and 10th Infantry Regiments, the horse artillery and the 1st division of heavy artillery under *General-Lieutenant* von dem Bussche. They reached the Duke of York's headquarters at Tournai on 29 April, with the exception of the 4th Infantry Regiment and the artillery. The 4th Infantry Regiment arrived on 7 May but *General-Major* von Mutio, the regiment's Colonel-in-Chief, had become ill and had to be left behind. He died on 8 May in his 51st year of service.[3] The remaining troops formed the second division, which marched out in three small columns starting from the beginning of April and reached Tournai between 11 and 24 May.

The Hanoverian troops had suffered greatly from a shortage of supplies on their march. The Duke blamed the Dutch for advancing earlier than agreed and taking all the available supplies, even though they had been informed of the route to be followed by the Hanoverians.[4] Later, he complained that his Commissary General,

---

1   Protocol of the Antwerp conference, TNA: WO 1/166, pp.125-32 and 'Considerations secretes Sur les Operations des Armées combines…' TNA: WO 1/166, pp.213-23.
2   Dundas to Murray 10 May 1793, TNA: WO 6/7, pp.45-7.
3   Anon., *Annalen der Braunschweig-Lüneburgischen Churlande* (Hannover: W. Pockwitz jun., 1793-5), 1793, p.715.
4   York to the King 23 April 1793, in Aspinall (ed.), *Later Correspondence*, vol. 2 p.30.

Brook Watson, had gained his experience in the American War, where almost all supplies had been sent from England. Watson was unsure how to proceed and, in his anxiety to do well, he acted so cautiously that contracts were not put in place quickly enough. He went on that the lack of supplies had prevented him from assembling the troops as quickly as he would have wished and that, unless Watson found a way of furnishing the necessary supplies, he would have to make a formal complaint against him. Fortunately, the problem was resolved and the Duke was able to write on the 31st that the necessary arrangements were now in place, although the lack of bread and forage had caused great distress and made it impossible to maintain discipline.[5]

Lieutenant von Ompteda of the Garde Regiment, serving with the 1st Grenadier Battalion, recorded in his diary that on 24 April he had been sent from Vilvoorde north-east of Brussels to the Duke of York's headquarters at Tournai, over 100 kilometres away, to deliver a report on the mutiny that had broken out among the troops on their march. He arrived in Tournai at 8.00 a.m. on the 25th, where the Duke's first words were 'I'll go there myself' and he set off with an aide-de-camp an hour later. The troops had been told that they were now in British pay on taking their oath of allegiance and had mistakenly believed that they would receive the higher British rates of pay. Trouble had broken out when it became clear that this was not the case. The Duke came upon the battalion at Halle, between Brussels and Tournai, where he assembled the troops and addressed them through *General-Lieutenant* von dem Bussche. He stated that he was not aware of the provisions of the treaty and that he was ashamed of their conduct, but he promised that they would receive whatever was due to them. Ompteda noted that the Duke's unexpected arrival had made a deep impression on the men and order was restored. Bussche was instructed to inform all of the regiments in his division that they would be given their entitlement, which he did by a general order on the 26th. The Duke also agreed with *Feldmarschall* von Freytag that the men's pay should be increased until the King's pleasure was known, as they could not survive on their current rates.[6] *Titulair Capitain* Gerhard von Scharnhorst, who later became famous for his role in the reform of the Prussian army, was serving with the artillery in the Hanoverian Auxiliary Corps. His letters home to his wife referred to the mutiny of the 1st Grenadier Battalion and noted that there was also unrest amongst the artillery and train.[7]

In addition to these difficulties, the relationship between the Duke of York and Freytag was strained from the start. The Field Marshal, a 73 year old veteran of the Seven Years War, was not happy to receive detailed orders from the young

---

5   York to the King, 17, 27 and 31 May 1793, in Aspinall (ed.), *Later Correspondence*, vol. 2 pp.31-45.

6   Regierungsrath von Ompteda, 'Hannoversche leichte Grenadiere im Feldzuge von 1793. Nach dem Tagebuche des Lieutenants von Ompteda, vom 1sten Grenadier-Bataillone', *Zeitschrift des Historischen Vereins für Niedersachsen*, Jahrgang 1862, pp.304-6 and York to the King 26 and 30 April 1793, in Aspinall (ed.), *Later Correspondence*, vol. 2, pp.31-4.

7   Scharnhorst to his wife 29 April and 5 May 1793 in J. Kunisch, M. Sikora and T. Stieve, *Gerhard von Scharnhorst Private und dienstliche Schriften, Band 1, Schüler, Lehrer, Kriegsteilnehmer (Kurhannover bis 1795)* (Köln, Böhlau Verlag, 2002), pp.207-9.

Duke, who had no practical experience of war, and a noticeable coldness developed between them.

After their difficult march to the front, the Hanoverian corps took part in the allied attack which drove the French from their entrenched camp at Famars on 23 May. The Duke wrote to the King, praising the conduct of the 4th Infantry Regiment and the Leibgarde. He singled out the example of *Lieutenant* Valentini, the riding master of the Leibgarde, and recommended him for promotion. Valentini had cut down six of the enemy and captured their standard, but he had then seen that his own regiment's standard was in danger. He left the one he had captured, rallied six men around his regiment's standard and carried it to safety, even though he had earlier suffered a severe wound to the face.[8] The Hanoverian losses in this action were 22 killed and 61 wounded and missing, with the greatest loss falling on the Leibgarde, who had two officers and 11 men killed, five officers and 38 men wounded and two officers captured.[9] The regiment had only 176 officers and men remaining on duty on 26 May, with a further 70 on command out of the full strength of 315.[10]

The army then moved to besiege Valenciennes, where the trenches were opened on 13 June. Again there were problems with the Hanoverian infantry, where men from the Garde Regiment left the trenches on two occasions, returned to their camp without their officers or NCOs and incited other regiments to follow them. The Hanoverian *General der Cavallerie* von Wallmoden-Gimborn had informed the Duke of York that two of their officers, *Capitaines* von Mecklenburg and von Bülow, had encouraged the men to leave and used expressions verging on mutiny and treason. After discussion with Freytag, the Duke had written to him to order the two officers to quit the camp immediately. This action had the desired effect and order was restored in the regiment.[11] The bad conduct of the Hanoverian infantry also attracted the attention of Lieutenant Powell of the British 14th Regiment of Foot, who recorded that the first time he saw them under fire during a French sortie 'it perfectly disgusted us with them, for every man got upon his Hands & Knees and ran out of the Trenches as hard as they could pelt'.[12] The King wanted to remove Prince Adolphus from his position as colonel in the Garde Regiment, but the Prince asked him not to do so because of the effect it would have on the regiment. He went on to explain to his father that their behaviour was not the result of cowardice, but of indiscipline owing to the number of peasants who had only recently joined the regiment and were not yet properly trained, made worse by the number of newly-appointed young officers and NCOs, who did not yet know their duty.[13]

Meanwhile, the march of the Hesse Cassel troops had been delayed. Although the treaty required the first division to be ready for review on 8 May and to march

---

8   York to the King 27 May 1793, in Aspinall (ed.), *Later Correspondence*, vol. 2, pp.43-4.

9   L. von Sichart, *Geschichte der Königlich-Hannoverschen Armee* (Hannover, Hahn'sche Hofbuchhandlung, 1871), Vol.4, pp.220-1.

10 Daily report, Famars 26 May 1793, Hann. 38 E Nr. 144, p.53.

11 York to the King 5 and 19 July 1793, in Aspinall (ed.), *Later Correspondence*, vol. 2, pp.57-8 and 61.

12 Diary of Lieutenant Powell 13 July 1793, NAM 1976-07-45, pp.7-8.

13 Prince Adolphus to the King 23 July 1793, in Aspinall (ed.), *Later Correspondence*, vol. 2, pp.64-5.

the following day, Major Gunn's commission to inspect them and establish their effective numbers before they left for the Netherlands was not issued until 30 May.[14] Kutzleben wrote to Grenville at the beginning of June to inform him that the first division had been ready to march on 8 May and the second would be ready on 8 June but, as no British commissary had arrived to muster them, they had remained near Cassel. The Duke of York had also written to the Landgrave, asking him to send the troops forward and confirming that a commissary would be sent to meet them en route, as had happened with the Hanoverians. The Landgrave replied on 8 June that he had issued orders for the troops to begin their march. He noted that the absence of a commissary to arrange the march route and the necessary supplies had caused problems, but he had sent an officer and commissariat staff to resolve the issues and he asked the Duke to send someone to meet his troops and take on these responsibilities without delay.[15]

The troops marched to join the Duke of York's army in two divisions. The first division, commanded by *General-Lieutenant* von Wurmb was made up of the 3rd Grenadier Battalion (von Wurmb), Infantry Regiments Prinz Carl and von Lossberg, and the Gens d'Armes. It began its march on 10 June and reached the allied camp on 10 July. The second division under *General-Lieutenant* von Buttlar, consisting of the 1st Grenadier Battalion (von Eschwege), Infantry Regiments Erb-Prinz and Kospoth, Jäger Battalion, Carabiniers, and Prinz Friedrichs Dragoon Regiment, set off on 17 June and arrived on 19 July.

The British commissary, Major Gunn, finally mustered the troops between 29 June and 12 July, around seven weeks later than intended in the treaty. He reported that the men were good but the horses were in poor condition. The Duke of York also reviewed the troops and commented on the poor quality of the horses, which were small and many with sore backs, although the men of both cavalry and infantry were fine, especially the Regiment Erb-prinz. He noted that the corps had suffered from desertion, but most had been caught.[16] The seriousness of the problem with the horses is shown by the return for 21 July, which records 111 sick horses for the Gens d'Armes, leaving only 292 fit for service, and the Prinz Friedrichs Dragoons with 303 sick and 354 fit. The Carabiniers were in much better shape, having 367 horses fit and only 39 sick.[17]

The treaty required the corps to be 'completely equipped, furnished with tents, and all necessary equipage', but this was soon found to be far from the case, as they had arrived without bread waggons and could not proceed without them.[18] It then became clear that they had brought inadequate supplies of ammunition, which came as an unpleasant surprise to the Duke of York, who had expected them to arrive fully equipped like the Hanoverians. Murray wrote to Dundas to request 600,000 musket

14   Gunn's commission signed by Henry Dundas, TNA: HO 51/147, p.84.
15   Kutzleben to Grenville 5 June 1793, York to the Landgrave of Hesse Cassel 29 May 1793 (copy) and Landgrave to York 8 June 1793 (copy), TNA: FO 31/5.
16   Gunn to Dundas with enclosures 18 July 1793 (copy), TNA: WO 6/7 pp.195-201 and York to the King 23 July 1793, in in Aspinall (ed.), *Later Correspondence*, vol. 2, pp.63-4.
17   Report dated 21 July 1793, HStAM 4h 3358, f. 16.
18   Article III of the treaty in Appendix II and Extract from a letter from Brook Watson 19 July 1793, TNA: FO 31/5.

cartridges, as the Hessian infantry had only brought 30 per man in their cartridge boxes and none in reserve, 50,000 carbine cartridges and 50,000 flints.[19] He reported that the infantry muskets were the same bore as those of the British infantry and the carbines the same as for British light dragoons. In fact, the shortage was no accident as the Hessian troops had been ordered to take with them only 30 cartridges for each infantryman and 20 for each cavalryman.[20] They had also only brought 100 round shot and 40 rounds of grape shot for each of their battalion guns and Murray asked for sufficient ammunition to bring them up to 300 rounds per gun. He sent a sample cannon cartridge, but this went astray and they had to proceed without the additional artillery ammunition.[21] The Duke of Richmond, Master General of the Ordnance, pointed out to Dundas that it was a pity that Murray had not thought to have the calibre of the Hessian guns measured, which would have been a simple matter for any of the British artillery officers with the army.[22]

The Hessians had arrived just in time for the final stages of the siege of Valenciennes, which surrendered on 28 July. The Hanoverian casualties during the siege had been 33 killed and 210 wounded, somewhat higher than the British losses of 23 killed and 127 wounded.[23] The Hesse Cassel losses were much lighter, with two privates killed and two officers and 13 privates wounded.[24]

While the siege had dragged on, the Austrian commanders had begun to draw up plans for subsequent operations. *Feldzeugmeister* Prince Hohenlohe-Kirchberg, who had replaced *Oberst* Mack as Coburg's chief of staff, put forward a plan dated 1 July for the allied forces, which were now estimated at 130,000 men in total. The British, Hanoverians, Hessians, and 15,000 Austrian troops were to march to the siege of Dunkirk and provide a covering force between Menin and Lille, while the remainder of the army would cover the line from Lille to Charleroi and Namur, besiege Maubeuge and/or Le Quesnoy, leaving 18,000 men to garrison Trier and Luxembourg.[25] Murray forwarded these plans to Dundas, who replied that 'His Majesty's Ministers according to the best information they are possessed of, see no reason to differ in opinion as to the propriety of any of the Operations therein proposed' and authorised the Duke to make arrangements to carry them out. He then added that he hoped that the 8,000 Hessians with the army might be released as they 'in various ways may very usefully be employed'.[26]

19 Murray to Dundas 19, 23 and 26 July 1793, TNA: WO 1/166, pp.583-6, 591-7 and 611-23.
20 Journal des Regiments Prinz Carl 9 June 1793, HStAM 10e II/8.
21 Murray to Dundas 26 July and 6 August 1793, TNA: WO 1/166, pp.611-623 and 695-702.
22 Duke of Richmond to Dundas 15 August 1793, TNA: HO 50/369, pp.279-84.
23 According to the return sent by Murray to Dundas, TNA: WO 166, pp.667-9. Sichart, *Geschichte*, p.235 gives the Hanoverian losses as 39 killed and 274 wounded.
24 M. von Ditfurth, *Die Hessen in den Feldzügen von 1793, 1794 und 1795 in Flandern, Brabant, Holland und Westphalen* (Kassel, Verlag von J. Bohné, 1839-40), Vol.1, pp.64-5.
25 'Considerations Qu'elles sont les Opérations, qui d'après les Principes & uniquement sous les Rapports militaires, pourrait être entreprises après la Conquête de Valenciennes et de Condé' and supporting papers, TNA: WO 1/166, pp.507-17 and 519-20.
26 Murray to Dundas 12 July 1793, TNA: WO 1/166 pp.493-505 and Dundas to Murray 19 July 1793, TNA: WO 6/7, pp.82-5.

Even before Valenciennes had fallen, the British government was planning a range of expeditions, seeking to juggle the limited resources available from one theatre of operations to another. Pitt sent a private and confidential letter to Murray on 19 July, which set out the government's ambitious, not to say confused and unrealistic plans. He expressed his wish to take the Hessians for another service 'if they can be spared without materially cramping your operations' as this 'may enable us to make an Impression in other quarters which might perhaps tend materially to shorten the Duration of the War'. He also wondered if it would be possible to take the three British line infantry regiments for the same purpose, to be replaced by an additional corps of cavalry, which he thought would be more useful for an army of observation. If this could be managed, he would be able to send what was required to the West Indies in the autumn and collect a force to be sent to the Mediterranean before the season was too advanced, which could be 'employed to the greatest advantage' using Britain's naval strength. His aim was to 'distress the Enemy on more sides than one, while their internal distraction continues', but he made it clear that did not wish 'to aim at this object at the expense of retarding or endangering your operations which I consider as more essential than any others'.[27]

In the same vein, Dundas wrote to Murray that the surrender of Valenciennes and of Mainz, which had capitulated after a long siege on 23 July, would allow Coburg to proceed with the next stage of operations and 'affords us the prospect of speedily withdrawing and applying to other important purposes, the Hessian Force in the Pay of Great Britain'. He went on that it was 'extremely material if the circumstances of the Campaign should justify it' that the Hessians were ready to embark by the beginning of September even though the siege of Dunkirk should be 'an object of immediate attention'.[28]

The allied commanders met again on 3 August to finalise their plans. Murray sent a copy of the protocol of the conference to Dundas, noting that the attack on Dunkirk had been finally determined upon, after a short delay while the French were driven from their current positions, and that the Duke had confirmed that he needed 15,000 Austrian troops to support his operations. He went on to express his view that the embarkation of the Hessians by the beginning of September would not interfere with the siege of Dunkirk and even that of Bergues. No time would be lost in carrying out the plan and it was expected that the army would reach Dunkirk between 20 and 22 August.[29]

Coburg tried to stop or at least delay the Duke's march and the Austrian diplomat Count Mercy-Argenteau put forward an alternative plan to postpone the attacks on Le Quesnoy, Maubeuge, and Dunkirk, while the army took Cambrai and moved towards Paris in an attempt to instil a 'consternation and terror in the inhabitants of Paris' and deter them from harming the French Queen Marie Antoinette.[30] Nothing came of this proposal and the allies continued with the agreed plan. They tried to bring the French to battle at Caesar's Camp, near Marquion north-west of Cambrai,

27 Pitt to Murray 19 July 1793, TNA: PRO 30/8/102, pp.212-15.
28 Dundas to Murray 1 August 1793, TNA: WO 6/7, pp.135-42.
29 Murray to Dundas 6 August 1793, TNA: WO 1/166, pp.695-706.
30 Lord Elgin to Grenville 12 August 1793, TNA: FO 26/21.

on 7 August but, although the French forces were driven from their positions, they slipped away without any serious fighting.

The Duke marched through Marchiennes on 11 August and camped near Orchies, where he assembled his forces for the attack on Dunkirk. The Austrians, who had been promised by Coburg to assist in the attack, arrived on the 14th under the command of *Feldmarschall-Lieutenant* Alvinczy. The combined army marched out in two columns the following day with an effective strength of around 35,000 men, slightly lower than the 38,000 men set out in Hohenlohe's plan.[31] The Duke divided the army into two parts on the 19th, keeping the siege army under his personal command and sending a corps under *Feldmarschall* Freytag to cover the left flank of the forces besieging Dunkirk, to maintain communications with Ypres and cover the French camps at Bergues, Cassel and Bailleul.

The decision to divide the allied armies has been much criticised. The French armies of the North and Ardennes had around 175,000 men available to defend the frontier between Longwy and Dunkirk – not counting the 9,500 men from the garrison of Valenciennes, who were forbidden to bear arms against the allies under the terms of their surrender – but were in no state to oppose a swift and vigorous attack by the allies.[32] Instead of following up their advantage after the fall of Valenciennes, the allies opted to besiege the two fortified towns of Le Quesnoy and Dunkirk, almost 150 kilometres apart, with the gap between them watched by 20,000 Dutch and Austrians in a cordon between Menin and Orchies. This static position played into the hands of the French, who were left in no doubt as to the allies' intentions, and allowed them time to reinforce and reorganise their armies, so that the only decision required was whether to move against Coburg or York. They were also granted a respite on the Rhine, where Austro-Prussian rivalry led to a period of inactivity, which allowed the French to transfer substantial numbers of troops from the armies of the Rhine and Moselle to reinforce their forces in the Low Countries.

The Duke's march to Dunkirk had been interrupted on 18 August, when he had to deal with a French force at Linselles, who had driven off the Dutch after they had come out of Menin to capture the French posts at Blaton and Linselles. This action, although successful, achieved nothing of lasting value and cost the British Foot Guards 183 casualties.[33] From there, the Duke marched to Furnes (Veurne) and then advanced to push back the French from their camp at Ghyvelde on the 22nd. He summoned Dunkirk to surrender on the 23rd but, when this was rejected, he advanced on the 24th to a line between Tetteghem on his left and the sea on his right and began the siege. His force was confined to this narrow strip of land by the Grande- and Petite-Moëre, a large area of marshland on his left which the French were able to flood. Murray reported that the French had made an opening in the dyke of the canal between Dunkirk and Bergues, allowing them to inundate a

---

31   Scharnhorst's estimate in Kunisch et al, *Gerhard von Scharnhorst,* pp.268-74 and Ditfurth, *Die Hessen.* p.73.

32   V. Dupuis, *La Campagne de 1793 à l'Armée du Nord et des Ardennes, de Valenciennes à Hondschoote* (Paris: Librairie Militaire R. Chapelot et Ce, 1906), pp.5-30.

33   Return of the killed and wounded…, TNA: WO 1/166, p.765.

considerable part of the country. It was hoped that the flooding would not increase sufficiently to inconvenience the siege operations against Dunkirk, although it would impair operations against Bergues and could lead to problems obtaining fresh water.[34] This flooding also disrupted communications between the Duke's army and Freytag's covering force, which now had to go by way of Furnes.

The siege could not proceed in earnest because the heavy guns and stores the Duke had requested from England had not yet arrived and he had no naval protection from the French gunboats, which were able to flank his positions on the seaward side. There were also worrying reports of French reinforcements coming towards Cassel from Lille and, in response to these, the Duke requested Coburg to send troops to take up the positions then occupied by the Dutch on the other side of the River Lys (Leie). This would allow the Prince of Orange to set up a camp of around 10,000 men between Poperinge and Roesbrugge, which would be of great assistance to the army.[35]

Meanwhile, *Général de Division* Houchard, who had taken over the command of the armies of the North and Ardennes, had decided to disrupt the Duke of York's operations by attacking the Dutch on the Lys, supported by a demonstration against Coburg's positions by the French troops at Maubeuge. The attack against the Dutch on the 27th drove them from their positions at Tourcoing and Lannoy, but the French troops gave themselves up to pillage and drunkenness, which prevented further progress. The Dutch retreated towards Mouscron and, instead of the hoped-for reinforcement, the Duke of York had to send the six squadrons of Hesse Cassel heavy cavalry towards Menin, without which the Dutch threatened to fall back to Tournai and Courtrai, leaving Ypres exposed. Coburg also replied that he could not detach a significant force, as requested by the Duke, until the siege of Le Quesnoy had been completed, which would probably be by mid-September, but that he would move to support the Duke then and if necessary delay the planned siege of Maubeuge.[36]

At the beginning of September the allied commanders still believed that things were proceeding in a satisfactory fashion. The siege guns, artillery men and stores were being brought forward and Admiral Macbride had arrived, although as yet without his naval squadron. Murray wrote to Dundas in a private letter on 3 September 'for my own part I think every thing is going on extremely well… I see nothing, but what offers a fair & reasonable expectation of the great purpose of the Campaign being accomplished'.[37]

---

34   Murray to Dundas 24 August 1793, TNA: WO 1/166, pp.781-5.
35   Murray to Dundas 28 August 1793, TNA: WO 1/166, pp.815-8.
36   Murray to Dundas 31 August 1793, TNA: WO 1/166, pp.823-33 and York to the King 31 August 1793 in Aspinall (ed.), *Later Correspondence*, vol. 2, pp.82-4.
37   Murray to Dundas 3 September 1793, TNA: WO 11/167, pp.21-3.

3

The Army of Observation

The composition of *Feldmarschall* Freytag's army of observation was announced in general orders on 19 August. It was made up of:

- All the Hanoverian cavalry and infantry, amounting to 15 battalions and 16 squadrons, as shown in Table 2;
- 10 squadrons of British cavalry, two each from the 2nd and 3rd Dragoon Guards and the 1st, 2nd, and 6th Dragoons;
- Two battalions of the Austrian Infantry Regiment Brentano, two squadrons of the Blankenstein Hussars and the *Freicorps* Grün-Laudon;
- Five squadrons of the Hesse Cassel Prinz Friedrichs Dragoon Regiment;
- The Loyal Emigrants, French émigrés in British service, when they had been relieved from their present post at Ostend.

The Austrian cavalry and the whole of the advanced posts were to be commanded by the Austrian *General-Major* von Fabri and the British cavalry by Lieutenant General Erskine, with Major Generals Harcourt and Mansel under him.[1] The corps was joined by the two companies of Hesse Cassel Jägers, which the Duke of York had originally intended to keep with the siege army as he expected them to be useful in the trenches.[2]

Estimates of the strength of this force vary, but it probably had a total of around 16,000 men. However, this includes a large proportion of cavalry, who would be of little use in the rough country in which Freytag was to operate, leaving fewer than 12,000 infantry. The number of infantrymen actually available for service was even lower once sick and the requirements for other duties are taken into account.

Freytag's corps marched to Ypres the same day and set up camp at Vlamertinge between there and Poperinge. He set off on the following day to drive the enemy advance posts from the area between the southern Furnes Canal and the river Yser. *Oberst* von Bothmer with the 1st Battalion of the Garde-Regiment remained at Vlamertinge and *Oberst* von Linsingen with the 1st Battalion of the 4th Infantry

---

1   Orderly book in the papers of Major General Charles Barnett, 3rd Foot Guards, 1786-1803, NAM 1985-12-15, and General-Ordres und Befehle aus dem Hauptquartiere des kommandierenden Generals, Hann. 38 E Nr. 72, f. 115.
2   York to the King 19 August, in Aspinall (ed.), *Later Correspondence*, vol. 2, pp.74-7.

Table 2: The Hanoverian Corps August-September 1793

	Sick	On Command	Other	On Duty
With the Advance Guard				
1st Grenadier Battalion	62	62	9	596
9th Light Dragoon Regiment	22	54	6	236
10th Light Dragoon Regiment	16	33	16	245
GM von dem Bussche				
2nd Cavalry Regiment	44	13	9	243
Leibgarde	54	23	20	221
5th Dragoon Regiment	55	23	21	213
GM von Oeyenhausen				
7th Dragoon Regiment	23	27	1	264
4th Cavalry Regiment	40	41	16	213
1st Leibregiment	47	41	8	221
GM von Hammerstein				
Garde Regiment	140	84	22	1,060
5th Infantry Regiment	124	53	29	1,100
10th infantry Regiment	140	401	19	746
GM von Diepenbroick				
4th Infantry Regiment	127	66	44	1,069
6th Infantry Regiment	93	53	21	1,139
11th Infantry Regiment	163	346	10	787
With the Reserve				
2nd Grenadier Battalion	47	14	6	662
3rd Grenadier Battalion	63	13	16	635
Total				
Cavalry	301	255	97	1,856
Infantry	959	1,092	176	7,794
	1,260	1,347	273	9,650

Sources:
Daily report for the Hanoverian infantry dated 13 August 1793 and report for the cavalry dated 18 September 1793, Hann. 38 E Nr. 144 pp. 19 and 57. The composition of brigades is based on Major [F.B.] von Porbeck, 'Feldzug der Verbündeten in Braband und Flandern 1793. Vorzüglich in Rücksicht des Antheils, welchen die Hessischen Truppen an demselben Hatten', *Neues Militairisches Magazin*, vol. 2 no. 2 pp. 34-5 and *Journal des Regiments Prinz Carl*, HStAM 10 e II/8 pp. 22-4.

Notes:
'Other' is made up of wounded, dead, under arrest, taken prisoner, deserted and wanting to complete.
Porbeck shows all three grenadier battalions as part of the reserve in the order of battle dated 17 August 1793 facing page 35, but includes the 1st battalion with *General-Major* von Fabri's Advance Guard shown on page 34.
The return for the cavalry is dated after the retreat of the army of observation but, as they were not heavily engaged during late August and early September, the figures give a reasonable picture of their strength when the army was divided.

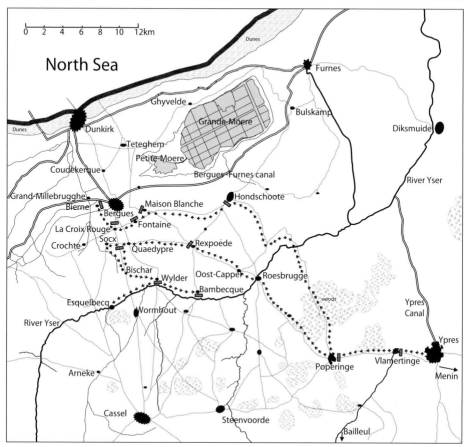

Map 2 Freytag's Advance, 19 to 25 August 1793. (Based on map No 3, Atlas des Cartes et Plans Relatifs au Memoire Historique et Militaire des Campagnes de l'Armée Britannique aux Ordres de Son Altesse Royale Monseigneur le Duc d'York Sur le Continent pendant les Années 1793-1794 et Commencement de 1795, TNA: MPH 1/139 and map 4 in V. Dupuis, *La Campagne de 1793 à l'Armée du Nord et des Ardennes, de Valenciennes à Hondschoote*)

Regiment and the two squadrons of the 10th Light Dragoons at Poperinge to cover Ypres and the left of his line.

The first objective was to take Roesbrugge, where the French had destroyed the stone bridges over the Yser. This attack was planned for daybreak on the 21st, but the main force was unable to arrive on time and the attack was made by a small column under the Hessian *Oberst* von Prüschenck, consisting of the 1st Hanoverian Grenadier Battalion with their two 3-pounder cannon, two companies of the *Freicorps* Grün-Laudon, *Capitain* Ochs's company of Hessian Jägers, and three squadrons of Hanoverian cavalry.[3] After driving back the French troops with ease, the bridge was repaired by laying planks over the stone pillars and Prüschenck

---

3   *Journal des Hauptmanns Ochs vom Feldjägerbataillon*, HStAM 10 e, II/18, p.56.

moved on to attack the French camp at Oost-Cappel. The French troops were again driven off and Fabri, commanding the advance guard, ordered Prüschenck to pursue the fleeing French as far as Rexpoëde. This attack was supported by the other Hessian Jäger company under *Capitain* von Thümmel and a Hanoverian horse artillery battery and was a complete success, forcing the French to give up their position and fall back to Bergues.

The French force at Oost-Cappel and Rexpoëde had consisted of three battalions under *Chef de Brigade* Fromentin, amounting in total to around 1,350 men.[4] They had been routed with a loss of 11 cannon, seven ammunition waggons, 150 killed or wounded including Fromentin mortally wounded, and around 150 prisoners. The allied losses had been insignificant, with no more than 40 killed and wounded according to a report to the Duke of York by one of Freytag's aides-de-camp.[5] The Hessian Jägers had played a major part in storming the French positions and were well rewarded for their efforts. *Capitain* Ochs and *Staabs-Capitain* Flies, who had particularly distinguished themselves, were awarded the order Pour la Vertu Militaire by the Landgrave and the Duke of York gave Ochs a significant cash sum for the capture of the cannon at Oost-Cappel, with smaller sums to the other officers and Jägers. On the other side, the French representatives of the people were indignant at the cowardice shown by their men, particularly the officers, and demanded exemplary punishment for the culprits. After this highly successful day, Freytag made camp at Rexpoëde and Wallmoden at Hondschoote.

On the following day Wallmoden's troops marched towards Bergues and took up the following positions around it:

- *General-Major* von Hammerstein with two battalions of the 11th Infantry Regiment, two squadrons of the 7th Dragoon Regiment, three squadrons of the Hessian Prinz Friedrichs Dragoon Regiment and a half division of artillery at Bierne;
- The Hessian *General-Major* von Schmied with the 2nd Battalion of the 4th Infantry Regiment and two squadrons of the Prinz Friedrichs Dragoon Regiment at La Croix Rouge;
- *General-Major* von dem Bussche with one battalion of the 5th Infantry Regiment and two squadrons of the 4th Cavalry Regiment at Fontaine;
- *General-Major* von Diepenbroick with one battalion of the 5th Infantry Regiment, two battalions of the 10th Infantry Regiment, two squadrons of the 1st Cavalry Regiment and a half division of artillery around Maison Blanche.[6]

---

4   Dupuis, *La Campagne de 1793*, p.228.
5   The French losses are given in Dupuis, *La Campagne de 1793*, p.230 and the allied losses in a letter from York to the King 19 August 1793 in Aspinall (ed.), *Later Correspondence*, vol. 2, pp.74-7, which also gives higher figures for the French casualties.
6   General-Ordres und Befehle aus dem Hauptquartiere des kommandierenden Generals, Hann. 38 E Nr. 72, f. 119 and Hauptmann Schwertfeger, 'Tagebuch-Auszeichnungen des nachherigen Königl. Hannoverschen Generalleutnants A.F. Frhr v.d. Bussche-Ippenburg aus den Revolutionskriegen 1793-1795', *Zeitschrift des Historischen Vereins für Niedersachsen*, Jahrgang 1905, pp.131-2.

Even though he did not have the heavy artillery necessary to reduce the fortress, Wallmoden summoned *Général de Brigade* Carrion, the French commander at Bergues, to surrender. This was rejected by Carrion, who in reality had little to fear as the garrison had ample supplies and Bergues was not even completely cut off by Wallmoden.

At the same time, Freytag marched to Socx, capturing two small cannon which some peasants fired at his men, and established his headquarters in the village. He then moved to the area between Socx and Quaëdypre, while the advance guard under Fabri advanced to Bischar and took up positions at Bambecque and Wylder, from which they observed the Yser and the French camp at Cassel. The advance guard took the French position at Esquelbecq on the 23rd and drove them back to Wormhout, cutting the road from Bergues to Cassel. After defeating French counterattacks, Freytag moved his headquarters to Wylder on the Yser on the 25th. He had now occupied the territory he wanted and he set about fortifying the outposts.

In spite of his early successes, Freytag's position was becoming increasingly precarious, as his troops were spread very thinly, and he was aware of the rapid buildup of the French forces facing him. He began to consider having to fall back to Hondschoote if he was forced from his current positions. He received modest reinforcements from the Duke of York, who sent two squadrons of the British 7th Light Dragoons from Furnes on 29 August and, more usefully, four companies of the Loyal Emigrants, who had marched from Ostend to Furnes on the 19th.[7]

As soon as he heard that Freytag's army had blockaded and summoned Bergues, the Duke of York went to tell him to forget about Bergues for the present, to draw back as many of Wallmoden's troops as possible, and to focus his attention on maintaining communications with his siege army and Ypres.[8] Freytag then reorganised his forces to face the French who were concentrating their troops at Cassel, Steenvoorde and Bailleul and along the canal.

Wallmoden's forces around Bergues were reduced, leaving:

- *General-Major* von Wangenheim with the 10th Infantry Regiment and the 4th Cavalry Regiment around Maison Blanche;
- *General-Major* von Hammerstein with the 11th Infantry Regiment, one battalion of the 4th Infantry Regiment, a company of the Loyal Emigrants, the 7th Dragoon Regiment, and two squadrons of the Prinz Friedrichs Dragoon Regiment holding the line from Croix Rouge to Crochte and from Crochte to Grand-Millebrugghe on the canal to the west of Bergues.

The remainder of the army covered the line from Crochte to Poperinge, a front of around 30 kilometres:

---

7   Journal of Lord William Bentinck (aide-de-camp to the Duke of York), University of Nottingham Manuscripts and Special Collections Pw Ja 611, f. 32 and letter from Ostend dated 21 August 1793, printed in *The Times* on the 24th.
8   York to the King 18 September 1793, in Aspinall (ed.), *Later Correspondence*, vol. 2 pp.97-101.

- The 5th Infantry Regiment, 2nd Cavalry Regiment, and three squadrons of the Prinz Friedrichs Dragoon Regiment from Crochte to Esquelbecq;
- The Austrian Infantry Regiment Brentano, 2nd Battalion of the Garde Regiment, 6th Infantry Regiment, and the 2nd and 3rd Grenadier Battalions from Esquelbecq to the position in front of the Yser;
- The advance guard under *General-Major* Fabri, consisting of the 1st Grenadier Battalion, two companies of the *Freicorps* Grün-Laudon, three companies of the Loyal Emigrants, the Blankenstein Hussars, 9th Light Dragoon Regiment, and British 6th Dragoons at Wormhout;
- *Oberst* von Prüschenck with the Hessian Jägers, two companies of Grün-Laudon and one squadron of the 5th Dragoon Regiment at Herzeele;
- Houtkerque and Watou were each held by two companies of Grün-Laudon and a detachment of Blankenstein Hussars;
- Oberst von Linsingen was at Poperinge with the 1st Battalion of the Garde-Regiment, the 1st Battalion of the 4th Infantry Regiment and the 10th Light Dragoon Regiment;
- Hondschoote was occupied by a detachment of infantry and cavalry under *Major* von Hugo.[9]

Captain Le Marchant, Harcourt's major of brigade, wrote on 26 August that the British cavalry were camped at Wylder, where they were attempting to clear the countryside of timber and hedges to make it more suitable for cavalry operations.[10] On 5 September, Freytag launched an attack on the village of Arnèke to the north-west of Cassel, from which the French had been troubling his position at Wormhout for several days. According to d'Arnaudin, one of a number of French émigrés who were attached to the Duke of York's headquarters, the intention was to carry out a reconnaissance in force of the area behind the enemy camp at Cassel.[11] The attack was to be made in two columns, with Diepenbroick marching against Arnèke from Esquelbecq with the 3rd Grenadier Battalion, the 2nd Battalion of the 5th Infantry Regiment, a squadron of the Prinz Friedrichs Dragoon Regiment, and a detachment of the Blankenstein Hussars, while Fabri moved with the 1st Grenadier Battalion and the other light troops from Wormhout to attack the enemy's right flank. The attack was badly thought out and Fabri struggled in the difficult terrain against greater French numbers than expected. Although Arnèke was captured, the French were able to get away, sustaining losses of about 200 men. The allies also lost around 200 men, including Fabri who was badly wounded. *Lieutenant* von Ompteda was also wounded in the attack and wrote to his brother while he was convalescing in Bruges, describing the fighting around the end of August, in which the troops had

---

9   Sichart, *Geschichte*, vol.4, pp.258-9. Sichart wrongly describes the British 6th Dragoons as light dragoons.

10 D. Le Marchant (ed.), *Memoirs of the Late Major General Le Marchant 1766-1812* (Staplehurst, Spellmount, 1997), pp.20-1.

11 In Dupuis, *La Campagne de 1793,* p.344. This was also Houchard's belief, as stated in his letter to Bouchotte, the Minister of War, on 5 September 1793 in E. Charavay (ed.), *Correspondance Général de Carnot* (Paris: Imprimerie Nationale, 1897), vol. III, pp.92-3.

to cut their way through the thick hedges, help each other hand in hand through the deep ditches and where it was impossible to maintain formation.[12] This was the first setback that Freytag's forces had suffered and he sent a request for support from the Duke of York.

In the meantime, Houchard had been concentrating his troops and taking the steps necessary to restore order and discipline in his army. He had been under pressure from the Minister of War and the Committee of Public Safety to relieve Dunkirk and destroy the Duke of York's army, although they made it clear that it was up to Houchard to decide how this should be achieved.[13] Houchard was an experienced, brave and loyal soldier, but he lacked the ability to command an army, particularly in the political environment of the Terror. He was aware of his short-comings and lacked confidence in his own ability. He was also disheartened by delays in the arrival of the promised reinforcements and even more by the news of the execution of Custine, his former chief, which led him to fear the same fate.[14] In practice, he relied completely on his two most senior staff officers, Berthelmy and Gay de Vernon, to draw up plans and direct operations and was under constant scrutiny by the Representatives of the People Delbrel and Levasseur, who were with his army and reported on his every move.

A council of war, including Delbrel and Levasseur, was held on 4 September and the attack on the allies was set for the 6th. After considering a direct attack on the Duke of York's siege army, it had been decided to attack Freytag's positions. It was considered that the rough terrain, intersected by numerous hedges, ditches, and streams, would favour the French troops and would allow them to rely on their courage and initiative, as they were not sufficiently trained for complex manoeu-vres.[15] After receiving his reinforcements, Houchard had a total of around 200,000 effectives, allowing him to assemble a strike force which would be sufficient to over-whelm Freytag's weak and widely dispersed army.[16]

The orders were issued on 4 and 5 September and preparations were made for the attack to commence on the morning on the 6th. Based on documents in the French archives, Dupuis shows the following dispositions and strengths of the various columns, which amounted in total to 45,800 men:

- The main column under *Général de Division* Jourdan, who had around 13,000 men assembled to the north of Cassel, on either side of the Hardifort road, with the objective of taking Houtkerque and Herzeele. He also had a pontoon train for the passage of the Yser;

---

12 Ompteda to his brother dated 16 October 1793 in Ompteda, 'Hannoversche leichte Grenadiere', pp.348-51.
13 Committee of Public Safety to Houchard 5 September in Charavay (ed.), *Correspondance*, vol. III pp.86-7.
14 The effect of these events on Houchard is described by Gay de Vernon in Baron Gay de Vernon, *Mémoire sur les Opérations Militaires des Généraux en Chef Custine et Houchard pendant les Années 1792 et 1793* (Paris: Librairie de Firmin Didot Frères, 1844), pp.246 and 249-50.
15 Baron Gay de Vernon, *Mémoire*, pp.252-3.
16 Dupuis, *La Campagne de 1793*, p.289.

- The advance guard under *Général de Brigade* de Hédouville, with 7,400 men was to move from Steenvoorde to take the positions at Poperinge and then Roesbrugge;
- A detachment of 4,400 men under *Lieutenant Colonel* Vandamme was assembled at Godewaersvelde with orders to take the position at Reningelst and then move against Poperinge to support Hédouville;
- *Général de Brigade Dumesny* had 9,000 men at Bailleul, who were to follow Vandamme's column, try to capture the citadel at Ypres and prevent the Dutch from sending help to Freytag from Menin;
- *Général de Division* Landrin's 6,000 men assembled at Mont Cassel on the Hardifort side were to march against Wormhout and tie down Wallmoden;

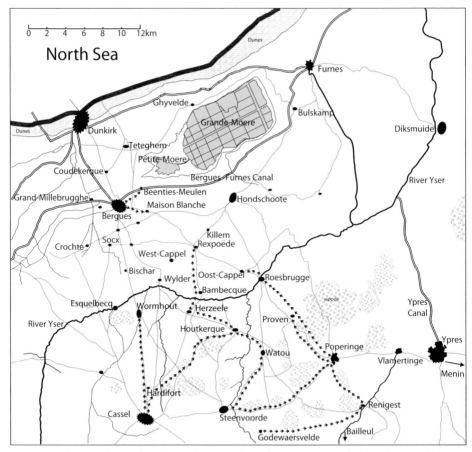

Map 3 The French Attack, 6 September 1793. (Based on map No 3, Atlas des Cartes et Plans Relatifs au Memoire Historique et Militaire des Campagnes de l'Armée Britannique aux Ordres de Son Altesse Royale Monseigneur le Duc d'York Sur le Continent pendant les Années 1793-1794 et Commencement de 1795, TNA: MPH 1/139)

- *Général de Brigade* Leclaire was to take his 6,000 men from Bergues to West-Cappel and Oost-Cappel, while keeping a strong force on his right on the Wormhout side.[17]

Houchard also requested the commander at Dunkirk to make a sortie around midday on the 6th to tie down the siege army. In spite of the dispersal of Houchard's troops over this wide front and communications between the columns being made difficult by the rough country, the French numerical superiority gave them every chance of success against Freytag's fragile cordon, which could expect no support from the Duke's army or the Dutch.

The French attack on the allied left met little resistance, as Hédouville and Vandamme had almost 12,000 men between them, whilst their opponents were no more than 1,000-1,500.[18] Vandamme drove the Hanoverians at Reningelst back into Ypres and proceeded to Proven, north-west of Poperinge, where he set up camp for the night. Hédouville also drove the allies at Poperinge back, some towards Ypres and some to Roesbrugge. He then moved on to take Roesbrugge, crossed the Yser and reached Oost-Cappel at about 9:00 p.m. Meanwhile, Dumesny remained inactive at Bailleul throughout the day, instead of following Vandamme to Ypres as planned, apparently unwilling to act on verbal orders passed on by Vandamme.[19]

Hédouville had detached a brigade under *Général de Brigade* Colaud, which moved through Watou to Houtkerque, where they pushed back the defenders and met Jourdan's advancing column. Houchard was with this column and intended to move through Roesbrugge to attack Hondschoote, but he was persuaded that this was too risky and he sent Jourdan to take Herzeele instead.

Herzeele was held by Prüschenck with around 500 men, consisting of two companies of the Hessian Jägers, two companies of the *Freicorps* Grün-Laudon and a squadron of the 5th Hanoverian Dragoon Regiment. True to character, Prüschenck attacked the head of Jourdan's advancing column and captured a cannon. He then put up a spirited defence of the village, taking advantage of the cover offered by the woods to the south-east. However, he could not stand against the overwhelming strength of the French, who were led forward by Jourdan, sword in hand, and was forced to retreat to Bambecque with heavy losses being suffered by Grün-Laudon.

After this success Houchard decided to attack Bambecque, which was held by *General-Major* von Dachenhausen with one battalion of the 6th Infantry Regiment, two squadrons of the 2nd Cavalry Regiment, and the remnants of Prüschenck's troops from Herzeele. This was to prove more of a challenge for the French, as they had to get across the Yser, where the bridge was defended by earthworks with cannon and a company of the 6th Regiment.[20] The French attack was delayed by a terrible storm and they were running short of ammunition, but a battalion of the 36th Line Infantry crossed a ford below Bambecque and attacked the flank of the defenders,

17 Dupuis, *La Campagne de 1793*, pp.420-9.
18 Ditfurth, *Die Hessen*, vol.1, p.110.
19 Baron Gay de Vernon, *Mémoire*, pp.263-4.
20 Two 3-pounders according to Scharnhorst, in Kunisch et al, *Gerhard von Scharnhorst*, pp.298-303.

while Houchard's chief of staff *Général de Brigade* Berthelmy led a bayonet charge against their front, and the bridge and village were taken. Dachenhausen retreated towards Rexpoëde and the other troops in this part of the line united at Wylder. The Hessian Jägers, who had previously escaped significant loss, suffered more than 40 killed and wounded in these actions, including Ochs and Prüschenck, who received four bullet wounds.

Houchard had now established himself on the left bank of the Yser, but it was 6:00 p.m., the troops were worn out after 13 hours of marching and fighting, and the roads were terrible. He wanted to stop for the day, satisfied with the success his troops had achieved, but he was overruled by the representatives of the people, who insisted that the army must continue its forward movement, so Houchard had no choice but to order the troops to march on to Rexpoëde.[21] As night came on and more rain fell, three of Jourdan's battalions and a regiment of cavalry occupied the village. Dachenhausen's infantry were dispersed in the woods and orchards around Rexpoëde and his cavalry was stationed behind a battery on the road to Killem and Hondschoote.

In the meantime, Landrin had followed his instructions to make a series of feints to tie down Wallmoden's forces at Wormhout. He had attacked the posts at Esquelbecq, Wormhout, and la Kruystraete, meeting strong resistance all along the front. A French column took the bridge over the Yser at Saint-Bonaventure to the west of Esquelbecq, but was driven back by a Hanoverian force commanded by Diepenbroick, consisting of the 2nd Grenadier Battalion, two companies of the 3rd Grenadier Battalion, the 5th Infantry Regiment, a squadron of the 1st Cavalry Regiment, and detachments of Hessian and British cavalry, supported by two heavy guns. The terrain in this area was unsuitable for cavalry to operate, so parts of the Hanoverian, Hessian, and British cavalry volunteered to fight on foot.[22] Le Marchant recorded that the French pushed so hard that the British 6th Dragoons were dismounted to act as infantry.[23] After failing to make any real progress, Landrin took up a position south of Wormhout, ready to renew his attack the following day.

Leclaire, having heard nothing by midday, began to deploy his forces on the glacis at Bergues. His right was covered by the flooded country and he moved forward against the allied fortified position at Beenties-Meulen (Benkies Mille) next to the Bergues-Furnes canal on his left and Maison Blanche on his right, but the allies stood firm and he faced considerable artillery fire. Still he heard nothing from the direction of Roesbrugge and Wormhout, although he could hear the sound of fighting from Dunkirk at 3:00 p.m. as the garrison launched a sortie supported by the guns on the ramparts and gunboats. Around 6,000 men attacked the Duke of York's positions, focusing mainly on his right. After a hard fight they were driven back with heavy casualties on both sides, including Colonel Moncrief, the British Chief Engineer and Quarter Master General, who was mortally wounded. At around 5:00 p.m. Leclaire was attacked by an enemy column from Socx and he retreated to Bergues.

---

21 Baron Gay de Vernon, *Mémoire*, pp.258-9. Houchard confirms this in his own account of the battle dated 11 September 1793, in Charavay (ed.), *Correspondance*, vol. III, pp.128-132.
22 Sichart, *Geschichte*, vol. 4, pp.287-8.
23 Le Marchant (ed.), *Memoirs*, p.23.

Freytag's position in the evening of the 6th was extremely serious. His right wing held firm, but the collapse of his left and the French possession of Bambecque and Oost-Cappel left him in danger of being cut off from Furnes and vulnerable to an overwhelming attack the following day. He therefore issued orders at 8:00 p.m. for his tired and battered army to fall back to Hondschoote. The troops around Bergues would go by way of Maison Blanche, while the rest of the army would retreat in two columns through Rexpoëde, which he still believed to be in allied hands, as the officers sent by Dachenhausen to warn Freytag that it was in fact occupied by the French had failed to reach him. Freytag went with the cavalry, artillery and the 2nd Battalion of the Garde-Regiment in the right hand column on the main road from Wylder to Rexpoëde, while Bussche took most of the infantry in the left column through West-Cappel.

Freytag was at the head of his column with his aides de camp and Prince Adolphus, *General-Major* von Trew who commanded the artillery, and a small escort of 24 dragoons and 100 men of the Garde Regiment.[24] As they entered Rexpoëde, they were taken by surprise and attacked by a squadron of French cavalry, who drove off the escort and both Freytag and Adolphus were wounded and captured. Adolphus managed to escape in the confusion with the assistance of his aide-de-camp *Lieutenant* von Wangenheim, who was severely wounded, but Freytag was taken into the village. The artillery at the front of the column blocked the road, preventing the cavalry from advancing and the battalion of the Garde-Regiment was driven back by heavy fire from the village.

Oberst von Spörken, the Hanoverian Adjutant General, and *Oberst-Lieutenant* Kunze, the Quarter Master General, went to find Wallmoden and informed him what had happened. As the main road was completely blocked, Wallmoden went to Bussche and ordered him to attack Rexpoëde with the 2nd Grenadier Battalion, a squadron of the 7th Dragoon Regiment, two companies of the Brentano Regiment, some men from the *Freicorps* Grün-Laudon, and two cannon. Bussche launched his attack on the north-west road into Rexpoëde at midnight in the rain and routed the French, who were taken by surprise by this attack on their flank. Jourdan tried in vain to rally his men and was ordered by Houchard to abandon Rexpoëde and fall back with his division to Bambecque.

Wallmoden's prompt action led to the rescue of Freytag, but the latter was suffering from the effects of his head wound and was taken to Furnes, handing over the command to Wallmoden. The allied forces continued their march to Hondschoote, where they began to arrive early the next morning, but the troops under Diepenbroick and Hammerstein, who were marching from Esquelbecq, Crochte, and Bierne, only reached Hondschoote at around noon and during the afternoon respectively.

Jourdan's troops were in a very poor state on the morning of the 7th, being without bread or eau-de-vie and almost out of ammunition, so they fell back to Herzeele to recover.[25] Houchard stayed with this division and did nothing to direct

---

24 Scharnhorst in a letter to his wife after 8 September in Kunisch at al, *Gerhard von Scharnhorst*, pp.257-60.
25 Baron Gay de Vernon, *Mémoire*, p.262.

The Relief of His Royal Highness Prince Adolphus and Field Marshall Freytag, at the Village of Rexpoede near Dunkirk on the 6th of Septr. 1793, engraving after M. Brown. (Anne S.K. Brown Military Collection, Brown University Library)

the operations of the other columns on that day. The French generals in command of the other divisions were unaware of the events of the previous night and, having received no new orders from Houchard, they continued their movements from the previous day.

Leclaire set off at about 10:00 a.m. and, finding that the camp at Maison Blanche had been abandoned by the retreating allies, continued his march and captured a convoy including many wounded and some women. He sent these back to Bergues, but had great difficulty in maintaining order and preventing pillage. His men also fired on the Hanoverians who were falling back from Esquelbecq, Crochte, and Bierne towards Hondschoote and then came upon Hédouville's column, which his advance guard almost opened fire on by mistake. The latter had left Oost-Cappel at 8:00 a.m. and had arrived too late to attack Wallmoden's rear guard under Erskine, which was retreating slowly along the road from Bambecque to Hondschoote via Rexpoëde. As night fell, Hédouville set up camp at Rexpoëde and Leclaire at Maison Blanche and along the canal.

Vandamme left Proven at 5:00 a.m. and advanced through Roesbrugge to Rexpoëde. Then, after a short break to restore order, he moved on to West-Cappel, where he captured a Hanoverian convoy and took some prisoners. He continued his advance and at around 4:00 p.m. came upon Diepenbroick's force, consisting of the 2nd and 3rd Grenadier Battalions and the 5th and 10th Infantry Regiments, holding the road from Killem into Hondschoote. Vandamme deployed his men out of range of the Hanoverian redoubts and there followed a fierce fire-fight, which lasted three hours. Diepenbroick then sent two battalions of grenadiers and the 2nd Battalion of the 10th Regiment forward in a bayonet charge, which pushed Vandamme back to Killem with the loss of three cannon, at which point Vandamme gave up his attack and stayed there for the night.

At the same time Landrin occupied Wormhout and Esquelbecq, which the allies had abandoned; Dumesny stayed put at Bailleul; and the Dunkirk garrison made another sortie in the afternoon, as the Duke of York fell back from his most advanced posts.

Wallmoden's position in front of the village of Hondschoote had his right resting on the Bergues to Furnes canal and his left extending to the gardens on the south of Leysele, with posts in the neighbouring villages, and had numerous ditches, hedges, and small farmsteads in front of his line. He set up abbattis, barricades, and entrenchments and constructed redoubts on the mounds of the windmills to his front and left and a small redoubt covering the road along the Canal on his right. The strongest of these redoubts was on the central mound covering the paved road from Killem, which was the only really practicable road after the recent heavy rain. He positioned a battery of eight cannon and four howitzers there and the redoubts on the left and right had six and two cannon respectively.[26] However, the broken terrain suited the French style of fighting and made it impossible for Wallmoden to use his cavalry, who were left in the rear. His total force was by now reduced to 13,000 men, including 9,000 infantry, and they were tired and short of

---

26 Baron Gay de Vernon, *Mémoire*, p.265.

ammunition.[27] Wallmoden was unwilling to defend this position seriously, as he feared that his communications with Furnes would be cut. He was persuaded to do so by the Austrian *General-Major* Werneck and the Marquis de Bouillé, who were sent by the Duke of York on the afternoon of the 7th to stress the danger to the siege army, whose left flank had to be covered while it withdrew.[28] Wallmoden sent the baggage back to Furnes under escort of the Prinz Friedrichs Dragoon Regiment, but the column was attacked by the French and 24 men were captured.

Wallmoden prepared his troops for the anticipated French attack and distributed the reserve ammunition from Furnes, which arrived on the morning of the 8th. He had also been reinforced by the two battalions of the Hesse Cassel Regiment Erb-Prinz under *General-Major* von Cochenhausen, who had been sent by the Duke, but had been forced to march by the road through Furnes because of the flooded countryside. Diepenbroick on the left was reinforced by a battalion of the 6th Infantry Regiment, the 1st Battalion of the 11th Regiment, and the 2nd Battalion of the Hesse Cassel Regiment Erb-Prinz with some of the Hanoverian heavy and horse artillery. The right was held by Hammerstein with the 2nd Battalion of the Garde-Regiment, 1st Grenadier Battalion, the 2nd Battalion of the 4th Regiment, the 2nd Battalion of the 11th Regiment and a battalion of the 6th Regiment. Cochenhausen was also on this wing with the rest of the Hessian troops and the Austrian Regiment Brentano.

Houchard drew up his plan for the attack to take place on the morning of the 8th as follows:

- Jourdan was to move against Hondschoote, with Colaud's brigade on his right and supported by Vandamme;
- Hédouville's column, less Colaud's brigade, was to move towards Bergues and join the battle if he did not meet the enemy there;
- Dumesny was to carry out the mission he should have completed on the 6th, to try to take Ypres and protect the right flank of the army from any movement by the Dutch;
- Landrin was sent to Dunkirk to reinforce the garrison and make sorties to prevent the Duke of York from sending help to Wallmoden;
- Leclaire was to complete his mission from the 6th and was advised by Houchard to make great use of the bayonet, as he himself intended to do, believing this was the only way to succeed and reduce casualties.[29]

This plan allocated almost half of his troops to secondary missions and left little more than 20,000 men available for the key objective of defeating Wallmoden's army and preventing its retreat to Furnes.[30]

---

27 Ditfurth, *Die Hessen*, vol. 1, p.114
28 Dupuis, *Campagne de 1793*, pp.458-9.
29 T.F.G. Leclaire, *Mémoires et Correspondance du Général Leclaire 1793* (Paris: Librairie Militaire R. Chapelot et Ce, 1904), pp.91-2.
30 Dupuis, *Campagne de 1793*, p.462 states 22,000, Baron Gay de Vernon, p.266, gives the total as under 21,000.

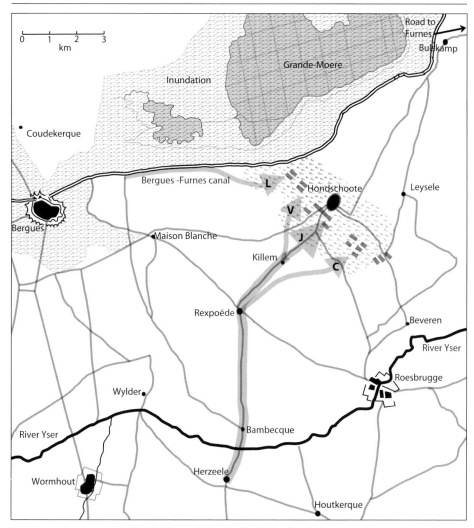

Map 4 The Attack on Hondschoote, 8 September 1793. The French columns are from left to right: L (Leclaire), V (Vandamme), J (Jourdan) and C (Colaud). (Based on map 14 in Comte P.H. de Grimoard and Général Servan, *Tableau historique de la guerre de la révolution de France, depuis son commencement en 1792, jusqu'à la fin de 1794*, Vol. III)

Vandamme set off along the road from Killem at 4:00 a.m. and sent his skirmishers towards Hondschoote, where they took cover behind the hedges on the west of the road. Jourdan's division had started their march at around 3:00 a.m. and the head of the column arrived at the cross roads to the south-west of Hondschoote, at about 7:00 a.m. Houchard was with this column and was surprised at finding no sign of the enemy. He halted and asked some peasants if Hondschoote was occupied by the enemy, but their reply was vague, suggesting that the allies had only left about 5,000 men and 15 cannon there. As this was not what he had expected, he sent Gay de Vernon to carry out a reconnaissance. Wallmoden had not thought it necessary to send advance posts forward, so Gay de Vernon was able to get close enough to see the allied dispositions, count the cannon in the various batteries and to identify the rough terrain on the allied left and the inundation on the right.

It was decided to make the main attack on the allied centre, even though it was covered by the battery on the windmill mound. Vandamme's skirmishers had already opened fire to the west of the Killem road, and this line was extended to their right by Jourdan's men. At this moment, the allied battery opened fire on Jourdan's main body, which was resting in column on the Killem road and Jourdan set up a battery of 10 cannon to return fire. The French troops formed up in attack columns on either side of the road, but Houchard would not launch the attack until Colaud's and Leclaire's troops were in position, so the skirmishing and artillery fire continued for two hours. The French battalions grew tired of waiting for the order to attack and began to disperse to act as skirmishers, taking cover and firing on the allied infantry, who remained drawn up in line just in front of the village and firing by platoon with little effect.

Wallmoden was concerned by the proximity of the French skirmishers and ordered Cochenhausen to drive them off with the first battalion of the Regiment Erb-Prinz and two companies of Brentano. This attack was successful at first, until the allied troops were stopped by a deep ditch topped by a hedge, from behind which the French were able to fire on Cochenhausen's men. At the same time French cavalry attacked the right flank of the detachment from Brentano and captured *Oberst* von Wolf and 100 men. The troops were forced to fall back to reorganise and replenish their ammunition. Another forward movement by Jourdan's men was halted when Cochenhausen charged again with his battalion of Erb-Prinz, this time supported by four companies of Brentano, and succeeded in recovering one of the battalion guns, which had been left behind in the retreat following the first attack. The allied troops suffered heavy losses during these attacks and Cochenhausen had both legs smashed by grapeshot. He was captured when the French occupied Hondschoote and died of his wounds two days later. The Duke of York's Hanoverian aide-de-camp *Hauptmann* von Marschalck was also killed while encouraging the men forward.

It was now around 10:00 a.m. and Houchard's situation was becoming critical. The infantry in the centre were losing ground and the artillery was in danger of being captured, but any attempt to pull it back risked causing the inexperienced troops to rout. Leclaire was only just arriving to attack the allied right, after being delayed in his march along the road beside the canal by the flooding and the vehicles abandoned by the allies in their retreat. Colaud had not been able to make any progress against Wallmoden's left and Houchard thought the battle was lost. According to Representative Delbrel, Houchard wanted to retreat and had to be persuaded by Delbrel, Levasseur, and by Jourdan to continue the fight. Gay de Vernon also confirms that Houchard thought the battle lost, but does not mention this intervention.[31]

---

31 Delbrel's account is in F.A. Aulard, 'Extraits des Notes Historiques du Conventionnel Delbrel', *Bulletin du Comité des Travaux Historiques et Scientifiques*, 1892 No. 2, p.274. Gay de Vernon's account is in Baron Gay de Vernon, *Mémoire*, p.268.

Houchard's plan for the next phase of the battle was for Jourdan to send forward three battalions, which had not yet been in action, to halt Cochenhausen's attack and to rally the rest of his division. At the same time, Houchard and Levasseur were to join Colaud's column on the French right and sound the charge as the signal to launch the general assault, which Jourdan would then join. An officer was also sent to Vandamme and Leclaire to tell them to move forward against the allied right in support of the attack.

Jourdan and Delbrel had managed to rally their troops as best they could and had succeeded in gaining a little ground, when the allies launched a third counterattack. This time the 2nd Battalion of the Regiment Erb-Prinz with 40 Hanoverian grenadiers advanced along the Killem road and the whole Hanoverian line moved forward. Once again the French fell back and Jourdan and Delbrel had to act quickly to prevent a rout. Jourdan proposed to bring forward a fresh battalion, which had been in reserve guarding the standards left by the battalions acting as skirmishers, and to send his cavalry to halt the fleeing troops and bring them back to the battle. However, he felt that his hands were tied by Houchard's order not to move forward until Colaud's troops on his right had begun their attack. Delbrel took the responsibility for the key decision, overruled Houchard and ordered Jourdan to attack at once. Delbrel went to send the cavalry to round up the fleeing troops and bring forward the reserve battalion, but when he returned a little before midday, he found that Jourdan had been wounded and forced to leave the field.[32]

The signal to attack was given from the right and the French columns moved forward in a series of bayonet attacks on the allied positions. Leclaire described his attack on the allied entrenchments supported by his artillery, with his men up to their knees in water, the fierce hand to hand fighting and terrible slaughter of the enemy. After driving off some allied cavalry, he pushed on and captured a body of 311 Hanoverians, who were sent back to Bergues.[33] While Leclaire was pushing back the allied right, Houchard led the 17th Cavalry Regiment forward to support Colaud, who was meeting stiff resistance on their left, and the infantry, spurred on by this movement and the encouragement of Levasseur, attacked the allied entrenchments. At the same time, Delbrel led forward Jourdan's column. *Chef de Bataillon* Lahure recorded that the attacks were preceded by swarms of skirmishers and that all the battalions became mixed up together, only reforming in the evening, after Hondschoote had been captured.[34]

Wallmoden ordered his troops to retreat at around noon as his men were exhausted and running out of ammunition and he feared that his line of retreat to Furnes would be cut by Colaud's advancing column. He had held on as long as he could to buy time for the siege army and now fell back in two columns to his chosen position at Bulskamp, about five kilometres south-west of Furnes. The French were too tired and disorganised to mount an immediate pursuit and were delayed by the allied rear guard. The 2nd Battalion of Regiment Erb-Prinz covered the road from

---

32 This is Delbrel's account, in in Aulard, 'Extraits des Notes Historiques', pp.275-6.
33 T.F.G. Leclaire, *Mémoires*, pp.94-5.
34 Baron P. Lahure, *Souvenirs de la Vie Militaire du Lieutenant-Général Baron L.-J. Lahure 1787-1815* (Paris: A. Lahure, 1895), pp.59-60.

Killem into Hondschoote until the allied troops on the right wing had passed and they were forced back by Vandamme's column with its supporting artillery. The road to the canal was held by *Capitain* von Lösecke with two companies of the 6th Infantry Regiment and a cannon. Scharnhorst also described his efforts to hold back the French advance with two 6-pounders, together with 150 men from the Garde Regiment under *Capitain* von Löw and a part of *Capitain* Hugo's company of the 10th Infantry Regiment.[35]

Hédouville's 5,000 men finally reached the battlefield after his pointless march to Bergues. Houchard wanted these fresh troops to pursue Wallmoden, but Hédouville found the bridge that he was to cross had been destroyed and stopped his march, as it was growing late. Houchard also declined to try to cross the Grande-Moëre with a force of cavalry and light infantry under Vandamme to attack the Duke of York, who was believed to be retreating to Furnes, and instead merely sent a weak reconnaissance. The Duke, faced by sorties from the garrison at Dunkirk and learning that Wallmoden had retreated from Hondschoote, ordered the baggage to retire to Furnes. At 8:00 p.m. he ordered his army to retreat and at midnight they started to fall back, arriving at Furnes the following morning.

Once again Dumesny showed a lack of energy. He advanced so slowly that he only reached Ypres at the end of the day, set up three batteries during the night and began his bombardment on the morning of the 9th. Even then, he took fright when a company of the Austrian Infantry Regiment Stuart with three guns from the garrison moved against his left flank and some Dutch troops from Menin appeared on his right. He fell back to Bailleul during the night, having achieved nothing. Similarly, Landrin failed to act decisively. He refused Leclaire's proposal to march with him to attack Hondschoote from the left and instead stuck to his orders to march to Dunkirk, where he arrived on the morning of the 9th.[36]

The much-criticised Hanoverian infantry had performed extremely well, but their losses had been very heavy. Sichart summarises the Hanoverian casualties over the four days from 5 to 8 September as 15 officers and 211 men killed, 52 officers and 1,092 men wounded and 28 officers and 933 men missing or captured, a total of 2,331. They had also lost two flags and six cannon. The 5th Infantry Regiment suffered the most, having lost 507 officers and men, including 375 prisoners, out of the 898 who had been fit for service on 3 September, together with two flags and two battalion guns.[37] Murray wrote in a private letter to Dundas 'The Hanoverians who really behaved with the greatest Gallantry are now entirely dispirited & by the confession of their own officers can be no longer depended upon.'[38] The Hessian Regiment Erb-Prinz had also suffered heavily, losing 13 officers, including Cochenhausen, and

---

35 Scharnhorst to his wife after 8 September 1793 in Kunisch et al, *Gerhard von Scharnhorst*, pp.257-60.

36 Leclaire, *Mémoires*, pp.92-3.

37 Sichart, *Geschichte*, vol. 4, pp.281-4 and daily report dated 3 September 1793, Hann. 38 E Nr. 144, f. 15

38 Murray to Dundas 9 September 1793, TNA: WO 1/167, pp.83-4.

152 men from the total of 1,057 fit for duty on 6 September.[39] The total allied losses over the three days were around 2,500 men.

Berthelmy sent a report to the Minister of War at the end of the day, in which he described the country there as 'abominable for war', with visibility no more than four paces. The battle had been long and very hot and had been finished, like those of the preceding days, with the bayonet, which he considered the infallible method of the *sans-culottes*.[40] French casualties are given by Gay de Vernon as 1,800 killed and wounded.[41]

Houchard had succeeded in raising the siege of Dunkirk and had inflicted heavy casualties on the allied forces, but he had not managed to destroy them, and the immediate relief amongst his political chiefs soon gave way to recriminations. His failure to follow up on his victory cost him his life; he was arrested on 20 September and executed on 17 November.

---

39 Ditfurth, *Die Hessen*, vol. 1, pp.120-1 and report dated 6 September 1793, HstAM 4h Nr 3358, f. 46.
40 Berthelmy to Bouchotte 8 September 1793 in Charavay (ed.), *Correspondance*, vol. III, p.123.
41 Baron Gay de Vernon, *Mémoire*, p.273

4

More Troops, but for What?

The Duke of York had to abandon his siege guns and much of his baggage when he was forced to raise the siege of Dunkirk after the defeat of Freytag's army of observation. The whole front appeared to be in danger of collapse when Menin was taken by the French, although it was soon recaptured, Ypres was threatened and there were fears that the allied communications through Nieuport (Nieuwpoort) and Ostend would be cut. In a panic, the British government sent eight regiments of infantry, which had been assembled for Sir Charles Grey's expedition to the West Indies, to protect Ostend. Luckily for the allies, the French did not follow up effectively on their victory at Hondschoote: the situation was soon stabilised and Grey's infantry was recalled.

Meanwhile, Coburg's army had also retreated and abandoned the siege of Maubeuge after his defeat at Wattignies on 15 to 16 October. The promising situation of the allied armies at the end of July had been frittered away and the majority of the troops went into winter quarters. The French continued to harass the allied forward positions throughout the winter, but there were no more major engagements in 1793.

The political negotiations to secure more troops, which had been making slow progress, were given added impetus by the problems in the Low Countries and the news that Toulon was in the hands of Admiral Hood's fleet. Troops were required urgently to shore up the front in the Low Countries, but even more for the expeditions being planned for the coast of France and the West Indies. As usual, the government tried to juggle the resources available, hoping to move all of these plans forward at once.

At the end of August, Yarmouth had sent Grenville the preliminary treaty that he had agreed with the Landgrave of Hesse Cassel for 4,000 additional troops on the same basis as the previous treaty. He noted that he had discovered that these men were already contracted to the King of Prussia until the end of the campaign, even though the Landgrave had tried to conceal this from the British. However, the Prussians had agreed to release them, provided that the Landgrave did not withdraw any part of his contingent currently serving with the Empire's forces, as he had previously attempted to do, and they wanted a secret article to this effect to be included in the treaty. Yarmouth reported that the muster was to begin on 25 August and the troops were to be ready to march the following week.[1] In spite of

---

1 Yarmouth to Grenville 23 August 1793 and enclosures, TNA: FO 29/1. The text of the treaty is in Debrett (ed.), *A Collection of State Papers*, Vol. 1, pp.12-13.

this timetable, he only sent instructions to Major Gunn on 1 September to proceed 'with all possible Expedition' to muster the 4,000 Hesse Cassel troops and to make arrangements for them to be supplied with new clothing and the other equipment necessary for an autumn campaign and to be sent down the Rhine.[2] Gunn replied that he would muster the infantry first, as the dragoons were not yet ready and they would have to follow later. He asked Yarmouth to write to the Duke of York to send a commissary to meet the troops at Cologne.[3]

Yarmouth also forwarded a letter he had received from the Landgrave to Grenville, in which the British request for 4,000 Hessian troops to be allowed to serve outside Europe was rejected. As an alternative, the Landgrave suggested that he could raise a body of foreigners for British service overseas. Yarmouth did not believe that this was the final word on the matter, but he would let it rest at present as he did not want to complicate the discussions that were underway to move the troops down the Rhine and on to Flanders. Yarmouth went on to suggest that the Landgrave's offer to raise this body of foreigners really meant recruiting French deserters and that, although he believed that it would be easy to collect such a 'Body of Vagabonds', they would probably disappear again once the bounty had been paid. He also expected that the Landgrave would try to get them at the lowest possible price and concluded that they would be of little value to Britain.[4]

At the same time as the arrangements for the Hesse Cassel contingent were being settled, Yarmouth continued his efforts to find other German auxiliaries. His brother went to Carlsruhe to follow up the possibility of hiring troops from Baden and, on his return, Yarmouth informed Grenville that the men were 'as fine troops as ever were seen, and were ready to take the field at an hour's notice'. A state of the troops which the Margrave was proposing to provide to Britain showed three battalions of infantry, light troops, cavalry, and artillery, amounting to 3,063 men in total. They had already been offered to Austria and, although this had been declined by General Wurmser, the Margrave was still waiting for formal confirmation from the Austrian court. The Margrave had requested that the Baden troops be left in Germany, where they could protect Baden's own territory. He suggested that Austria could provide an equivalent number of men for service in the Low Countries, but had been informed that this was not acceptable to the British.[5]

Grenville also authorised Yarmouth to negotiate for 3,000 men, who were offered by the Landgrave of Hesse Darmstadt on the same terms as those agreed with Hesse Cassel, provided that the Landgrave had not already concluded an agreement with the Austrians. He stressed that 'the most immediate measures should be taken for the March of these Troops'.[6] He also informed Yarmouth that the King had agreed to the proposal to take the three battalions of Baden troops into British pay and confirmed that the proposed restriction on their use was unacceptable, although the government would agree to the troops not serving in Britain or Ireland. He gave

2   Yarmouth to Gunn 1 September 1793, TNA: FO 29/2.
3   Gunn to Yarmouth 2 September 1793, TNA: FO 29/2.
4   Yarmouth to Grenville 5 September 1793 and enclosures, TNA: FO 29/2.
5   Yarmouth o Grenville 13 August 1793, TNA: FO 29/1.
6   Grenville to Yarmouth 16 August 1793, TNA FO 29/1.

full powers to Yarmouth to conclude the treaty and asked him to give directions to hold the muster and for them to march to join the Duke of York's army.[7] However, the Margrave was not satisfied with the British proposal and his minister, Baron von Edelsheim, made it clear that the he was not prepared to send the three battalions to the Low Countries, but would agree to send a regiment of five companies.[8]

Grenville continued to press Yarmouth to push for some of the Hessian troops to be made available for service outside Europe and declined the Landgrave's alternative proposal to provide a 'body of foreigners'. He also asked for the Hesse Cassel contingent to be restored to 5,000 rather than 4,000, but stated that the proposed secret article to satisfy Prussian concerns should not be accepted. Yarmouth was instructed to get the troops on the march to the Low Countries as soon as possible and to conclude the arrangements for the Baden and Darmstadt troops.[9]

Yarmouth was able to inform Grenville that the King of Prussia had agreed to drop his request for the secret article in the Hesse Cassel treaty, but reported that the Landgrave was impatient to ratify the treaty. He urged that this be done immediately, as otherwise the Landgrave would stop their equipment and new clothing, so that they would not be available for service in the Low Countries in the current year. He apologised for the delay in finalising the subsidy treaties, noting that 'the Courts of Germany are proverbially slow in their proceedings, and it has been impossible for me to induce them to amend their Pace'.[10]

Yarmouth's report to Grenville on the progress of the negotiations expressed his fear that the Landgrave of Hesse Cassel would not allow his troops to proceed down the Rhine until the treaty had been ratified, even though he had been assured that this would be done. Yarmouth had again pushed for some of the Hessian troops to be allowed to serve outside Europe and for the total of 5,000 to be reinstated. He was also trying to get confirmation from the Austrians of their intentions with regard to the Darmstadt troops and he was seeking to finalise the treaty with Baden. In order to move things along, he pressed Gunn to complete his business in Carlsruhe and to induce Edelsheim to fix an early date for the signature of the Baden treaty, 'as every hour is of consequence in the present state of things'. Gunn was then to return to Cassel and get the Hesse Cassel troops on the move, as their arrival in the Low Countries was 'prodigiously wanted'.[11]

Yarmouth wrote to Grenville to confirm that the Landgrave of Hesse Cassel would allow his troops to begin their march as soon as ratification of the treaty was received, but not before then. He noted that Gunn believed that the Landgrave would consent to some of his troops being sent to the West Indies and that a definite answer was expected soon. He also reported that the Austrian minister, Count

---

7   Grenville to Yarmouth 24 August 1793, TNA: FO 29/2.
8   Edelsheim to Yarmouth 6 September 1793 and Yarmouth to Grenville 7 September 1793 enclosing a copy, TNA: FO 29/2.
9   Grenville to Yarmouth 12 and 14 September 1793, TNA: FO 29/2.
10 Yarmouth to Grenville 17 September 1793, TNA: FO 29/2.
11 Yarmouth to Grenville 18 September 1793, TNA: FO 29/2 and Yarmouth to Gunn 19 September 1793, in Badische Historische Commission, *Politische Correspondenz Karl Friedrichs von Baden, 1783-1806* (Heidelberg: Carl Winter's Universitätsbuchhandlung, 1892), Vol.2, p.62.

Lehrbach, had informed him that the Darmstadt troops had been engaged by the Imperial Treasury but, for reasons of economy, they would not be put in motion until the following April. Yarmouth had suggested that half of the troops be ceded to Britain and the remainder sent at once to join the Austrian army. The court of Vienna had agreed to this arrangement and he hoped to conclude matters in a few days.[12]

Yarmouth also enclosed the treaty signed with the Margrave of Baden on 21 September, which followed the model of the Hesse Cassel treaty, amended so as to reflect the size of the contingent, which was now fixed at 754 men including officers, and the proportional reduction in the annual subsidy. The troops were to be ready to be reviewed by the British commissary on 10 October and to march the following day. The article in the Hesse Cassel treaty, which covered the payments to be made if the troops were not required, was omitted as no longer relevant, but a secret clause was added that the troops would not serve in Great Britain, Ireland, or Gibraltar.[13] Yarmouth asked Grenville to write to Sir James Murray to send a commissary to Cologne to meet them and the Hessians.

The delay in ratifying the Hesse Cassel treaty was starting to cause serious problems. Gunn sent Yarmouth copies of letters, expressing the Landgrave's impatience at the delay and stating that the troops would be sent to their former garrisons unless ratification arrived immediately. Gunn also expressed disappointment that he had not received confirmation that a commissary was at Cologne to receive and supply the troops and that he had written to Murray to arrange this. He feared that this delay would lead to desertion and confusion, as the troops were 'already becoming troublesome' and went on to ask Yarmouth to write to headquarters to back up this point. He also stated that he had been informed that the Landgrave had given the British government and Yarmouth a flat refusal to their request to allow any of his troops to serve outside Europe, although he was prepared to raise troops in his own dominions and officered by Hessians on the same terms as his own troops, if required.[14]

Grenville finally sent the ratification of the Hesse Cassel treaty to Yarmouth on 26 September and asked him to arrange for the exchange with the Landgrave to take place as soon as possible, so that the troops could march to join the Duke of York. He wrote again on 4 October enclosing the King's ratification of the Baden treaty, including the secret article, and instructed Yarmouth to lose no time in organising the exchange.[15]

Yarmouth sent Grenville the preliminary treaty he had just concluded with the Landgrave of Hesse Darmstadt, along with supporting papers, at the beginning of October.[16] The treaty for 3,000 men included the changes made in the Baden treaty,

---

12 Yarmouth to Grenville 22 September 1793, TNA: FO 29/2.

13 The text of the treaty is in Debrett (ed.), *A Collection of State Papers*, Vol. 1, pp.21-5. The secret article is not included here, but is in TNA: FO 95/1/5, p.388 and in Badische Historische Commission, *Politische Correspondenz*, Vol.2 pp.67-8, along with the rest of the treaty.

14 Gunn to Yarmouth 27 September 1793, TNA: FO 29/2.

15 Grenville to Yarmouth 26 September and 4 October 1793, TNA: FO 29/2.

16 Yarmouth to Grenville 5 October 1793 and enclosures, TNA: FO 29/2. The text of treaty is in Debrett (ed.), *A Collection of State Papers*, Vol. 1, pp.27-31.

but did not have the additional secret article. The troops were to be ready for review by the British commissary on 17 October and to begin their march on the following day. He noted that the treaty allowed the troops to be sent to Britain or Ireland if necessary and expressed his belief that they could also be sent to Toulon, if that was permissible under the Hesse Cassel treaty. He advised that if that was the intention, it should not be stated until after ratification, in case it caused difficulties and that he trusted and hoped that at least one English commissary would meet the various contingents at Cologne. Grenville sent the King's ratification of the treaty two weeks later.[17]

Having resolved the issue of ratification of the treaties, the march of the troops was now delayed further by the failure of the British government to make the payments which were due under the treaties. Yarmouth asked Grenville for the accounts to be set up to pay the amounts due in respect of the Hessian and Baden troops. He explained that their rulers had been reluctant to allow their men to march until this was done and had only agreed because of the critical situation in the Low Countries. Grenville's reply was that he had again applied for the information requested with regard to payments for the German troops, which he would forward as soon as it was received.[18]

As the matter had still not been resolved over two weeks after his request, Yarmouth was obliged to write to Grenville that he was 'very sorry to have been under the necessity of troubling Your Lordship so often respecting the Darmstadt and Baden troops – They are perhaps the finest Corps, that was ever sent to any Army'. He feared that, unless the matters dealt with in his former letters were resolved, 'Mutiny, Desertion, and perhaps their entire Dissolution may take place'. He went on that their rulers were making scant provision for the troops until they knew what they were to receive from Britain, and this was leading to great dissatis-faction among them and they were suffering from desertion. He also noted that the Landgrave of Hesse Cassel 'has a direct Interest in keeping the British Monopoly in his own Hands, and with that View, has uniformly endeavoured to disgust other Courts from assisting His Majesty with Troops' and that he retained part of the allowances made for the pay of the soldiers, making a further profit in addition to his subsidy.[19]

Yarmouth's distrust of the Landgrave of Hesse Cassel had been growing for some time. He had written to Grenville the previous month, warning him of an offer made by the Landgrave to provide an additional 1,000 men to Britain. Yarmouth's view was that the Landgrave had already given all of the troops he could, whilst main-taining his obligations to the Empire, so that any troops offered to Britain would be taken from his contingent serving on the Rhine. Instead of providing troops for the Imperial army, he would make cash payments into the Imperial Treasury at a lower rate than the British subsidy and keep the difference. The result would be that no additional men would be serving with the allied forces and Yarmouth was

---

17 Grenville to Yarmouth 19 October 1793, TNA: FO 29/3.
18 Yarmouth to Grenville 5 November 1793 and Grenville's reply 14 November 1793, TNA: FO 29/3.
19 Yarmouth to Grenville 22 November 1793, TNA: FO 29/3.

concerned that, if Britain agreed to this practice, then other princes would follow the example. He had told the Landgrave's minister that, far from recommending acceptance of this proposal, he would do everything in his power to warn Grenville against it and he now feared that an approach would be made to the British government through Kutzleben 'to recommend this coarse and mischievous Job'.[20]

After the delays in finalising the arrangements for the new contingents from Hesse Cassel, Baden, and Hesse Darmstadt, the troops were finally on the march to the Low Countries. The Hesse Cassel division under *General-Major* von Hanstein marched to the front on 17 October and reached Tournai on 16 November, where they were reviewed by the Duke of York. Major Gunn noted in his report on the muster that, in addition to the 3,991 men in the new contingent, the Landgrave had also sent 50 recruits to help replace the losses suffered by the Regiment Erb-Prinz during the siege of Dunkirk.[21] The Hesse Darmstadt brigade, with a total strength of 3,226 men, set off on 24 October, arrived on 22 November and was immediately sent to the outposts around Menin. The Duke reviewed them and commented on their fine appearance, but 156 men had already deserted by 1 December and a further 53 by 1 January 1794.[22] The Baden battalion of 760 men began its march to join the Duke's army on 29 October and reached Tournai on 1 December, where they were reviewed by the Duke and his entire staff, and sent to join the garrison of Ypres.[23] Although it had been at full strength at the muster, the battalion suffered heavily from desertion and the number of sick was rising, so that by 20 December 1793 it had one musician and 144 privates missing and 35 men sick.[24]

Even before these troops had assembled, the British government was planning where to deploy them. Grenville sent a confidential letter to inform Yarmouth that, following receipt of the news that Toulon was in British hands, the King had issued directions for 5,000 Hessians, who were currently serving with the Duke of York, to embark immediately for Toulon. They were to be replaced by eight British battalions, but Grenville explained that these troops were also needed for another 'indispensable service', the expedition to the West Indies, for which they would have to leave at the beginning of October. The additional Hesse Cassel division was therefore needed urgently to replace them.[25] The King saw more clearly than the government ministers that 'The misfortune of our situation is that we have too many objects to attend to, and our force consequently must be too small at each place'.[26]

The situation became even more complicated when the government became excited by the success of the Royalists in the west of France and began to prepare a force to support them. The original plan to embark 5,000 Hessian troops for Toulon was shelved and Dundas informed the King that ministers proposed to send the

20 Yarmouth to Grenville 20 October 1793, TNA: FO 29/2.
21 Gunn to Yarmouth 27 October 1793, TNA: FO 29/3.
22 *Monathliche Tabelle* 1 December 1793 and 1 January 1794, HStAD E8 B No 271/1, ff. 10-11.
23 Anon., *Aus dem Leben des Freiherrn Ludwig Christian Heinrich Gayling von Altheim* (Freiburg im Breisgau: Friedrich Wagner'sche Buchdruckerei, 1864), pp.19 and 23-44.
24 Report 20 December 1793, NLA HA Hann. 38 E Nr. 144 p.114.
25 Grenville to Yarmouth 14 September 1793, TNA: FO 29/2.
26 George III to Pitt 14 September 1793, in J.H. Rose, *Pitt and Napoleon: Essays and Letters* (London: G. Bell and Sons, 1912), p.225.

eight regiments of British infantry, who were intended for the West Indies, to Jersey instead. They were to be used to take Saint-Malo, before being sent to Toulon.[27] Pitt also wrote to the King, expressing the hope that these regiments, together with the 'disposable foreign troops', would be sufficient to take advantage of the favourable opportunity on the French coast and then to proceed to Toulon, where they were much needed.[28]

Major General Francis, Earl of Moira, received a commission from the King on 20 November 1793 as 'Lieutenant General in Our Army on the Continent of Europe only' and was appointed 'General and Commander in Chief of all and singular our forces Employed or to be Employed on a particular service agreeable to such Instructions as we shall think proper to give you for that purpose'.[29] His instructions of the same date confirmed that this 'particular service' was to support the Royalist uprising by attacking the coast of Brittany and adjacent areas, and that his force was to include troops provided under the subsidy treaties with the Landgraves of Hesse Cassel and Hesse Darmstadt and the Margrave of Baden, in addition to the British troops under his command.[30]

Dundas informed Murray that 4,000 Hesse Cassel troops, together with those of Hesse Darmstadt and Baden, would probably be employed on the coast of Brittany or Poitou in two divisions, the first of which consisted of the Hesse Cassel troops. In view of the advanced season, he wanted these troops to be ready to march to Ostend at short notice and it was intended to bring together two or three British regiments and a corps of emigrants to complete the force.[31] He wrote shortly afterwards that the transports would sail for Ostend on the first favourable wind, so the Duke was asked to order the troops to Ostend to be ready to embark. Captain Bisset of the Royal Navy had been sent to Ostend to supervise the embarkation.[32]

The plan immediately ran into difficulties. The Duke of York informed the King that he had written to the commanding officers of the Hessian troops to advise them that they were to march as soon as possible to Ostend, to be embarked for an expedition. He had not yet received any answer from the general in command of the Hesse Cassel troops, but *General-Major* von Düring, the commander of the Darmstadt brigade, informed him that he had instructions not to allow a single one of his troops to be embarked without acquainting the Landgrave first. Düring had sent an officer to the Landgrave for instructions and had expressed concern that there would be disorder or mutiny if the troops were ordered to embark.[33] Murray reported this 'Circumstance of a very unpleasant nature' to Dundas on the same date and noted that the Duke had written to the Landgrave of Hesse Darmstadt,

27 Dundas to the King 16 November 1793, in Aspinall (ed.), *The Later Correspondence*, Vol. 2, p.123.
28 Pitt to the King 17 November 1793, in Aspinall (ed.), *The Later Correspondence*, Vol. 2, p.125.
29 Commissions signed by Dundas 'By His Majesty's Command,' TNA: HO 51/147 pp.150-1 and 159-61.
30 Draft instructions annotated with the King's amendments, TNA: HO 42/27, ff. 227-236.
31 Dundas to Murray 16 November 1793, TNA: WO 6/8, pp.98-100.
32 Dundas to Murray 21 November 1793, TNA: WO 6/8, pp.100-103.
33 York to the King 25 November 1793, in Aspinall (ed.), *The Later Correspondence*, Vol.2, p.128.

urging him to allow his troops to embark without delay.[34] Meanwhile, Dundas wrote to Murray that most of the transports for the expedition had been assembled and were only delayed from sailing to Ostend by adverse winds. It would now be possible to include the Baden infantry and their bat horses with the Hesse Cassel troops in the first embarkation and the Duke was therefore requested to order them to Ostend immediately.[35]

Dundas now faced a major problem, as it appeared that the German princes might not allow their troops to be sent to join Moira and the King had already informed Pitt that he would not allow the Hanoverians to be used in operations outside of Flanders.[36] Dundas told Murray that, if the Germans would not agree to join the expedition, it would be necessary to make up the shortfall by taking the British guards, line infantry, and light cavalry from the Duke of York's army, and he was therefore to hold this force in readiness to march to Ostend for embarkation. He also sent strongly-worded messages to be forwarded to the three rulers, setting out the government's belief that the treaties allowed the troops to be used anywhere in Europe, except for the secret clause with Baden excluding Gibraltar, Toulon, and Marseilles. Dundas was in error here as the secret clause did not refer to Toulon or Marseilles, although Yarmouth informed Grenville that the Margrave had made it clear that he would not allow his troops to be sent there. Dundas threatened to cease subsidy payments to the Landgraves if they would not meet their obligations, but in the case of Baden this was replaced by a statement that the King 'would feel it a matter of great accommodation on the part of the Margrave' if the Baden troops were allowed to embark for the Coast of Brittany.[37]

The Duke of York managed to resolve matters without having to resort to these threats. *General-Lieutenant* Friedrich Wilhelm von Wurmb, who had taken over the command of the Hesse Cassel corps, had written to him on 12 December in response to the Duke's order for a fourth of his corps to be held ready for embarkation, pointing out that he had instructions from the Landgrave to obtain a written assurance from the Duke that the troops would not be sent to the West Indies or to any place out of Europe.[38] The Duke had therefore given a 'positive Declaration, signed with Our own hand' that to the best of his knowledge the Hesse Cassel troops ordered for embarkation were to serve in Europe under the Command of the Earl of Moira, and that the government had no intention of sending them to the West Indies or anywhere out of Europe.[39] He was also able to tell the King that the Landgrave of Hesse Darmstadt had consented to his troops being used in the Vendée, so that he would not have to give up any of his British regiments. The Hesse Cassel regiments which were to be embarked were already at Ostend and Nieuport awaiting

34   Murray to Dundas 25 November 1793, TNA: WO 1/167, pp.707-712.
35   Dundas to Murray 27 November 1793, TNA: WO 6/8, pp.105-106.
36   George III to Pitt 5 December 1793, in Rose, *Pitt and Napoleon*, p.226.
37   Dundas to Murray 5 and 8 December 1793 with enclosures, TNA: WO 6/8, pp.107-115 and Yarmouth to Grenville 22 September 1793, TNA: FO 29/2.
38   Wurmb to York 12 December 1793, TNA: WO 1/167, p.861.
39   York to Wurmb 12 December 1793, TNA: WO 1/167, p.849.

the transports, but the Duke stated that the Darmstadt troops had begun to desert so fast that they had to be confined at Ypres.[40]

While the negotiations with the German princes were under way, the Austrians had also agreed to send a contingent of 1,084 men, consisting mainly of hussars, artillery, infantry, and Jägers, to join Moira's force and the preparations for the expedition were progressing.[41] The Duke reported to Dundas on 21 December that he had not sent the latter's messages to the Landgraves of Hesse Cassel and Darmstadt, as they had consented to the embarkation of their troops, and that he would give the assurances they required that the troops would not be sent out of Europe or be required to serve as marines on the fleet. He was confident that this would stop the desertions which had occurred, especially among the Darmstadt troops, since they had heard that they were to embark. He also informed Dundas that Captain Bisset had told him that morning that the transports for the first division had arrived at Ostend. Orders had been given to start embarking the Hessians and the Austrian artillery immediately and it was expected that the Austrian hussars would arrive by the time this was completed. He had also authorised Bisset to take on additional ships if necessary to make up for the lack of sufficient tonnage for the horses.[42]

Although there were delays in assembling the transports at Ostend, Bisset was able to write to Evan Nepean, Under-Secretary of State for the Home Department, on 27 December enclosing the embarkation returns for the Hessians, who were all expected to be on board by the following day. He noted that the transports that had been sent were only sufficient for 1,000 horses, but that he had two ships ready to take the stores and the extra Hessian baggage that could not be fitted on the transports.[43] He wrote again the following day to inform Nepean that he had not yet been able to complete the embarkation of the Hessians, but they would get away on the following day. He complained again that the horses were overcrowded with only two spare stalls per ship, instead of the four required, and expressed his fear that 'those poor officers will lose the half of their horses'. He suggested that it would be cheaper for the second division to dispose of their horses before embarkation and receive compensation for them.[44]

In the end, the orders for the Austrians to join the expedition were countermanded and the second division was never embarked. The only German troops sent to join Moira were the Hesse Cassel contingent, which was commanded by *General-Major* von Borck and made up of the Gens d'Armes, the Infantry Regiments Prinz Carl and Lossberg, and the Fusilier Battalion, with a small staff, reserve artillery, general hospital, and commissariat. The division had just over 2,500 men fit for duty, but was accompanied by a large number of non-combatants and baggage. The embarkation return shows a total number of 3,151 persons, including 95 pack horse

---

40   York to the King 17 December 1793, in Aspinall (ed.), *The Later Correspondence*, Vol.2, pp.135-136.
41   Return of the Imperial detachments 14 December 1793, TNA: WO 1/167, p.913.
42   York to Dundas 21 December, TNA: WO 1/167, pp.909-11.
43   Bisset to Nepean 27 December 1793, TNA: WO 1/167, pp.1,013-14.
44   Bisset to Nepean 28 December 1793, TNA: HO 42/27, ff. 705-708.

and waggon drivers, 155 officers' servants, 59 women, and 16 children. They had 1,033 horses, eight 3-pounder regimental cannon, 16 ammunition waggons, and 117 waggons and carts to carry the baggage, medicine chests and the pay chest.[45] The men and horses were crammed onto the ships, around 240 men to an infantry transport and 40 horses and 40 men to a horse ship, and there was great difficulty getting the large waggons on board.[46]

The convoy sailed on 1 January 1794 and arrived off Cowes on the Isle of Wight on the 4th, where the ships carrying the British infantry were already waiting. They were to wait there for news from the French Royalists and be ready to launch the expedition to support them. In the meantime, the troops waited on board the crowded transports. An issue of two pounds of fresh beef per man was made on 11 January, the first they had received since embarking, although regular supplies of fresh meat were provided from the 22nd. The health of the men and horses was suffering from their confinement on board ship and it was only towards the end of January that groups of men were allowed short spells ashore to exercise. The horses were also landed with one man to look after every three horses, but their food and fodder had to be brought from the ships.[47] The Cowes Customs Collector reported on 10 February that 903 horses had been landed and that many were offered for sale by the officers who owned them.[48]

The arrival of the Hessian troops on British soil created a political storm. The King sent messages to the House of Commons on 27 January and to the Lords on the 29th, informing them that a body of Hessian troops in British pay, who were intended for foreign service, had reached the Isle of Wight. He had ordered them to be disembarked, in order to prevent sickness among the troops from their remaining on the transports.[49] This provoked an outcry in both Houses of Parliament. On 10 February, a motion was introduced in the Commons that the landing of the Hessian troops was 'clearly unconstitutional and undeniably illegal... the King had no power to introduce them without the consent of Parliament', but the motion was lost after a lengthy debate.[50] Other attempts to challenge the legality of the decision to allow the Hessian troops to disembark were also defeated.

A hospital had been established at East Cowes on 29 January to treat the growing number of sick and some of the men began to be landed in February and put into barracks in West Cowes. On 12 February, one officer, one NCO, one drummer, and 29 men from each battalion were put into these barracks, which were in reality no more than outbuildings at Dallimore's farm, and they were joined by further detachments later in the month. On 19 March, Moira also ordered that each man

---

45 Embarkation return 27 December 1793, TNA: WO 1/167, p.1,019.
46 Lieutenant Home Popham, Royal Navy, to Nepean 24 December 1793 with embarkation arrangements, TNA: WO 1/167, pp.1,005-11.
47 Oberst von Geyso, 'Über die Expedition hessischer Truppen nach der Insel Wight', *Hessenland*, 1906, p.215.
48 http://www.customscowes.co.uk/1792-1794.htm, accessed 13 May 2016.
49 Anon. *Journals of the House of Commons* Vol. 49, p.24.
50 W. Woodfall and assistants, *An Impartial Account of the Debates that occur in the Two Houses of Parliament* (London: T. Chapman, 1794), Vol.1, pp.316-47.

was to be given an allowance of three pints of porter a day in a measure designed to promote the health of the troops.[51]

Borck was not happy with the conditions his men were living under and complained to Baron von Kutzleben, the Hessian minister in London. Kutzleben eventually took up these complaints with Grenville, informing him that he had received a letter from Borck dated 19 February, complaining that they were 'immensely crowded in their bad Quarters' and with the greatest part still on board their ships, so that between 3 and 400 men were already ill and that the number would increase unless their situation improved. The cavalry had also lost 39 horses because of their want of proper accommodation. Kutzleben went on that he had not troubled Grenville when Borck had written about these issues some time ago, but had referred him to Lord Moira. However, he now understood that Borck had informed the Landgrave of the situation and he 'should esteem it a particular favour if Your Lordship (when at leasure) would honor me with a few lines in answer', so that he could tell the Landgrave that he had taken up Borck's concerns.[52]

Grenville was sent a copy of a letter which Dundas had received from Moira in reply to Kutzleben's note. This stated that Moira was 'exceedingly happy' that Dundas was 'satisfied with the exertion that has been used to render the situation of the Hessian Troops as comfortable as circumstances will admit'. He went on to add that Doctor Hayes had come from Southampton to examine the Hessian sick. He had reported that their condition was not as bad as that of the British troops and that 'Out of the five hundred Sick, very few have the Fever, and even in those cases it does not appear malignant'. His conclusion was that 'the other Distempers are of a nature to be speedily cured, with the present accommodation & treatment'.[53]

After repeated failures to make contact with the Royalists, the planned landings on the French coast were finally abandoned and Moira wrote to Dundas that he had ordered the Hessian troops to hold themselves ready to leave for Flanders at short notice. He continued to play down the level of sickness affecting the Hessians and noted that, although their sick list numbered 800, they did not have 'that formidable malady [the malignant fever referred to by Doctor Hayes] which has fallen so heavy upon the British' and many of their cases would not be admitted to a British sick list.[54] The order was given on 25 March that the Hessians would embark on the following day.

Before they left, Moira ordered that *Staabs-Capitain* von Lossberg of the Regiment Prinz Carl should receive the pay applicable to one of his aides de camp from the date the Hessians had arrived at the Isle of Wight. He explained that it had been his intention to appoint a Hessian aide-de-camp when the army landed on the Continent but, as that would not now be possible, he wanted to make this

---

51 Unless otherwise stated, these details are taken from the campaign journals of the regiments, principally Prinz Carl and Lossberg, HStAM, 10 e, II/4 and 8.
52 Kutzleben to Grenville 22 February 1794, TNA: FO 31/6.
53 Moira to Dundas 25 February 1794 (copy), TNA: FO 31/6.
54 Moira to Dundas 22 March 1794, TNA: HO 42/29, ff. 167-170.

payment as 'a Testimony of esteem, and acknowledgment' of Lossberg's 'Diligence and Punctuality' in his service as Borck's major of brigade.[55]

The convoy set sail on 29 March and returned to Ostend, where they were disembarked at the beginning of April. In spite of Moira's reassurances concerning the health of the troops, 375 men were too ill to travel and had to be left in the hospital in East Cowes. In addition, 84 men, two soldiers' wives, and two children had died and were buried in the nearby Whippingham churchyard. A plaque commemorating the 84 men who died was placed in St Mildred's Church by the Landgrave of Hesse in 1906, although it does not mention the women and children who also died.[56]

The force, particularly the infantry, was much reduced by sickness, as shown in Table 3, and the Gens d'Armes had only 309 troop horses fit for service out of the 355 they had taken with them.[57] The Regiments Prinz Carl and Lossberg were too weak to take the field and were sent to join the garrison at Ypres to recover, while the Gens d'Armes were ordered to Nieuport and the Fusilier Battalion to Menin. The sick from the Cowes hospital reached Ostend at the beginning of May and Major General Stewart, the British commander there, reported that upward of 400 convalescents of the Hessian corps had arrived, where he was ordered to keep them until further orders.[58]

The British government agreed to some financial compensation for the losses suffered by Borck's brigade, on what had turned out to be a futile expedition. Moira informed Stewart that Commissary General Davison had sent a draft for £1,500, being a gratuity allowed by the King to the division of Hessian troops who had been attached to his command. This had been granted to the Hessian officers as damages to cover their losses on the expedition, but by the time the Hessian commissary presented his authority to receive and distribute the money, the majority of the men had been taken prisoner when Ypres surrendered.[59] The Treasury also issued a warrant for £1,537 in respect of the 101 horses that had died, described as 15 officers' horses, 44 cavalry horses, and 42 artillery, bat, and draught horses.[60]

55 Order book associated with William Stuart 28th Regiment of Foot 26 March 1794, NAM 85-12-9.
56 A list of the dead is given in Anon., 'Eine Gedenktafel für Hessen-Kasselischer Krieger in der Kirche zu Whippingham auf der Insel Wight (England)', *Hessenland*, 1906, pp.146-7.
57 Reports dated 30 December 1793 and 1 April 1794, HStAM, 4 h, 3360, ff. 2 and 34.
58 Craig to Stewart 9 May 1794, BL Add MS 40634, f. 68.
59 Moira to Stewart 19 May 1794 and commissary Heuser to Stewart 19 August 1794, BL Add MS 40634, ff. 79-80 and 197-8.
60 Warrant dated 22 July 1794, TNA: T 52/81 p.302.

Table 3: *General-Major* von Borck's Division December 1793 and March 1794

	Full Strength	30 December 1793		1 April 1794	
		Fit for Duty	Sick	Fit for Duty	Sick
Cavalry					
Regiment Gens d'Armes Infantry and Artillery	439	374	41	336	62
Regiment Prinz Carl					
1st Battalion	556	464	59	311	182
2nd Battalion	549	468	33	333	142
Regiment von Lossberg					
1st Battalion	556	481	48	287	211
2nd Battalion	549	500	31	274	231
Fusilier Battalion	224	210	10	197	19
Artillery Detachment	91	89	1	80	8
	2,525	2,212	182	1,482	793
Total	2,964	2,586	223	1,818	855

Source:
Rapporte vom Auxiliarkorps in Flandern unter G. v. Borck, 1794, HStAM, 4 h, 3360 ff. 2 and 34.

Notes:
The totals shown for full strength are the establishments (*Sollstärke*) for officers, NCOs, squadron/company surgeons, musicians, and privates. They do not include the middle and junior staff, drivers, and servants.
Other reasons for absence, such as men on command, wounded or taken prisoner, and those wanting to complete, are not listed above.

5

High Hopes for 1794

After the disappointing end to the 1793 campaign, the Austrians drew up an ambitious plan to assemble a total force of 340,000 men for operations in the spring of
1794. The main body was to move towards Paris after taking the French border
fortresses and leaving sufficient troops to guard the frontier. The force provided
by Britain and its German auxiliaries was to be increased from 20,000 to 40,000
men and a siege train was to be added to reduce the French fortresses. The Duke
forwarded a summary of the plan to Dundas and it was agreed that Mack, who
had been reinstated as Coburg's chief of staff, would come to London to discuss the
details of the plan.[1]

Mack arrived in London in February, where he held a series of meetings with the
British ministers and the King on the 13th and 14th. He wrote a detailed report on
these conferences, dealing first with his successful opposition to Pitt's suggestion
that Lord Cornwallis, who had recently returned from India, should replace the
Duke of York in command of the Anglo-Allied Army. Having resolved this sensitive
issue, he then proposed that Freytag should be removed from the command of the
Hanoverian troops, citing the harmful effects of his failure to respect the Duke of
York's authority, especially at Dunkirk, his lack of military talent, and his failure to
win the love and confidence of his troops. This matter had to be agreed by the King,
who gave his consent after a separate meeting with Mack.

It was agreed that the majority of the Duke's army would take part in an offensive
in East Flanders, leaving part with the Austrians under *Feldzeugmeister* Clerfayt to
defend West or maritime Flanders. The augmentation of the Anglo-Allied Army
to 54,000 men in total, or 40,000 muskets, was to be achieved by sending 5,000
additional British troops and 5,000 Hanoverians, with the balance to come from a
further 1,500 to 2,000 British troops and by taking over the 3,000 Brunswick troops
in Dutch pay. It was also hoped to raise 4,000 to 6,000 light troops from German free
corps and possibly some troops from the Elector of Cologne.[2]

Grenville's report to the King on the conferences confirmed that Mack's plan had
been agreed, and suggested that Cornwallis be given the command of the forces
in West Flanders. He also noted that Coburg was likely to be replaced in overall

---

1   York to Dundas 2 February 1794, TNA: WO 1/168, pp.247-53.
2   Dr H. Ritter von Zeissberg, *Quellen zur Geschichte des Politik Oesterreichs während der
    Französischen Revolutionskriege (1793-1797)* (Wien: Wilhelm Braumüller, 1885), Vol.2, pp.89-
    96.

command of the army by either the Emperor himself or his brother, the Archduke Carl. The King was eager to preserve the Duke of York's leading role and insisted that the Hanoverians had to serve under him, but was happy for the Hessians, Brunswick, and Baden troops to form part of the corps in West Flanders. He also expressed doubt that the Austrians would allow Cornwallis to have the overall command there, in which he was proved correct, as Clerfayt, albeit reluctantly, retained the command.[3] In spite of the difficulty the government had found in assembling the ordnance required for the siege of Dunkirk, it also agreed to provide the siege train requested by Mack, although it was never actually sent.

Yarmouth's mission had ended and he took no further part in the engagement of German auxiliaries, but the negotiations with German princes for additional troops had continued. The Hanoverian contingent was increased by 5,299 men under an 'Article of Agreement relative to an additional Body of his Majesty's Electoral Troops to be taken forthwith into the Pay of Great Britain' dated 7 January 1794.[4] The terms were the same as in the 'Preliminary Articles' and it was agreed that their pay would commence on 22 January 1794, so that they could join the army in Flanders by March to be ready for the new campaigning season.

Discussions also took place at the end of 1793 between the Duke of York and *General-Lieutenant* Friedrich Wilhelm von Wurmb, the commander of the Hesse Cassel troops, to add two or three batteries of heavy artillery and howitzers to the corps, to overcome the disadvantage they faced compared with the heavy guns of the French.[5] Following the government's approval of the proposal, the Duke began detailed negotiations with the officer appointed by the Landgrave, his aide-de-camp *Brigadier* and *General-Adjutant Oberst* Ludwig Johann Adam von Wurmb. The main sticking points were the proposed cost and the Hessians' wish to include the drivers in the calculation of levy money but, after some hesitation, the terms were agreed on the same basis as the earlier treaties. The subsidy was calculated as the equivalent of 100 men for each howitzer and 12-pounder and 80 men for each 6-pounder. The *Article séparé*, to add two brigades of artillery with 20 cannon and howitzers and 535 men to the Hessian corps in British pay, was signed at Courtrai (Kortrijk) on 23 March 1794.[6] Article 6 of the agreement specifically provided that Britain was responsible for the replacement of horses lost as a result of exceptional circumstances, such as the cavalry and artillery horses lost in their transport from Ostend to the Isle of Wight.

Once again the march was delayed by British failure to set up the appropriate financial arrangements. Major Gunn wrote to Dundas in June that the artillery brigade had been ready to march for some time, but the Landgrave had not let them go until the British paid the 100,000 crowns to cover the cost of fitting it out, which was due to be paid immediately after the signature of the agreement.[7]

---

3   Grenville to George III 16 February 1794 and the King's reply 17 February 1794, Historical Manuscripts Commission, *Manuscripts of J.B. Fortescue*, pp.505-7.
4   Debrett (ed.), *A Collection of State Papers*, Vol. 1, pp.42-3.
5   Undated note of proposal by Wurmb, possibly around 12 December 1793, TNA: WO 1/167 pp.865-6.
6   Signed copy of the agreement, TNA: WO 1/168 pp.577-86.
7   Gunn to Dundas 8 June 1794, TNA: WO 1/898 p.1.

The Duke of York returned to Courtrai from England at the beginning of March and wrote to the King that he had met Freytag, who had informed him of his recall and replacement by Wallmoden as commander of the Hanoverian corps. This had obviously affected him a great deal and the Duke expressed his sympathy for him, even though they had not always agreed.[8]

The Duke was pressed by the Austrians to confirm the actual strength of his corps and when the promised reinforcements were expected to arrive, so that the plans for the campaign could be finalised. He wrote to Dundas, asking to be informed of the status of the British reinforcements and also stressed the importance of concluding the arrangements for the additional German troops, especially those from Brunswick, who he had been informed 'do not as yet know, that it is His Majesty's Intention to take them into Pay, and are therefore selling off their Horses and Equipage as fast as possible'.[9]

Dundas's reply set out the steps taken by the government to provide the reinforcements promised at the London conferences in February. As the departure of troops from Ireland had been delayed by lack of shipping, ministers had recommended to the King that the Hesse Cassel infantry with Lord Moira (estimated at 2,500 men) should immediately return to the Duke's army and the 3,000 Darmstadt troops who were to have joined Moira were now to stay with the Duke. The additional Hanoverian troops engaged in January, except for the horse artillery, were already on the march to join the army. Dundas also pointed out that the return which he had received for the Hanoverian corps which was currently with the army for 1 February showed only 537 infantry and 178 cavalry 'wanting to complete' from the original force of 13,000 men, and that 409 infantry and 200 cavalry had been sent to join them on 21 February. He acknowledged the shortfall caused by around 1,000 prisoners of war and stated that a proposal would be made to the King to take on additional men to replace them. He also informed the Duke that Grenville had instructed Lord Malmesbury and William Eliot, the British minister at The Hague, to try to engage the Brunswick troops.[10]

There are a number of problems with Dundas's figures. No agreement was reached to replace the Hanoverian prisoners of war and no allowance was made for over 2,000 sick among their infantry at the beginning of April.[11] The Hesse Cassel troops recalled from the Isle of Wight were reduced to 1,818 men and the Hesse Darmstadt Brigade had only 2,245 men fit for duty as at 1 April, although this was brought up to 2,454 during the month as replacements for the losses during the previous autumn and winter arrived.[12]

The government also failed to engage the Brunswick troops or the other German troops suggested at the London conference. Grenville had written to Eliot that the Dutch Government had declared that it did not intend to renew the treaty with

---

8   York to the King 8 March 1794, in Aspinall (ed.), *Later Correspondence*, Vol.II pp.183-5.
9   York to Dundas 9 March 1794, TNA: WO 1/168, pp.397-8.
10 Dundas to York 15 March 1794, TNA: WO 6/11, pp.43-56.
11 Report for 1-14 April 1794, Hann. 38 E Nr. 213.
12 For the Hesse Cassel troops see Table 3, for the Hesse Darmstadt brigade Reports dated 1 April and 1 May 1794, HStAD, E 8 B No 271/1.

Ludwig Graf von Wallmoden-Gimborn, drawn from life and engraved by J.G. Huck. (Anne S.K. Brown Military Collection, Brown University Library)

Brunswick for the corps of troops in its service. It was believed that the treaty was to expire at some time in April and the King wished to open negotiations to engage these troops on the same terms as those already in place for the other German troops in British pay. Eliot was therefore to put this proposal to the commander of the Brunswick troops and request that it be passed on to the Duke of Brunswick as soon as possible. In order to avoid loss of time, the troops should be put in a state of readiness to march as soon as a treaty was concluded and the Dutch government was to be asked to consent to them marching to join the British before the expiry of their treaty, if the negotiations could be concluded quickly.[13]

Eliot replied that he had discussed the matter with the Dutch Stadtholder, who had no objection to the British proposal, and confirmed that the treaty expired on 5 April. He had also written to the commander of the Brunswick troops at Maastricht and pressed him to agree the arrangements necessary for them to be ready to march as soon as the treaty was signed. However, he later had to report that he had received a letter notifying him of the Duke's rejection of the proposal, on the grounds that he could not ignore the protests of the Estates against the further absence of the troops at the end of the Dutch treaty.[14]

While efforts were being made to engage the Brunswick troops, Dundas wrote to the Duke of York authorising him to negotiate for the provision of 4,000 or more Prussian light troops and instructing him to send Colonel Craig, who had replaced Murray as Adjutant General to the Duke's army, to Berlin to progress this. Craig was also to visit Cassel to investigate reports that the Landgrave of Hesse Cassel had 'a Battalion of Yagers [sic], one of Light Infantry and a third of Hussars, totally unemployed' who might be taken into British pay.[15] Far from being 'totally unemployed', these were the troops serving on the Rhine, about whom Yarmouth had written to Grenville in October 1793. Grenville wrote to Craig on the same date, advising him that a similar proposal had been made by the Landgrave the previous autumn, but its validity had been doubted. He suggested that Craig go to Cassel on his way back from Berlin to see if there were in fact any troops available who could be taken into British pay, without reducing the number of recruits who were needed to complete the corps already serving with the Duke of York or the Landgrave's contingent with the Imperial army. Craig was authorised to engage any men who were available for immediate service.[16]

Craig replied to Grenville that on his arrival in Cassel he had been informed that the light troops could only be provided if the current treaties were extended for a further three years, the pay of the new corps doubled, the officers allowed bat and forage money, and an immediate advance of 200,000 Crowns was made. Craig had stated that he was not authorised to enter into such negotiations, but made it clear that he thought it highly unlikely that the British government would agree to the proposed terms, which the Landgrave had attempted to justify by the threat posed

---

13 Grenville to Eliot 4 March 1794, TNA: FO 37/52.
14 Eliot to Grenville 12 March 1794 and Eliot to Grenville 2 April 1794 and enclosure, TNA FO 37/52.
15 Dundas to York 7 March 1794, TNA: WO 6/11 pp.37-40.
16 Grenville to Craig 7 March 1794, TNA: FO 31/6.

by the French to his own territories and the need to raise additional troops at considerable expense.[17] Nothing came of Craig's missions to Berlin and Cassel.

As usual, ministers overestimated the effective strength of the army and the Duke was left far short of the 40,000 men originally intended. Even more serious for the allied plan was Prussian inactivity and the growing evidence that its commitment to the war was waning, as its attention was increasingly turning to the situation in Poland.

The composition of the armies to be commanded by the Duke of York and Clerfayt and the dispositions for the defence of West Flanders were agreed at a conference at Valenciennes on 17 March 1794, which included the Duke, Coburg, Clerfayt, and Mack.[18] It was agreed that Clerfayt would have all of the Hanoverian troops, including the seven battalions expected to arrive at the end of March or early April, the Hesse Darmstadt brigade, the Baden Regiment, five battalions and two squadrons of Brunswick troops then in Dutch pay at Maastricht, and the Loyal Emigrants in British pay, as well as 14 battalions and 12 squadrons of Austrians. It was hoped that the King would allow some of the Hesse Cassel troops with Lord Moira to be sent to garrison Ostend, and the Duke of York was to leave six Hesse Cassel battalions and two squadrons with Clerfayt until the Hanoverian and Brunswick troops arrived. The Duke was to have the British and the remainder of the Hesse Cassel troops under his command, together with 12 battalions and 12 squadrons of Austrians. On paper the allied forces in the Low Countries amounted to 187,000 men, but the effective force in the field was little over 120,000.[19]

At the end of March the Anglo-Allied army was split up between Clerfayt's corps and the corps under the Duke of York, which was attached to Coburg's main army. Contrary to the King's wishes, the Duke was obliged to leave the Hanoverians with Clerfayt on account of their 'extreme Sicklyness', which made them unfit to march.[20] He explained to the King that only one brigade of infantry was able to serve, but the cavalry were in good order and he meant to take them with him, although it was later decided to leave the whole body behind until they were all recovered. He stated his view that a major cause of their sickness was the failure to supply and cook meat on a regular basis.[21] Prince Adolphus described the sickness afflicting the troops as a kind of fever, which pulled them down immediately and from which it took them a long time to recover their strength.[22]

The Duke found it necessary to complain again to the King about the conduct of the Hanoverian infantry. They had shown a spirit of mutiny, with the 2nd and 3rd Grenadier Battalions at first refusing to go into their barracks and then setting fire to them, and the recruits from Hanover behaving 'most riotously' on their march.

17   Craig to Grenville 17 March 1794, TNA FO 31/6.
18   Disposition For the defence of West Flanders…., TNA: WO 1/168, pp.485-496.
19   G. von Scharnhorst, 'Stärke, innerer Zustand, und Krieges-Theatre der verbundenen Armeen, in den Niederlanden, im Jahr 1794', *Neues militairisches Journal*, Vol.8, pp.281-2.
20   York to Dundas 19 March 1794, TNA: WO 1/168, pp.497-9.
21   York to the King 12 March and 19 March 1794, in Aspinall (ed.), *Later Correspondence*, Vol.2, pp.185 and 186-7.
22   Prince Adolphus to the King 26 January 1794, in Aspinall (ed.), *Later Correspondence*, Vol.2, pp.149-50.

He pointed out that there were no such problems with the cavalry and artillery. He wrote again in response to Wallmoden's claim that the Hanoverians had been given hard duties. He explained that he had sent the four Hessian battalions which had previously been with Lord Moira into garrison in Ypres, as their lack of horses made them unfit to take the field immediately, omitting to mention their high level of sickness, and had put two Hanoverian battalions into Ostend to recover. The whole of the Hanoverian infantry was now in cantonments, except for three battalions who were, together with four Hessian battalions, covering the works at Menin. When the works were completed, they would be relieved and sent into cantonments near Mouscron.[23]

Soon afterwards, he informed the King that the additional Hanoverian troops had arrived at Tournai and that from the reports he had received they were very fine, especially the 14th Light Infantry and Jägers. He went on that the 14th Regiment lacked tents, so Wallmoden had sent them into Menin to relieve the Garde Regiment and the 2nd Grenadier Battalion, who had been sent to join him at Tournai. Prince Adolphus, who was serving with the Garde Regiment, gave a different explanation, that Wallmoden would not allow him to face the risks of joining the garrison at Menin.[24]

In mid-April the allied forces were organised as follows:

- Clerfayt with 32-34,000 men defended West Flanders. After deducting the garrisons at Nieuport, Ostend, Ypres, and Menin, he had at most 24,000 men available, with his main force around Marquain and Tournai and a weak cordon covering the line of around 110 kilometres from Nieuport to Marchiennes, where a small force kept his corps in contact with the troops at Denain;
- *General-Lieutenant* von Wurmb with 5,500-6,500 Hesse Cassel and Austrian troops at Denain linked Clerfayt's corps with Coburg's army;
- The main army under Coburg was assembled between Valenciennes and Bavay, and was divided into three elements: the Austrian army of 42,900 men under Coburg's personal command; the Austrian, British, and Hessian corps commanded by the Duke of York with 23,600 men; the Prince of Orange's 19,000 Austrian and Dutch troops.
- The left of the army was covered by *Feldmarschall-Lieutenant* Kaunitz, observing Maubeuge and defending the Sambre as far as Namur, and *Feldmarschall-Lieutenant* Beaulieu holding the line to Arlon and on towards Luxembourg.[25]

The Emperor arrived at Valenciennes on 14 April and took over the command of the main allied army, which he reviewed on the 15th, and set in motion the planned

23 York to the King 26 March and 4 April 1794, in Aspinall (ed.), *Later Correspondence*, Vol.2, pp.188-9 and 191-2.
24 York to the King 11 April 1794 and Prince Adolphus to the King 8 April, in Aspinall (ed.), *Later Correspondence*, Vol.2, pp.194-5.and 192-3.
25 J.B. Schels, 'Der Feldzug der kaiserlich-östreichischen und der alliirten Armee in den Niederlanden 1794', *Oestreichische Militärische Zeitschrift*, 1818 Vol.2, pp.80-84 and Ditfurth, *Die Hessen*, Vol.2, pp.35-43.

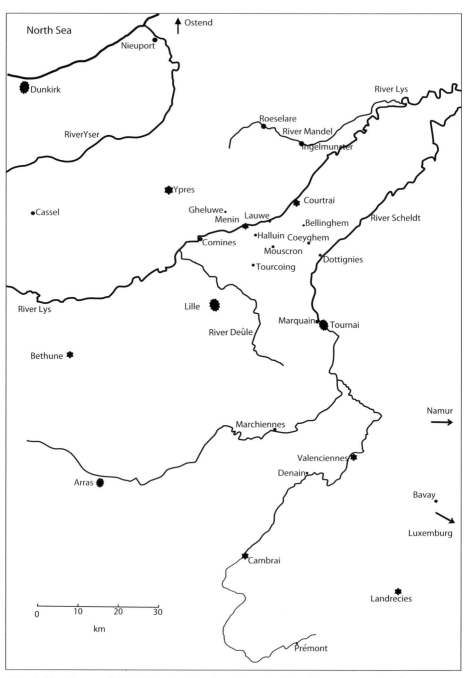

Map 5 The Theatre of War in Flanders, March to July 1794. (Based on map 1 in the atlas to A. von Witzleben, *Prinz Friedrich Josias von Coburg-Saalfeld, Herzog zu Sachsen*)

offensive against the French positions from Landrecies to Prémont. A Dutch and Austrian force under the Prince of Orange was to attack Landrecies, while the corps under Coburg and the Duke of York covered the siege army. At first the allied attack went well, and the French were pushed back, so that Landrecies was invested on 21 April and surrendered on the 30th.

While the allies were acting cautiously and never fielded the numbers that they hoped for, the French had been busy mobilising additional forces, under the law for the *levée en masse*, which the Convention had passed on 23 August 1793, and were preparing to attack. The Armies of the North and of the Ardennes, which were now commanded by *Général de Division* Pichegru, had around 160,000 men available for offensive operations after allowing for garrisons, and they made a series of attacks against Coburg and Wurmb's position.[26] Although these attacks were unsuccessful, they drew off part of the force defending West Flanders. Clerfayt marched with nine battalions and 13 squadrons to Denain, where he took over the command and repulsed a French attack on 23 April. The Hesse Darmstadt brigade also marched from Courtrai on the 23rd and camped at Brillon, between Orchies and Saint-Amand, where they remained until ordered back to Marquain on the 28th.

The French launched a general attack along the whole front on 26 April. The attack on Coburg and the Duke of York's forces was defeated and *Général de Brigade* Chapuis (also known as Chapuy) was captured, and with him Pichegru's orders for the campaign. Having discovered that a major attack was to be made on West Flanders, Clerfayt was ordered to march back to Tournai immediately, reinforced by six battalions and 10 squadrons from the Duke of York's army and six battalions from the siege army at Landrecies.

Craig wrote to Nepean on 28 April, expressing his surprise at the French attack on the 26th, and noting that he was being sent to West Flanders by the Duke to assess the situation. He stated that the works at Menin were sufficiently complete to allow the garrison to hold out for a few days, which should be sufficient until Clerfayt arrived. As long as Ypres did not fall, he did not think the French attack would have serious consequences.[27]

The forces remaining to defend West Flanders on 26 April were thinly spread in the following garrisons and positions:

- *General-Major* von Diepenbroick was at Nieuport with the two battalions each of the Hanoverian 5th and 10th Infantry Regiments and a detachment of Hessian cavalry, in total around 2,000 men;
- One battalion of the Loyal Emigrants and two squadrons of British cavalry were at Ostend;
- The Austrian *General-Major* Salis was at Ypres with six battalions of Hesse Cassel infantry, four battalions of Austrian line infantry and two companies of light troops, together with detachments of Hanoverian and Hessian cavalry, in total about 6,500 men;

---

26 H. Coutanceau, C. de la Jonquière and H. Leplus, *La Campagne de 1794 à l'Armée du Nord* (Paris: Librairie Militaire R. Chapelot et Ce, 1903-8), Part II, Vol.1, pp.103-4.

27 Craig to Nepean 28 April 1794, TNA: WO 1/168, pp.785-6.

- Two squadrons of the Hanoverian 10th Light Dragoons and three squadrons of Hesse Cassel Gens d'Armes were between Ypres and Nieuport;
- *General-Major* von Hammerstein was at Menin with two battalions of the Hanoverian 14th Light Infantry Regiment, the 1st Grenadier Battalion, a battalion of the Loyal Emigrants, a small detachment of Hanoverian cavalry and a half battery of Hanoverian artillery;
- Two squadrons each of the Hanoverian 1st and 9th Cavalry Regiments and three horse artillery guns, with the Uhlans Britanniques and York Rangers, two units of foreign troops in British service each around 150 strong, were also near Menin;
- The Hanoverian headquarters were at Courtrai, which was held by a battery of heavy artillery, 150 convalescents from the infantry, and a guard drawn from the Hanoverian infantry in Menin;
- *General-Major* von Wangenheim with two battalions each of the Hanoverian 1st and 4th Infantry Regiments, two squadrons of the 7th Dragoon Regiment, the two Jäger companies of the 14th Light Infantry Regiment, and five guns from the heavy artillery was in position around Mouscron;
- Two battalions each of the Hanoverian Garde Regiment and 9th Infantry Regiment, two squadrons of the Leibgarde, a battery of heavy artillery and a half battery of horse artillery, with two battalions each of the Austrian Infantry Regiments Wenkheim and Clerfayt were stationed around Marquain.[28]

Wallmoden commanded the forces from Courtrai to the sea and the Austrian *Feldmarschall-Lieutenant* Sztáray those at Mouscron and Marquain in Clerfayt's absence.

Pichegru had assembled nearly 70,000 men with supporting artillery in West Flanders, which were positioned as follows on 24 April:

- *Général de Brigade* Osten with 7,822 officers and men covered the right of the army, south of Lille;
- *Général de Division* Souham with 31,856 officers and men was on the River Lys and around Lille;
- *Général de Division* Moreau had 15,948 officers and men around Cassel;
- *Général de Division* Michaud commanded 13,943 officers and men around Dunkirk.[29]

The French forces moved into position on the 24th and 25th, ready to begin their attack on the unsuspecting allies on the 26th. Souham moved forward towards Courtrai with the main body and, as his troops were mostly inexperienced, he intended to use his numerical superiority to turn the allied positions, which would be fixed in place by light frontal attacks. He had no difficulty in driving back the allied posts to the east of Menin as he advanced, forcing the Uhlans Britanniques

---

28 G. von Scharnhorst, 'Feldzug der verbundenen Armeen in Flandern im Jahre 1794', *Neues militairisches Journal*, vol.9, pp.358-61.
29 Coutanceau et al, *La Campagne de 1794*, Part II, Vol.2, p.65.

and York Rangers from their position covering Halluin and then a company of the Hanoverian 14th Infantry Regiment from Lauwe. After leaving part of Daendels' brigade as a flank guard to cover Menin, he occupied Courtrai, which was virtually undefended, and moved on with Macdonald's 15,000 men to attack Mouscron. Wangenheim was in turn forced to retreat from there towards Dottignies and the French took up a position between Belleghem and Courtrai. At the same time, Moreau's division, with 11,000 infantry and 200 cavalry, had advanced to Comines where they spent the night of the 26th to 27th, with his right on the Lys and his left threatening Menin and covering the flank facing Ypres.[30]

The French attack was renewed on the 27th, with Vandamme's brigade of Moreau's division marching in three columns and encircling Menin, while Souham took up his position to defend Courtrai. *General-Major* von Oeyenhausen took over the command of the allied forces around Mouscron from Wangenheim, who had been seriously ill for some days and who died at Tournai on 1 May. Even though he was facing around 45,000 enemy troops around Menin, Courtrai and Lille, Oeyenhausen planned to attack Bertin's brigade of 5,000 men at Mouscron on the 28th. He was reinforced during the night of the 27th to the 28th by the two battalions of the Hanoverian 9th Infantry Regiment and the two squadrons of the Leibgarde. He also expected the 6th Infantry Regiment, but they did not appear, although the 4th Cavalry Regiment arrived unexpectedly. On the following morning he attacked with his force of around 3,600 men in two columns and pushed Bertin back to Tourcoing with the loss of around 300 men, two 8-pounders, a howitzer, and two 4-pounder battalion guns.[31] Oeyenhausen now found himself in the middle of a semi-circle formed by Moreau and Souham's divisions and Bertin's brigade. He set up a chain of posts around his position, although he knew that he could not hold it with such a weak force and he intended to retreat under cover of night.

On the same day, Clerfayt had arrived at Dottignies with his corps. He sent two battalions and two squadrons to Coeyghem to strengthen the front facing Courtrai, left a battalion at Dottignies, and brought the other three battalions and 10 squadrons to reinforce the corps at Mouscron, where he took over the command. That evening, *General-Major* Kollowrat also arrived with four Austrian battalions, bringing the total force at Mouscron to 10,000 men.[32] Clerfayt held a conference of his generals at 6:00 a.m. on the 29th and announced his intention of marching towards Menin to cut off Souham from Lille, but this would be delayed until 10 am the following morning because of the tiredness of the troops.

Clerfayt did not expect to be attacked and made no preparations to defend Mouscron. He was therefore surprised by Souham, who had assembled a force of 24,000 men to remove the allied threat to his lines of communication and who encouraged Moreau to press on with the capture of Menin as quickly as possible. Bertin's troops were still shaken by their earlier defeat and he was ordered to restrict his activity to making feints from Tourcoing, while Macdonald attacked the

30 Coutanceau et al, *La Campagne de 1794,* Part II, Vol.2, pp.79-80.
31 Coutanceau et al, *La Campagne de 1794,* Part II, Vol.2, p.112.
32 Schels, 'Der Feldzug', *Oestreichische Militärische Zeitschrift,* 1818, Vol.2, pp.336-7.

Hanoverians on the allied right at the mills at Castrel and Daendels pushed forward to attack the Austrians at Mouscron on the left.

The attack began between 9:00 and 10:00 a.m. on the 29th, but Bertin's demoralised troops were routed and Macdonald's attack was held up by the difficult approach to the allied position – which was through terrain cut up by ditches, hedges, and abbattis – and by heavy artillery and musket fire. The defenders left their position and pushed Macdonald back twice, while Daendels was also unable to make progress. At 1:00 p.m. Clerfayt believed that the French were retreating, but at 2:00 p.m. Souham ordered Macdonald forward a third time. Souham and Macdonald advanced at the head of their inexperienced troops to encourage them, supported by the well-directed fire of their artillery. The allied artillery at the mills was forced to fall back and the Hanoverian infantry, without this support and surprised by the renewed French attack after thinking that the two previous checks had decided matters, began to retreat towards Mouscron. The allied cavalry launched a charge to cover this movement, but, after initial panic, the French troops regained their order and pursued the retreating Hanoverians. The Austrians were then forced to abandon Mouscron and the allies fell back towards Dottignies. Souham's men were in no condition to follow up on their victory and camped on the field of battle for the night.

The Hanoverian losses between 26 and 29 April were 58 killed, 232 wounded, and 527 missing or captured, making 817 in total, together with five flags (one of the 1st Infantry Regiment and four from the 6th), 12 battalion guns, one from the heavy artillery, and 16 ammunition waggons.[33] The Austrians lost 903 men and 11 cannon, while the French losses were in excess of 2,000 men, mainly from the new levies.[34]

With Clerfayt's defeat, the situation of Menin became hopeless. The fortifications had been partly demolished by the Emperor Joseph II, although the Dutch had made some repairs in the spring of 1793 and work had started in 1794 to put up thick earthworks and palisades. However, delays in providing the 6,000 workmen required, and shortage of timber, meant that the works were not yet complete when the siege began. The cannon and munitions requested from England for its defence were awaited in vain, and the artillery actually in place only consisted of 10 6-pounders, six 4-pounders, four 1-pounders, two 30-pound howitzers, and four 7-pound howitzers. The garrison of little over 2,000 men was commanded by the Hanoverian *General-Major* von Hammerstein and consisted of:

- 62 cavalrymen from the 1st and 9th Hanoverian Cavalry Regiments;
- 1st Grenadier Battalion with 354 muskets;
- 14th Infantry Regiment with 1,148 muskets;
- One battalion of the Loyal Emigrants with around 400 muskets;
- An officer and around 40 muskets from the Hesse Cassel Regiment Erb-Prinz;
- 2nd Hanoverian artillery division with three companies and around 160 men;
- An NCO and 16 men from the Austrian artillery.[35]

33 L. von Sichart, *Geschichte der Königlich-Hannoverschen Armee*, Vol.4, p.376.
34 Schels, 'Der Feldzug', *Oestreichische Militärische Zeitschrift*, 1818 Vol.2, p.340.
35 G. von Scharnhorst, 'Die Vertheidigung der Stadt Menin und die Selbstbefreiung der Garnison unter dem Königlich Grossbrittannisch-Chur-Hannöverschen General-Major von

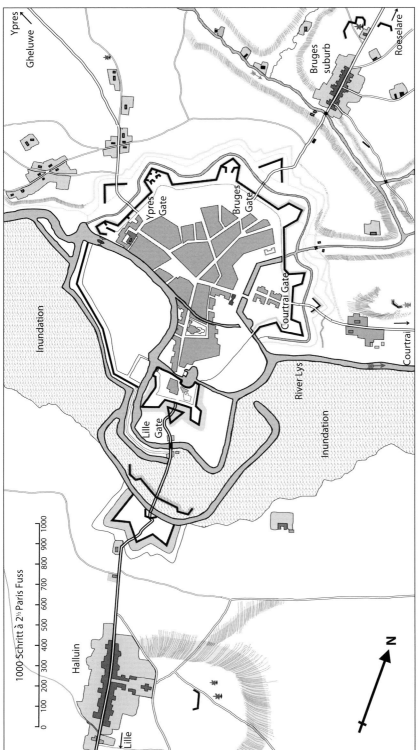

Map 6 Menin, April 1794. (Based on the plan in G. von Scharnhorst, 'Die Vertheidigung der Stadt Menin und die Selbstbefreiung der Garnison unter dem Königlich Grossbrittannisch-Chur-Hannöverschen General-Major von Hammerstein, im April 1794', *Neues militairisches Journal*, 1803, Vol.11). The scale is as shown by Scharnhorst, '1000 Schritt à 2½ Paris Fuss' is 812 metres.

Ammunition for the artillery and infantry was so short that it had to be saved in case of an assault or an approach by the French to the fortifications. Moreau's force surrounding them had 14,000 effectives according to papers later captured from the French.[36]

The bombardment had begun on the night of the 27th and became more effective when mortars were brought into action. It continued on the night of the 28th to 29th and the artillery and small arms fire intensified the following morning, so that much of the town was set on fire. Moreau was under pressure to move the siege on and, believing the garrison to be sufficiently demoralised, ordered a ceasefire at 10.00 a.m. on the 29th and summoned the allied commander to surrender the fortress. Hammerstein's defiant reply was 'We are accustomed to do our duty; we will not surrender.'[37] On being informed of this, Pichegru ordered Moreau to increase the pressure, using red-hot shot, so that not a single house would remain standing.

Knowing that he could not hold Menin and uncertain of the outcome of the action at Mouscron, Hammerstein held a council of war at 10:00 p.m. on the 29th, at which it was agreed that 1,800 men would attempt to break through the French lines at 1.30 a.m. on the 30th. As the south bank of the Lys was largely flooded, was commanded by the enemy batteries at Halluin and, in any case, did not lead to the best route back to the allied lines, it was decided to break out on the north bank. The enemy were strongest before the Ypres gate, so it was planned that the Loyal Emigrants, preceded by 20 cavalry, would cut a way through the palisade, as the Courtrai gate had been barricaded, and then enter the Bruges suburb, which was held by the enemy. At the same time a company of the 1st Grenadier Battalion would leave the Bruges gate and attack the battery positioned there, while the Loyal Emigrants tackled the enemy in the suburb. They would be followed by the 1st Battalion of the 14th Infantry Regiment, then by the artillery and the 2nd Battalion of the 14th Infantry Regiment. The other three companies of the 1st Grenadier Battalion and the remaining cavalry would form the rear guard. The main threat to the escape was seen to come from the French camp at Gheluwe, so a howitzer and two cannon were to remain in the bastion on the left of the Bruges gate to take them in flank.

A force under *Titulair Oberst-Lieutenant* von Spangenberg of the 14th Infantry Regiment was to try to hold the town until the following morning. He had one artillery and six infantry officers, 13 NCOs, 30 gunners, and 200 infantry, with the heavy howitzers and four 4-pounders. The infantry men were drawn from all the battalions in the garrison, except for the Loyal Emigrants, who would be executed by the French if captured.[38]

At first things went well, with the Loyal Emigrants succeeding in driving off the French troops in the Bruges suburb after a bloody hand to hand combat, supported by *Capitain* Hugo's company of the 1st Grenadier Battalion. They then moved to

---

Hammerstein, im April 1794', *Neues militairisches Journal,* 1803 Vol.11, pp.185-6 and Ditfurth, *Die Hessen,* Vol.2, p.449.

36 Scharnhorst, 'Die Vertheidigung der Stadt Menin', p.223.

37 Scharnhorst, 'Die Vertheidigung der Stadt Menin', p.320b.

38 Scharnhorst, 'Die Vertheidigung der Stadt Menin', p.303.

attack the two French battalions camped further along the road and pressed on through, opening the way to the allied lines at Roeselare.

However, the attack by the main column soon ran into difficulties. The 1st Battalion of the 14th Infantry Regiment, which was to take up a position to the left of the road from the suburb to the Bruges gate, came under heavy fire before the men had been able to form up. To make matters worse, the officer commanding the two 1-pounder amusettes at the head of the battalion set about deploying them as soon as they came under enemy fire as they passed the barrier, which disrupted the battalion's march. The allied battery placed to fire on the flank of the enemy did nothing. Meanwhile, the artillery, which should have been following the battalion into the Bruges suburb, had failed to take its opportunity and only two cannon with their caissons had passed through. The French attacked the left flank of the battalion, forcing it back, and took possession of the road between the barrier and the gate. The Loyal Emigrants were now cut off from the rest of the garrison, Hugo had been wounded and captured and his grenadier company dispersed by the French.

At this critical moment, Hammerstein refused to fall back into Menin and ordered the three companies of the 1st Grenadier Battalion in the rear guard to move forward, although they had to get round the artillery blocking the Bruges gate and then reform under enemy fire. Hammerstein harangued them and led them forward in a bayonet charge which drove back the French. Eventually, after great difficulties, the allied troops were able cut through the French lines to Roeselare and safety.

Spangenberg's men surrendered that morning and became prisoners of war, along with the wounded men of the 14th Infantry Regiment in the hospital, while the French killed any wounded men they found from the Loyal Emigrants. The cavalry and infantry lost a total of 704 officers and men, including 55 during the bombardment and 234 captured when the town surrendered. On top of this, the artillery and train lost 103 officers and men, bringing the total to 807, 40 percent of the total garrison. The heavy artillery division lost two 30-pounder howitzers, three 7-pounder howitzers, and two 6-pounder cannon. The 1st Grenadier Battalion lost its two 3-pounder battalion guns and the 14th Infantry Regiment lost a 1-pounder amusette.[39] The bravery of the garrison in making their escape received glowing praise in letters to Hammerstein from the Emperor, Clerfayt, and the King.[40]

While the allied operations were having mixed fortunes, the British government finally sent part of the promised reinforcements to the Duke of York's army. Three additional British infantry regiments, the 12th, 38th, and 55th Foot, and the 8th Light Dragoons were sent from Ireland, in addition to the drafts of recruits sent to reinforce the British regiments who were already in the Low Countries. They arrived at Ostend at the end of April and beginning of May, where they were put under the command of Major General Whyte and sent to join Clerfayt's corps. Major Calvert,

---

39 Report by Hammerstein in Sichart, *Geschichte der Königlich-Hannoverschen Armee*, Vol.4, pp.407-9.

40 Scharnhorst, 'Die Vertheidigung der Stadt Menin', pp.320b-h.

The Sally made by the Garrison of Menin, in the night of 30 April 1794, painted and engraved by J.G Huck. *General-Major* von Hammerstein is on horseback in the centre with his staff and senior officers on the left. The Hanoverian 1st Grenadier Battalion is advancing, led by *Capitain* von Alten (Garde) in the left foreground and *Capitain* von Hugo (10th Infantry Regiment) behind the cannon. (Anne S.K. Brown Military Collection, Brown University Library)

one of the Duke of York's aides de camp, wrote that these troops were 'said to be in a shocking state, badly clothed and some without firelocks'.[41]

At the end of April, the Duke of York received a request from the Emperor to march to Tournai. He set off with around 18,000 men to support Clerfayt's 19,000 in attempting to drive the French from West Flanders, with a further 6,000 under Wallmoden positioned between them near Courtrai.[42] The Duke's army repulsed a French attack on 10 May, but Clerfayt's attempt to retake Courtrai was defeated on 10 to 12 May. Taking part in the latter action, the Hesse Darmstadt brigade was heavily engaged at Ingelmunster, where Düring reported their losses to be one officer and 26 NCOs and men killed, 12 officers and 169 NCOs and men wounded, and one of the wounded officers and 20 NCOs and men captured. The 1st Leibgrenadier Battalion also lost its two battalion guns.[43]

After this setback, Mack drew up an elaborate plan to envelop and annihilate the French forces. The main army was to attack the French around Tourcoing in five columns on 17 May, while Clerfayt's corps was to move to attack them in the rear. *General der Infanterie* von dem Bussche, who had been promoted on 13 December 1793, had taken over the temporary command of the Hanoverian corps in Wallmoden's absence due to illness. He commanded the first column, made up of the Leibgarde, 2nd, 4th, 5th, and 7th Cavalry regiments, 2nd Grenadier Battalion, Garde Regiment and 1st, 4th, 6th, and 11th Infantry Regiments.[44] The Hesse Cassel troops were divided between *Feldmarschall-Lieutenant* Otto's second column, the Duke of York's third column, *Feldmarschall-Lieutenant* Kinsky's fourth column, and Clerfayt's corps, which also included the other Hanoverian troops and the Hesse Darmstadt brigade.

From a combination of poor planning and coordination, and the lack of activity of some of the column commanders, only the second and third columns were fully engaged on the decisive second day of the battle and the attack ended in a costly defeat. Two of the German regiments suffered particularly heavy losses: the Hanoverian 1st Infantry Regiment had *Oberst-Lieutenant* von Dachenhausen killed, an officer and 15 men wounded, and seven officers and 250 men captured when Bussche was pushed back from Mouscron on the 17th;[45] and the Hesse Cassel Leib-Regiment which was left by the Duke of York to hold Lannoy had seven men killed, three officers and 54 men wounded, and 11 officers and 254 men captured or missing.[46]

41 Calvert to Dalrymple, 11 May 1794, in Sir H. Verney (ed.), *The Journals and Correspondence of General Sir Harry Calvert* (London: Hurst and Blackett, 1853), p.206.
42 Figures given by Craig in a letter to Nepean 6 May 1794, TNA: WO 1/169, pp.21-2.
43 Düring's report on the action of 11-12 May in Scharnhorst, 'Feldzug der verbundenen Armeen in Flandern im Jahre 1794', *Neues militairisches Journal*, 1801 Vol.10, pp.243-4 and Rittmeister Zimmermann, *Geschichte des 1. Grossherzoglich Hessischen Dragoner-Regiments (Garde-Dragoner-Regiments) Nr. 23, I. Theil Geschichte des Landgräflich und Grossherzoglich Hessischen Garde-Regiments Chevaulegers von 1790 bis 1860* (Darmstadt: Arnold Bergsträsser, 1878), pp.37-8.
44 Schwertfeger, 'Tagebuch-Auszeichnunge', p.306.
45 Sichart, *Geschichte der Königlich-Hannoverschen Armee*, Vol.4, pp.449-50.
46 Ditfurth, *Die Hessen*, Vol.2, Table facing p.157.

Although the allies defeated the French forces at Pont-à-Chin near Tournai on 22 May, the defeat at Tourcoing was to prove decisive. The Austrians were disheartened and the British, feeling badly let down by their ally, complained bitterly of the 'folly and ignorance' of the Austrian commanders.[47] The Emperor called a council of war of the senior allied commanders to consider the options for future action, but the Austrians were by now ready to give up the defence of the Austrian Netherlands. The Duke of York reported to Dundas on the 29th that the Emperor had unexpectedly declared his intention of returning to Vienna as soon as possible and that he would quit the army the following day, leaving Coburg in command. He also noted that Mack had resigned as chief of staff, to be replaced by the Prince of Waldeck, and that over two thirds of the Austrian officers had expressed the wish to retire.[48]

Apart from having to deal with these unwelcome events, the Duke had to address another unpleasant matter. In general orders on 7 June, he announced that the French National Convention had passed a decree that their men should give no quarter to the British and Hanoverian troops. He doubted that the French troops would pay any attention to the decree and urged his men not to allow their resentment at it to lead to any acts of cruelty against the enemy.[49] The Duke was right in believing the French would ignore the decree, which was in any case repealed when Robespierre fell from power.

Meanwhile, Pichegru had moved forward and began the siege of Ypres on 1 June. It had once been a very strong fortress, but part of the fortifications had been demolished by Joseph II and, although it had 110 cannon of all calibres on the walls and outworks, many were in very poor condition and the fortress only had enough ammunition for 14 days. The Austrian *General-Major* Salis commanded the garrison, which was made up of:

- Two battalions of the Austrian Infantry Regiment Stuart Nr 18 with 1,600 men;
- 120 men of the *Freicorps* O'Donell;
- Two battalions each of the Hesse Cassel Infantry Regiments Erb-Prinz, Prinz Carl, and von Lossberg, with 2,173 men between them;
- The Leib Squadron of the Hesse Cassel Gens d'Armes with 116 men;
- A detachment of 24 men from the Hanoverian 9th Light Dragoons;
- A company of Austrian artillery and the artillery detachment serving the Hesse Cassel battalion guns with 111 men.

Two more weak Austrian battalions from the Infantry Regiments Callenberg Nr 54 and Carl Schröder Nr 7, with a combined strength of around 900 men, were sent to reinforce the garrison, bringing the total to a little over 5,000 men.[50]

47   Craig to Nepean, 19 May 1794 TNA: WO 1/169, pp.97-100.
48   York to Dundas 29 May 1794 TNA: WO 1/169, pp.203-6.
49   R. Brown, *An Impartial Journal of a Detachment from the Brigade of Foot Guards, commencing 25th February, 1793 and ending 9th May, 1795*, (London: John Stockdale, 1795) pp.156-63.
50   'Beschreibung der Westflandrischen Festung Ypern, deren Belagerung und Einnahme im Feldzug von 1794', *Neue Bellona*, 1801 Vol.1 pp.92-3 and 102, Ditfurth, *Die Hessen*, Vol.2, pp.473-4 and Report of Borck's corps for 25-31 May 1794 in HStAM 4 h 3360, p.53.

Clerfayt made several half-hearted attempts to relieve Ypres but, when these failed, the garrison surrendered on the 17th, leaving maritime Flanders open to the French. The Hesse Cassel contingent lost *General-Majors* von Borck and von Lengercke, with 120 officers and 3,193 men, including the sick, staff and servants. They also surrendered 30 infantry flags, a cavalry standard and 12 battalion guns.[51] In one of the attempts to relieve Ypres, *General-Major* von Düring was wounded in the neck and shoulder by a cannon ball, while leading a charge at Beveren on 13 June. The command of the Hesse Darmstadt Brigade was taken over temporarily by *Obrist* von Werner of the Chevauxlegers.

The end of Austrian attempts to save the Austrian Netherlands came with the failure of Coburg's attack on the French around Charleroi. Although the Battle of Fleurus on 26 June was tactically indecisive, Coburg's retreat left the Duke of York's army exposed. A conference was held on the 30th, at which Coburg announced his intention to defend the Austrian Netherlands, but soon afterwards he continued his retreat. This left the Duke no option but to fall back. The British government was, as usual, anxious to protect Ostend and rushed Lord Moira with the British infantry regiments, which had been held back from the spring campaign in case of an attempted French invasion, to join the other troops assembled there. Moira arrived on 28 June and, finding Ostend to be indefensible, he marched to join the Duke of York's army. With these reinforcements, British troops for the first time formed around half of the Duke's army.

As the British retreated, they left a weak garrison to hold Nieuport, which was considered of great importance by the government. The garrison was left there until it was too late to evacuate them and Moreau arrived at the town with 8,000 men on 4 July, encircled it and began the bombardment on the night of the 5th. By 15 July, the Hanoverian *General-Major* von Diepenbroick, who commanded the garrison, had only 2,085 officers and men under arms, including 329 artillery men serving the battalion and fortress guns. His motley force was made up two battalions each of the Hanoverian 5th and 10th Infantry Regiments, a battalion of the Loyal Emigrants, 140 men from Captain Wilson's ship's company, small detachments from the Hesse Cassel Gens d'Armes and of British infantry and cavalry, 65 Hanoverian and Austrian artillerymen, 15 officers and men of the engineers, and a corps of 125 volunteers. He also had 280 non-combatants, made up of staff, commissariat personnel, servants, drivers and women, and 259 sick, making 2,624 in total.[52]

The defences were far too weak to withstand a siege and Diepenbroick surrendered on 18 July. Moreau was aware of the decree that no quarter should be allowed to British or Hanoverian troops, but had been authorised by the representatives of the Convention on the 15th to allow a capitulation to the Hanoverians, but not to the émigrés. This authority was revoked on the 18th, but the letter informing Moreau of this did not arrive until after the capitulation had been signed and it was honoured

---

51 Ditfurth, *Die Hessen*, Vol.2, p.501.
52 Return of the effective strength of the garrison on 15 July 1794 in Hann 38 E Nr 189, p.44. The name of Wilson's ship is not given.

Map 7   The Theatre of War in the United Provinces and Northern Germany, 1794-5. (Based on map
24 in the atlas to The Hon. J.W. Fortescue, *A History of the British Army*, Vol. IV)

by the French.[53] The garrison, excluding the Loyal Emigrants, were allowed to march
out as prisoners of war, but the 264 officers and men of the Emigrants were massa-
cred, including Lieutenant Colonel Marquis de Villaines, who had commanded the
battalion at Menin.

It had been agreed at a further conference of the allied commanders at Waterloo
on 5 July to hold the line from Antwerp to Namur but, by the 7th, Coburg had
ordered the whole of his army to fall back upon Tirlemont. By the end of July,
Antwerp had been abandoned and the Duke of York had been obliged to retreat
into the United Provinces. The French, advancing from Nieuport besieged the port
of Sluis (l'Écluse), which surrendered on 25 August. Its garrison, mainly Dutch, also
included a battalion each of the Hanoverian 11th and 14th Infantry Regiments, who
became prisoners of war. Meanwhile, part of the French army was sent to recapture Valenciennes, Condé, Le Quesnoy, and Landrecies, which were still held by the
Austrians.

---

53   R. Bittard des Portes, *Les Émigrés à Cocarde Noire* (Paris, Émile-Paul, 1908), p.197.

At around this time, Baron von Barkhaus, Director of the Hesse Darmstadt War Department, was sent to London by the Landgrave and wrote to Grenville that, although it was necessary for the Landgrave to keep substantial numbers of troops in Germany, he could offer Britain an additional 2,242 men for the following year's campaign. These would comprise two battalions of infantry, a corps of chasseurs, four squadrons of cavalry, and a battery of artillery and could be ready by 1 March 1795. These new troops would be volunteers drawn from the battalions intended for the defence of the Landgrave's own territories, and chasseurs from his territories in Alsace, which had been seized by the French. The British government did not take advantage of this proposal at this time, nor when Count von Jenison Walworth, the Hesse Darmstadt Minister in London, raised it again in September.[54]

---

54 Barkhaus to Grenville 22 July 1794 and Jenison Walworth to Grenville 30 September 1794, TNA: FO 31/6.

6

Defending the United Provinces

The Duke of York resisted Dutch requests for him to place garrisons in their fortresses and to send an expedition to relieve Sluis. By the end of August he had fallen back to a position behind the River Aa, which covered the route into Holland and would allow him to march to support any of the Dutch fortresses which were attacked, as well as re-establishing communications with the Austrians.[1] He assembled his troops there, leaving the Hesse Cassel Regiment von Kospoth and the British 87th and 88th Foot to garrison Bergen op Zoom. The army had been reinforced by the two new batteries of Hesse Cassel artillery which arrived on 10 August with eight 12-pounders, eight 6-pounders, and four howitzers, but the horses had suffered greatly on the march.[2] The total strength of the Duke's army fit for duty was a little over 10,000 cavalry and 30,000 infantry, including the 2,000 at Bergen op Zoom, as shown in Table 4. However, as explained in Appendix VI, the actual number of men under arms was considerably lower, for example the Hanoverian cavalry and infantry only had 1,674 and 4,411 of all ranks under arms respectively.[3]

The Austrian *Feldmarschall-Lieutenant* Beaulieu arrived at the Duke's headquarters on 31 August with a letter from Clerfayt, who had been appointed to command the Austrian forces in the Low Countries following Coburg's resignation. He had come to arrange a meeting between Beaulieu, the Duke, and the Hereditary Prince of Orange to discuss a forward movement for the relief of the French fortresses in Austrian hands and the re-occupation of Flanders. The meeting took place at Bois-le-Duc ('s-Hertogenbosch) the following day and it was agreed that the Duke was to take Antwerp with 25,000 men of the Anglo-Allied Army and 5,000 Dutch troops, supported by the Austrians. The army was then to move to relieve Condé and Valenciennes, but the operation could not begin until Austrian troops moving towards Trier to resupply Luxembourg had re-joined the army, which was not expected until 15 September.[4] The Duke received news on the 6th that the Austrian garrisons at Condé and Valenciennes had surrendered, but he still thought the

---

1   York to Dundas 31 August 1794, TNA: WO 1/170, pp.279-82.
2   H.R.P. von Porbeck, *Kritische Geschichte der Operationen welche die Englisch-combinirte Armee zur Vertheidigung von Holland in den Jahren 1794 und 1795 ausgeführt hat* (Braunschweig: Friedrich Bernhard Culemann, 1802-4), Vol.1, p.386.
3   Reports of the Hanoverian cavalry and infantry for 15-31 August 1794, Hann. 38 E Nr. 213, pp.75 and 78.
4   Secret letter from York to Dundas 2 September 1794, enclosing the protocol of the conference, TNA: WO 1/170, pp.287-95.

Table 4: Anglo-Allied Army at the End of August 1794 – Total Fit for Duty

	Officers	NCOs	Musicians	Rank & File	Total
Cavalry					
British	132	255	60	3,105	3,552
Foreign troops	70	116	23	2,040	2,249
Hanoverian	160	252	51	1,798	2,261
Hesse Cassel	51	170	32	1,384	1,637
Hesse Darmstadt	19	41	8	348	416
	432	834	174	8,675	10,115
Infantry					
British	464	814	446	14,272	15,996
Foreign troops	75	107	47	1,484	1,713
Hanoverian	276	654	184	6,322	7,436
Hesse Cassel	156	459	148	3,008	3,771
Hesse Darmstadt	61	128	43	1,391	1,623
	1,032	2,162	868	26,477	30,539
Total					
British	596	1,069	506	17,377	19,548
Foreign troops	145	223	70	3,524	3,962
Hanoverian	436	906	235	8,120	9,697
Hesse Cassel	207	629	180	4,392	5,408
Hesse Darmstadt	80	169	51	1,739	2,039
	1,464	2,996	1,042	35,152	40,654

Sources:
Monthly Return of the British Troops 1 September 1794, TNA: WO 1/170 pp.555 and 689;
Monthly Return of the Foreign Troops in the Service of Great Britain 1 September 1794, TNA:
WO 1/171 p.289; Return of the German Troops 31 August 1794, TNA: WO 1/170 p.563.

Notes:
The figures shown above are for the total fit for duty from the returns submitted by the British
Adjutant General's department, which were compiled on a consistent basis. The returns
prepared by the German contingents themselves are lower.
The Baden battalion was behind the lines guarding French prisoners of war and is not included
above.

attack to recover West Flanders should go ahead and that he should then establish
his winter quarters there.[5]

Colonel Craig reported to Nepean that everything was quiet and that they had
not seen anything of the enemy. However, he was concerned that the army had not
been able to establish dependable lines of intelligence and estimates of the enemy

---

5   York to Dundas 7 September 1794, TNA: WO 1/170, pp.337-40.

strength varied between 60,000 and 80,000.[6] He also expressed his doubts that the Austrians would act in good faith and, contrary to the Duke's opinion, whether it would be possible to establish winter quarters in Brabant and Flanders, without the protection of the fortresses they had held in 1793. Hammerstein, who commanded the advance posts, had sent out cavalry patrols to gather information about enemy numbers and movements. On 12 September, the Duke received a report that one of these patrols had captured two French officers, one of whom stated that he was an aide-de-camp to General Souham, and that the army under Pichegru's personal command was marching to carry out a strong reconnaissance and then attack the allied positions.[7]

The heavy baggage was sent away to safety but, in spite of the obvious danger posed by the greatly superior French forces, Hammerstein's exposed posts were not pulled back closer to the main army. His troops were strung out along a front of almost 40 kilometres behind the River Dommel, up to 14 kilometres in front of the main army behind the Aa. The line stretched from Sint-Michielsgestel and Boxtel on his right, through Olland and Sint-Oedenrode, where he had his headquarters, and Breugel to Aarle on his left. The allied commanders knew that it was not a good position, with the right not extending as far as the inundations of Bois-le-Duc, the left uncovered and open to being turned by the enemy, and even the river in front was 'not capable of being converted into a line of defence'.[8]

The Duke contented himself with sending some minor reinforcements, which were not sufficient to have a significant effect on Hammerstein's position. He sent two squadrons of the Hesse Cassel Prinz Friedrichs Dragoons and two of the Hanoverian 1st Cavalry Regiment to Sint-Oedenrode, and a battalion of British infantry with its battalion guns towards Vught to defend Sint-Michielsgestel. The post at Boxtel was reinforced by 40 men from the Hanoverian 2nd Cavalry Regiment from Sint-Oedenrode; Irvine's Hussars and the Hompesch Jägers, two of the newly raised foreign regiments in British service, were ordered to Boxtel.

After receiving these reinforcements, Hammerstein had around 10,000 men fit for duty, over half of them cavalry, but with probably fewer than 9,000 under arms.[9] They were positioned behind the Dommel as follows:

Right Wing
- Boxtel: *General-Major* von Düring with the Hesse Darmstadt Chevauxlegers, 1st Leibgrenadier Battalion, 1st Battalion Regiment Landgraf, Light Infantry Battalion and Feldjäger-Corps, Choiseul Hussars, Hompesch Hussars and York Rangers;
- Olland: Hesse Cassel Leib Dragoon Regiment and Fusilier Battalion.

---

6   Craig to Nepean marked 'Private & confidential' 8 September 1794, TNA: WO 1/170, pp.375-8.
7   York to Dundas 12 September 1794, TNA: WO 1/170 pp.429-30 and Porbeck, *Kritische Geschichte*, Vol.1, pp.447-8.
8   Craig to Nepean 19 September 1794, TNA: WO 1/170, pp.471-4.
9   The number fit for duty is taken from the returns listed in Table 4

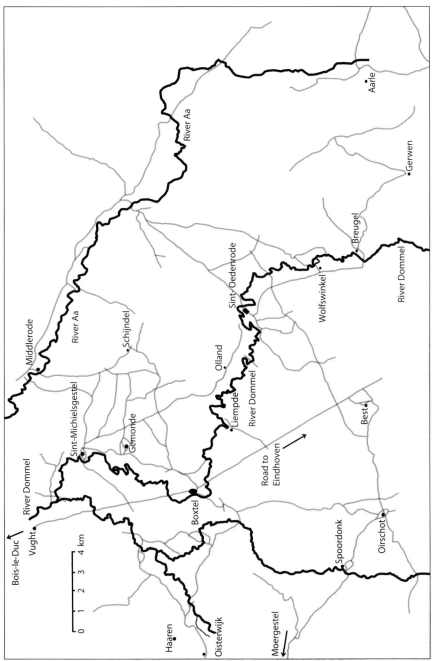

Map 8 Boxtel and the Dommel, September 1794. (Based on Map 10 of the Atlas Part II to F.H.A. Sabron, *De Oorlog van 1794-95, op het Grondgebied van de Republiek der Vereenigde Nederlanden*)

Centre
- Sint-Oedenrode: *General-Major* von Hammerstein and Major General Sir Robert Laurie with the Hanoverian 2nd and 3rd Grenadier Battalions, 2 squadrons of Hanoverian cavalry and a horse artillery battery, the Hesse Cassel Jäger Battalion, and two squadrons each of the British 7th, 11th, 15th, and 16th Light Dragoons;
- Breugel: Hanoverian 9th Light Dragoons, a company of Hanoverian Jägers, and a battalion of the Loyal Emigrants.

Left Wing
- Aarle: *General-Major* von Linsing with the Hanoverian 10th Light Dragoons, 1st Grenadier Battalion, a company of Jägers and a half battery of horse artillery, Rohan Hussars, Salm Hussars and Rohan Light Infantry.[10]

The Hanoverians had suffered greatly from sickness and losses in the earlier part of the campaign, with the three battalions of grenadiers having only 671 officers and men under arms between them.[11] Even the Hesse Darmstadt troops, who were considered among the best in the army, were worn down by their continuous service on the advance posts. *Obrist* von Werner, who was commanding the brigade in Düring's absence, wrote to the Duke of York and *Major* von Löw, the Duke's *Flügel-Adjudant* and effectively adjutant general for the German troops, to request that they be withdrawn from the advance posts and allowed time for the men and horses to recover, so that they would be fit for future service. The reply on 10 September was that they must hold their current positions for the next eight to 10 days, but that the Duke hoped to be able to relieve them after that and allow them a period of rest.[12] Unfortunately for them, the French attacked before this could happen.

Pichegru's reconnaissance found that the Dommel was only held weakly, and he decided to attack the enemy right and centre on 14 September with four divisions, in total over 40,000 men supported by strong artillery:

- *Général de Division* (provisional) Bonnaud with 9,400 infantry and 1,600 cavalry was ordered to march at 9:00 a.m. passing by Oirschot and Best towards Breugel and Sint-Oedenrode.[13] His advance guard was to cross the river when the rest of the army was in position;
- On his left *Général de Division* Despeaux with 5,600 infantry and 600 cavalry was to go by Moergestel and then march parallel to Bonnaud and execute the same manoeuvre;

---

10 Hammerstein's disposition for the advance posts in HStAD, E 8 B No 269/1 and Anon., 'Relation des Gefechts bey Boxtel an der Dommel, am 14ten und 15ten September 1794', *Neue Bellona*, Vol.2, 1802, pp.260-1.
11 Report of the Hanoverian infantry for 15-31 August 1794, Hann. 38 E Nr. 213 p.78.
12 Werner to York and Löw 7 September 1794 and reply by Löw 10 September 1794, HStAD, E 8 B No 267/2.
13 Bonnaud's appointment was made provisionally by the Representatives of the People with the army and was only confirmed officially later.

Rudolph Georg Wilhelm von Hammerstein, drawn from life and engraved by J.G. Huck. (Anne S.K. Brown Military Collection, Brown University Library)

- *Général de Division* Delmas with 4,600 infantry and 400 cavalry was to follow the same road as Despeaux as far as Oirschot and then move left to take part in the attack on Boxtel. When that position was taken he was to follow the Dommel to the left of Despeaux;
- The main mission was entrusted to *Général de Division* Souham's division of 15,400 infantry and 3,600 cavalry, which was to set off in two columns at 9:00 a.m. The first under *Général de Brigade* (provisional) De Winter was to go by Oisterwijk and to deploy on the heath before Boxtel after crossing the river. He was to wait until the enemy had been driven from that area and then take up position behind the Dommel. *Général de Brigade* Macdonald's second column was to march to the left of De Winter, and his advance guard under Jardon was to take Boxtel. Souham directed that Boxtel was to be attacked from both the left and right.[14]

Hammerstein reported that Düring had returned and taken over the command of the post at Boxtel on 13 September. Düring had allocated the responsibility for the defence of key posts to his senior officers, made wise dispositions of the troops in case of attack, and had then taken up a position from which he could oversee and direct operations. He was to hold his post for as long as possible, or as stated by Keim 'to the last man', according to the Duke's direct orders.[15]

Obrist von Werner commanded the forces at Boxtel, which consisted of the Hesse Darmstadt 1st Leibgrenadier Battalion and the battalion of Regiment Landgraf with their four 3-pounder battalion guns, the Feldjäger-Corps, and a squadron of Chevauxlegers, together with Irvine's and Hompesch's Hussars and the Hompesch Jägers. His total force amounted to 1,116 infantry and 528 cavalry.[16] Werner placed a company of infantry with two battalion guns to defend each of the two bridges over the Dommel, one on the road to Oirschot the other on that to Eindhoven. The routes leading into Boxtel were covered by the Jägers with detachments from the infantry battalions, and the remaining infantry were held as a reserve in the village. The cavalry was drawn up behind and pickets were placed to watch the river and the roads leading to the enemy.

Meanwhile, Düring took three squadrons of Hesse Darmstadt Chevauxlegers, the Choiseul Hussars, and a half battery of Hanoverian horse artillery onto the heath to the west of Boxtel to cover Werner's right flank. Three companies of the Hesse Darmstadt Light Infantry Battalion were at Sint-Michielsgestel, which was

14 L. Jouan, 'La Campagne de 1794 das les Pays Bas, Deuxième Partie', *Revue d'Histoire*, Vol.51, 1913 pp.429-30. The strengths of the divisions are taken from Tableau général des forces de l'Armée du Nord au 1er Septembre 1794 (15 Fructidor An II) in F.H.A. Sabron, *De Oorlog van 1794-95, op het Grondgebied van de Republiek der Vereenigde Nederlanden Nederlanden* (Breda: Van Broese & comp., 1891-3), Vol.I, Appendix 1, pp.III-XIV.

15 Hammerstein's report to the Duke of York, HStAD, E 8 B No 269/1; Anon., 'Relation des Gefechts bey Boxtel', pp.265-8 and A. Keim, *Geschichte des Infanterie-Leibregiments Grossherzogin (3. Grossherzogl. Hessisches) Nr. 117 und seine Stämme 1677-1902* (Berlin: Ernst Siegfried Mittler und Sohn, 1903), p.125.

16 Ditfurth, *Die Hessen*, Vol.2, p.252.

commanded by *Obristlieutenant* von Canngieser of the Chevauxlegers, with the other company posted at Gemonde between there and Boxtel.

After small enemy patrols had been seen on the morning of the 14th, the French attack began in earnest at around 2:00-2:30 p.m. They advanced in three columns from Oisterwijk, Moergestel, and Oirschot and attacked the advance posts at Boxtel, driving back the pickets, while their cavalry advanced onto the large heath between Haaren and Boxtel. At first things seemed to be going reasonably well for the defenders, with *Major* von Schäfer's Feldjäger-Corps at the front of the position receiving reinforcements and pushing back the French attacks, while Düring's cavalry and horse artillery held back the enemy cavalry.

At 4:00 p.m. another strong French column, believed by Jouan to be Despeaux marching to the sound of the guns, advanced along the Eindhoven road, cutting off and capturing a Hessian detachment and threatening the allied left flank.[17] The French were able to cross the shallow river in a number of places and, although the guns defending the bridges kept up a fierce fire, Werner was in danger of being completely surrounded and ordered his troops to fall back behind the village and retreat towards Sint-Michielsgestel. The movement began in good order, but the retreating column was attacked from both sides and had the French cavalry following its rear. Irvine's Hussars were covering the retreat, but were driven back into the infantry, throwing them into disorder and the majority of the troops were forced to surrender.[18]

When Boxtel was clearly lost, Düring fell back towards Sint-Michielsgestel and the remnants of his command retreated to the allied position at Middelrode on the Aa, which his rear guard reached at 11:00 p.m.. The losses of his brigade had been enormous: 20 officers, 35 NCOs, two company surgeons, 11 musicians, 667 men and 12 drivers, making 747 in total. The heaviest losses had fallen on the troops driven out of Boxtel, with the Leibgrenadier Battalion losing a total of 327 officers and men, Regiment Landgraf 303, and the Jägers 63. The artillery detachments lost its two officers and 31 NCOs, gunners and drivers.[19] They also lost the four battalion guns and their ammunition waggons, although they were able to save their flags from falling into enemy hands. The losses of the foreign troops in British service at Boxtel were 14 dead and 40 prisoners of war for Irvine's Hussars, eight dead and 30 prisoners for Hompesch's Hussars, and one dead and 97 prisoners for Hompesch's Jägers.[20]

A little over an hour later than the attack on Boxtel, the enemy attacked Hammerstein's centre at Sint-Oedenrode, Wolfswinkel, and Breugel with a strong force of cavalry on the plain and a column of infantry advancing along the road from Best. The allied forces here, including the Hesse Cassel Jägers under *Capitain* Ochs who again distinguished himself, managed to hold their positions until nightfall,

---

17 L. Jouan, 'La Campagne de 1794', p.432.
18 Reports by Düring, Schäfer and Hammerstein, HStAD, E 8 B No 269/1.
19 Report of the losses of the 1st Hesse Darmstadt Brigade at Boxtel on 14 September 1794, dated 17 September 1794, HStAD, E 8 B No 271/2 p.60.
20 Monthly Return of the Foreign Troops in the service of Great Britain 1 October 1794, TNA: WO 1/171, p.291.

although the troops at Olland had been forced to fall back by the enemy cavalry. With the loss of Boxtel and Olland, Hammerstein's position was now untenable. He ordered his troops to fall back towards the Aa but, on their way, they received orders to return to their former positions. After doing nothing on the 14th, the Duke of York sent Lieutenant General Abercromby with a force of British infantry and cavalry to try to retake Boxtel on the morning of the 15th, but he found the enemy forces before him too strong and called off the attack.

The Duke of York now believed that the enemy forces advancing towards him 'could scarcely be less than eighty Thousand Men'. He also received reports that they were moving against his left and decided that he could not risk an engagement on such unequal terms. He decided to retreat across the Meuse and the army began its march at 3:00 p.m. on the 15th, crossing the river at Grave.[21] In order to cover his retreat, three companies of the Hesse Darmstadt Light Infantry Battalion under *Obristlieutenant* von Stosch were ordered to join the garrison of Fort Crevecoeur, on the Meuse to the north of Bois-le-Duc. They were captured when the fort surrendered on 28 September, but were released on condition that they swore not to take up arms against the French until they were exchanged for French prisoners. Thus, by the end of September the Hesse Darmstadt brigade had virtually ceased to exist, as shown in Table 5. This, coming on top of the months of hard campaigning and his serious wound at Beveren, was too much for Düring, who took his own life on 19 May 1795 at the age of 39.

Table 5: State of the Hesse Darmstadt Brigade 30 September 1794

	Full Strength	Sick	Effectives Under Arms
Cavalry			
Chevauxlegers	508	210	126
Infantry			
1st Leibgrenadier Battalion	711	131	96
Regiment Landgraf (1st Battalion)	715	120	121
Light Infantry Battalion	708	89	67
Feldjäger-Corps	150	12	26
	2,284	352	310
Total	2,792	562	436

Source:
Reports of the Hesse Darmstadt cavalry and infantry 16-30 September 1794, HStAD, E 8 B Nr 271/3 pp. 66-8.

Note:
The totals include staff and the artillery detachments with the battalion guns.

---

21   York to Dundas 17 September 1794, TNA: WO 1/170, pp.437-41.

The description of events given above is based on the reports by Hammerstein, Düring, and Schäfer, and is consistent with that given by Ditfurth, Porbeck, and the regimental histories of the units involved, and followed by Jouan and Sabron. They all describe the small force at Boxtel holding their positions until overwhelmed by the much stronger enemy columns. Hammerstein stated that they faced an enemy 20 times stronger, whilst estimates in the regimental histories of the French troops engaged vary between 15 and 20,000.[22] These figures are certainly reasonable in relation to the movements and strengths of the French columns that attacked them.

As Jouan noted, there are virtually no accounts of the fighting from the French side, but the Representatives Bellegarde and Lacambe with the Armée du Nord sent a report which was published in *Le Moniteur*. Not surprisingly, it overstated the scale of the French victory and described how the French troops had attacked Boxtel, which they claim had entrenchments bristling with artillery and 5,000 infantry and cavalry defending it. It stated that, after an hour and a half of combat, the enemy fled, losing 2,000 prisoners and eight cannon with their ammunition waggons, and went on to relate how 30 men from the 8th Hussars had forced two battalions of Hessians to lay down their arms.[23] 'Citizen David' claimed to be a witness to most of the events during the campaigns of the Armies of the North and of the Sambre and Meuse from March 1794 to March 1795. He wrote that Pichegru attacked the allied advance post of 6 to 7,000 men at Boxtel, and that the attack took place from 3:00 to 6:00 p.m. He described how the French troops crossed the river, some by swimming and some on planks, and forced the allied troops to surrender. He also repeated the story that 30 hussars from the 8th Hussars forced two Hessian battalions to surrender and added that an unarmed drummer had taken 10 prisoners.[24]

The Duke of York sent a secret report to Dundas, which was picked up by Fortescue and has been accepted by most subsequent British historians.[25] In this letter, the Duke gave a number of particulars 'for His Majesty's Information', which he did not consider it advisable to include in his public letter. After stating that 'It does not appear that the attack at first was very severe', he went on to blame the defeat on 'a sudden Panick' which affected the two battalions of Hesse Darmstadt infantry who, he conceded, had previously shown the greatest courage on all occasions. Not only had this led to the loss of Boxtel, but he also blamed them for cutting down the bridges while the cavalry was engaging the enemy on the other side of the river, causing 'confusion and loss in that Corps'. He went on that, having begun their retreat in great confusion, the Hessians were overtaken by a few French hussars, who had crossed the river by an unguarded ford, and laid down their arms. He finished by praising the conduct of the new foreign corps, who had 'conducted themselves

---

22 Hammerstein's report to the Duke of York, HStAD, E 8 B No 269/1 and Anon., 'Relation des Gefechts bey Boxtel', p.268.

23 Report by the Representatives Bellegarde and Lacambe from the headquarters of the Armée du Nord 30 Fructidor An II (16 September 1794) in *Le Moniteur* No 1, 1 Vendémiaire An III (22 September 1794) in Anon., *Réimpression de l'Ancien Moniteur*, (Paris: Henri Plon, 1862). Vol.22, pp.3-4.

24 Citoyen David, *Histoire Chronologique des Opérations de l'Armée du Nord et de celle de Sambre et Meuse* (Paris: Guerbart, 1796), pp.78-9.

25 York to Dundas marked 'Secret' 17 September 1794, TNA: WO 1/170, pp.453-5.

with great Spirit', but noted that the two companies of Hompesch's Jägers, who had defended themselves at Boxtel to Düring's satisfaction, had been 'nearly cut to pieces'.

The Duke did not give his source of information, and this account is completely at odds with the reports from his commanders on the spot, ignoring their praise for the officers and men, who had defended the post with courage and skill. It is also difficult to understand the Duke's claim that the cavalry, who were fighting the enemy on the other side of the river, suffered 'confusion and loss' because of the premature destruction of the bridges. He may have meant the foreign hussars who were positioned behind Boxtel and were to cover the withdrawal of the infantry. It seems more likely that he was referring to the Hesse Darmstadt Chevauxlegers and Choiseul Hussars under Düring, who were resisting the French advance to the west of Boxtel. However, these troops did not suffer any great loss in the action: the total loss of the Chevauxlegers, including the squadron at Boxtel, was 11 officers and men and the return dated 1 October does not record any men either dead or captured for the Choiseul Hussars. In addition, Düring reported that his retreat to Sint-Michielsgestel, away from Boxtel and its bridges, was conducted in good order.[26] It may just be that the Duke was trying to shift the blame for the defeat onto the Hessian infantry, and to avoid criticism for having left the troops at Boxtel exposed and unsupported, in the face of greatly superior enemy forces.

Once again, the French did not follow up on their victory and the Duke took up a position behind the Meuse. He agreed with Prince Frederick of Orange to cover the stretch from Heusden, west of Bois-le-Duc, to Venlo, on the condition that the Duke would recall the troops in British pay who were currently in Flanders and Bergen op Zoom, and that the Dutch would put in place the artillery necessary to defend the Bommelerwaard, reinforce the garrisons of Graves and Venlo and, if possible, relieve the Darmstadt troops in Crevecoeur.[27] As Craig observed, 'It is now our business to defend the Meuse along an extent which is by much by too great for our numbers.'[28]

The Duke rejected Clerfayt's suggestion that the British should attempt to relieve Maastricht, and he was obliged to retreat and cross the River Waal at Nimeguen, when he learned that the Austrians had been defeated and fallen back behind the Rhine, uncovering his left flank.[29] For the rest of October the French set about besieging Bois-le-Duc, Venlo, and Maastricht, all of which had surrendered by early November, after which the French crossed the Meuse. The allied forces around Nimeguen (Nijmegen) were pushed back and the siege began on 1 November.

As the allies' military position deteriorated, Grenville wrote to Lord St Helens, who had taken over as ambassador at The Hague, that the situation in the United Provinces had become 'so embarrassing and alarming' that it was 'necessary to

---

26   Report of the Hesse Darmstadt losses in HStAD, E 8 B No 271/2 p.60 and Monthly Return of the Foreign Troops in the service of Great Britain 1 October 1794, TNA: WO 1/171, p.291.
27   York to Dundas 19 September 1794 enclosing minutes of the conference on the 18th, TNA: WO 1/170, pp.457-62.
28   Craig to Nepean 19 September 1794, TNA: WO 1/170, pp.471-4.
29   York to Dundas 3 October 1794, TNA: WO 1/170, pp.637-8.

have recourse to the most immediate and decisive measures'. The Duke of York had been instructed to make proposals to the Austrian and Prussian commanders for their cooperation to protect the Dutch Republic. It was also considered necessary to appoint a commander in chief for all of the allied forces in the Republic, and St Helens was to propose to the Dutch government that the command should be offered to the Duke of Brunswick, with the Duke of York and the Hereditary Prince of Orange retaining the 'interior management' of their respective forces. He informed St Helens that Eliot had been instructed to proceed to Brunswick 'as expeditiously as possible' to offer the command of the British and Dutch forces defending the United Provinces to the Duke, and St Helens was to press the Dutch government to authorise Eliot to act on their behalf or to appoint their own representative.[30]

St Helens reported to Grenville that the Prince and Princess of Orange and the senior officials of the Dutch government all 'highly approve and relish' the idea of offering the overall command to the Duke of Brunswick, and that Eliot had left for Brunswick accompanied by Major General Bentinck, the Quarter Master General of the Dutch army, who had been appointed to conduct negotiations on behalf of the Dutch government.[31] Later in the month, St Helens sent a confidential letter to Grenville, informing him that the Princess of Orange had received a letter from the Duke of Brunswick, her father in law. The Princess had previously informed the Duke of the proposal to be made to him and, although it appeared that he would decline to give a definitive answer, it was hoped that he was prepared to offer his advice for the defence of the Republic. St Helens believed that the Princess would ask the Duke to come to The Hague for that purpose and to facilitate negotiations.[32]

However, the Duke refused to accept the command. Lord Malmesbury had been sent to Brunswick in November to agree the terms of marriage between the Duke's daughter, Princess Caroline, and the Prince of Wales. He noted in his diary that the Duke had declined the command because of the 'want of unanimity amongst the Combined Powers' and later that Eliot had informed him that the Duke had explained to him that he did not wish to displease the Prussians.[33]

Although the Duke could not be persuaded to take the command of the allied armies, or even to go to The Hague to give advice, Eliot was at last able to conclude a subsidy treaty with the Duke's Minister of State. The treaty was signed on 8 November for a corps of 2,289 men to serve for three years in any part of Europe, but not on board the fleet. The corps was to be ready to march by 1 January 1795, if necessary in two divisions, with the second to be ready by 1 February, and the levy money and three months' pay were to be paid immediately after the signature of the treaty to cover the expenses of their march to join the allied army.[34]

---

30 Grenville to St Helens 12 and 15 October 1794, TNA: FO 37/55.
31 St Helens to Grenville 16 and 21 October 1794, TNA: FO 37/55.
32 St Helens to Grenville 27 October 1794, TNA: FO 37/55.
33 J.H. Harris, Third Earl of Malmesbury (ed.), *Diaries and Correspondence of James Harris, First Earl of Malmesbury* (London: Richard Bentley, 1844), Vol. 3, pp.150, 152 and 156-7.
34 Debrett (ed.), *A Collection of State Papers*, Vol.II, pp.14-19. The text of the treaty is in Appendix III.

Meanwhile, the strain of the campaign and the succession of retreats were having a serious effect on the officers and men. Craig sent a pessimistic letter to Nepean, stating that Wallmoden and all of the Hanoverian and Hessian officers were in favour of abandoning Nimeguen. Although he acknowledged Wallmoden's ability, Craig thought that he commanded with 'an ill will and' was being swayed in his opinions by others. He went on that 'the Hessians are clearly tired of their business and they are commanded by a J_ F_', a *jean-foutre*, or good-for-nothing. He explained that he was referring to Dalwigk, as his subordinate, *General-Major* Ludwig Johann Adam Wurmb, 'was a brave & a good Man'.[35] Prince Ernest also wrote to his brother, the Prince of Wales, that the troops looked 'wonderfully ill' and that he had never seen anything like the change that had come over Wallmoden.[36]

The garrison of Nimeguen, which included both men from the Duke of York's army and Dutch troops, made a sortie on 4 November which delayed the progress of the siege, but it was clear that the city could not be held. The British and German troops were evacuated on the night of the 7th, but the floating bridge on which the Dutch troops were attempting to cross the Waal was damaged and they surrendered, rather than risk it being sunk by French artillery fire.

After this, things remained quiet and Craig told Nepean that he did not expect the French to try anything further that year. However, he noted that there were reports of them collecting boats, so the possibility of their crossing the Waal made it necessary to keep the regiments in cantonments in the villages along the river and between the Waal and the Lek. They had to use churches and barns as there were not enough houses and the army was suffering greatly, with the sick list increasing to 7,000. The army now had only 22,000 infantry of all ranks, including the German infantry who were in a much reduced state, with only 4,300 effectives for the Hanoverians and 3,041 for the Hesse Cassel troops. The Hesse Darmstadt infantry, with only 384 rank and file, had been in cantonments since the crossing of the Meuse and the Baden troops were in the rear, guarding French prisoners.[37]

At this point Dundas wrote to the Duke of York, ordering him to return to England as soon as possible, to confer with government ministers on the critical situation in Holland and the state of the army. His 'short absence' was announced in general orders on 2 December.[38] In fact the government ministers had finally persuaded the King to recall the Duke and he left the army on the Continent shortly afterwards, never to return. The command of the army passed to Wallmoden, although the Duke was instructed to leave 'the command of His Majesty's British Forces in the hands of such British Officer as may be next in Seniority to Your Royal Highness', and this task was undertaken by Lieutenant General Harcourt. This division of command was bad enough, but communications between the government

---

35   Craig to Nepean marked 'Confidential' 28 October 1794, TNA: WO 1/170, pp.889-90.
36   Prince Ernest to the Prince of Wales 6 November 1794, in A. Aspinall (ed.), *The Correspondence of George, Prince of Wales 1770-1812* (London: Cassell, 1964), Vol.2, pp.481-2.
37   Craig to Nepean 27 November 1794 and Return of the actual strength of the infantry 27 November 1794, TNA: WO 1/171, pp.333-6 and 325.
38   Dundas to York 27 November 1794, TNA: WO 6/11, pp.579-80 and General Order signed by Don, Deputy Adjutant General, 2 December 1794, Hann. 38 E Nr. 198, f. 56.

and the commanders in the field became even more erratic and confused, with Dundas usually sending orders and instructions to the Duke of York to pass on to them, but sometimes writing direct to Harcourt.

French activity increased in early December and Harcourt reported to the Duke of York that both he and Wallmoden expected an attack. In anticipation of this, the sick and the heavy baggage were being sent back to safety, as quickly as the availability of waggons would allow. The French crossed the Waal in boats on the 11th and attacked the battery in front of Gendt under cover of thick fog and supported by their batteries on the opposite bank. They were eventually driven back by the Hanoverians but, at the end of the action, *General der Infanterie* von dem Bussche was struck by a cannon ball on his right side, which shattered his arm, and he died a few minutes later.[39]

The allied line along the Waal in mid-December was divided into sectors, with the Hesse Cassel troops under *General-Lieutenant* von Dalwigk on the right from Heesselt to Tiel, the British in the centre from Tiel to Lent opposite Nimeguen, and the Hanoverians under *General-Major* von Hammerstein, who had succeeded von dem Bussche, on the left from Lent to the Pannerden Canal, which connects the Rivers Waal and Lek.[40] The Dutch held the Bommelerwaard on the right of the line, with the left was covered by a corps of Austrians under Alvinczy. The infantry were posted in two lines, one near the Waal and the second in reserve, with most of the cavalry further back. Orders were issued to be ready for a French attack: half of the troops along the Waal had to maintain a chain of pickets and send out patrols to observe the enemy, with artillerymen stationed in each battery, to be ready to fire on the enemy before they could land; alarm posts were set up and communications maintained between the first and second line, so that the latter could support the first line if it came under attack; the posts were to support each other in case of attack and the second line was to retake any posts captured by the enemy, without waiting for further orders.[41]

Wallmoden and Harcourt reported to the Duke of York that although things remained quiet, the frost had become very severe and that ice was forming on the river. By 25 December it was expected that the river would be frozen over during the night, which would enable the enemy to cross. Wallmoden promised that they would 'do everything their feeble means allowed to dispute the ground foot by foot for as long as they could' if this happened. However, the infantry now had fewer than 16,000 combatants, insufficient to hold the position along the Waal.[42] At this critical time, the government, far from sending help to the army, informed Harcourt that it had been decided to withdraw seven British infantry regiments from the

---

39 Harcourt to York 8 December 1794 and Wallmoden to York 11 December 1794, TNA: WO 1.171, pp.407-12 and 435-8.

40 Cantonments of the army 19 December 1794 issued by Fox, TNA: WO 1/171, pp.579-82 and MFQ 1/1269.

41 Porbeck, *Kritische Geschichte*, Vol.1, pp.804-8 and translated copies of Wallmoden's *Disposition for the Defence of the first Line* and *General Plan of Defence in the case of an Attack from the Enemy*, TNA: WO 1/171, pp.569-71 and 573-5.

42 Wallmoden to York 22 December 1794, Wallmoden and Harcourt to York 23 December, Harcourt to York 25 December 1794, TNA: WO 1/171, pp 587-90, 635-6 and 643-5.

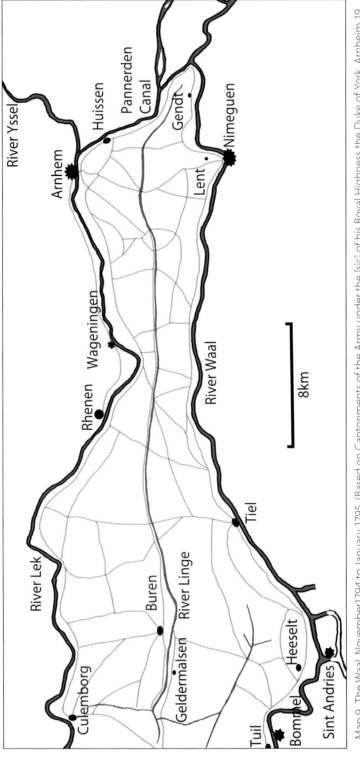

Map 9 The Waal, November1794 to January 1795. (Based on Cantonments of the Army under the [sic] of his Royal Highness the Duke of York, Arnheim 19 Dec. 1794, TNA: MFQ 1/1269)

Continent, the first three of which were to proceed to Helvoetsluys immediately to embark on transports. Harcourt was advised that the King was anxious to leave 'as much as possible the means in your hands of defending the passage of the Waal, and of otherwise opposing the progress of the Enemy', so he was instructed to ask Clerfayt to provide troops to replace the British infantry. Harcourt wrote to the Duke, informing him of this and of reports that the Dutch were seeking a separate peace with France, and requested instructions as soon as possible.[43]

The French crossed the Meuse over the ice on 27 December and drove off the Dutch defenders and occupied the Bommelerwaard. In their pursuit, they also crossed the frozen Waal at Bommel (Zaltbommel) and captured the Dutch post at Tuil on the right bank. The few troops on hand were unable to repel the French, who were reported to be at least 1,500 strong, so plans were drawn up for a major counter-attack on the 30th. The allied force was to be commanded by Major General David Dundas, and was to include the Hesse Cassel troops under *General-Major* von Wurmb, comprising the three grenadier battalions, Garde-Grenadier-Regiment, small detachments from the Jägers and Fusilier Battalion, and four squadrons of dragoons. The attack was a success and the French were driven back over the Waal, but the situation of the army remained critical, with the river still frozen and the troops worn down by sickness, cold and exhaustion.

Wallmoden complained that they had received no orders, news or instructions for three weeks and he sent the Duke a memorandum on the state of the army and the need for a change in its position, which was signed by him and the senior British officers. They warned that the line was already too long to be defended by the forces available, and was made completely untenable by the loss of the Bommelerwaard. They feared that the army would cease to exist in a few weeks as a result of the hard service and growing sickness. Therefore, they proposed to withdraw behind the Lek, continuing to observe the Waal and ready to attack the French if they attempted to cross, unless the enemy's numbers were too great.[44] By 31 December the Hanoverian infantry with the army was reduced to 2,302 of all ranks under arms, including the remaining men from the regiments which had been taken prisoner and who were now serving with other battalions, and had 3,190 sick. The Hesse Cassel infantry still had 3,582 of all ranks on duty and 468 sick, while the Hesse Darmstadt infantry only had 461 on duty and 191 sick.[45]

The temperature continued to drop and Dundas's troops were ordered to pull back to a position on the River Linge, which they did on the night of the 3rd, leaving advance posts on the Waal. The French crossed the frozen Waal near Bommel again on the 4th and retook Tuil. Dundas found them too strong to attack and was himself attacked at Geldermalsen on the morning of the 5th. After some initial success,

43 Dundas to Harcourt 13 December 1794 and Harcourt to the Duke of York 23 December, TNA: WO 6/11, pp.639-42 and WO 1/171, pp.651-5.
44 Wallmoden to York 1 January 1795 and copy of memorandum dated 31 December 1794, TNA: WO 1/172, pp.1-16.
45 Report of the Hanoverian infantry for 15 to 31 December 1794, Hann. 38 E Nr. 213, p.51, report of the Hesse Cassel infantry for 21 to 31 December 1793, HStAM, 4 h, 3361, f. 86, Report of the 1st Hesse Darmstadt Brigade 1 January 1795, HStAD, E 8 B No 271/3, f. 84

including the capture of two British guns, the French were driven back and the guns recaptured. After this, Dundas was ordered to fall back behind the Lek, as there was not enough shelter for the troops in his current position. There was a hope of some respite from French attacks with a thaw on 6th, but this was succeeded by the return of the freeze on the 7th. By this time Harcourt reported that the British army had little more than 10,000 men, was short of supplies, and without the means to transport the sick, ammunition, and stores. He complained again that his letters remained unanswered and took the opportunity to protest against the embarkation of the British infantry regiments.[46]

When the thaw had come on the 6th, it had been hoped that the line of the Waal could be held again. Abercromby and Hammerstein were ordered to march back towards Tiel and Bommel, and Dundas was sent to occupy Buren and the surrounding area. It was too late to countermand these orders when the frost returned, and the French were found to be in considerable force near Buren. The planned general attack did not take place on the 8th, but the French were again pushed back beyond Geldermalsen. However, the French crossed the Waal in force again on the 10th and attacked the allied line at several points, forcing them to retreat. The Hanoverian troops in Hammerstein's corps suffered 158 casualties and lost three 3-pounder battalion guns and two 1-pounder amusettes in this action.[47]

The French launched another general attack on the 14th and, although they were repulsed, Wallmoden and the British generals now decided that they had no choice but to retreat eastwards behind the river Yssel (Ijssel). The terrible march began that night, in bitter cold and through a bleak landscape offering little shelter, and the army reached the banks of the Yssel on the 18th. Fortunately for the allies, the French were as much in need of rest and shelter as they were, and did not pursue the retreat aggressively, although many stragglers either froze to death or fell into enemy hands. In these harsh conditions, tensions between the allies were revealed. An example of the strained relations was given by Corporal Brown of the Coldstream Guards, who recorded in his journal for 16 January that the guards were refused shelter in Bickborge (Beekbergen), where every house was already full of Hessian infantry. The Hessians were not friendly towards the English and would not let them near the fires, and even posted sentries to prevent the inhabitants from selling them liquor.[48]

The attempt to defend the United Provinces had never been a realistic proposition, given the lack of support from the Austrians and Prussians and growing unrest among the Dutch people. The army now had no choice but to retreat into Germany, both to protect Hanover and to allow access to ports from which the British troops could be evacuated.

---

46   Harcourt to York 6 January 1795, TNA: WO 1/172, pp.55-8.
47   Return of the killed and wounded in Hammerstein's corps in the action of 10 January 1795, TNA: WO 1/172, p.509.
48   Brown, *Impartial* Journal, p.222.

7

Back in Germany and the Return Home

The army took up quarters on the line of the River Ems in Munster and Osnabrück to allow the troops to recover. The British were on the right, well placed for their intended evacuation, and the German troops on the left, meeting the right of the Austrians. Wallmoden wrote to the Duke of York to explain the situation of the army as he saw it. After complaining again about the lack of news from England, he made his well-known comment that 'this army is destroyed', having no more than 6,000 combatants remaining.[1] Harcourt, also clearly dispirited, expressed his wish 'that some one more capable than myself may soon be fixed upon to relieve me'. He referred to Wallmoden's 'partiality to German politicks' and over-eagerness to fall in with suggestions from the Prussians, although he still believed him to be 'most perfectly attached to the great cause for which we are all contending'. He also complained that the British troops had been left exposed, with the Germans in better cantonments and with a shorter line to defend.[2] Meanwhile the British government's attention was focussed on the best place to embark their troops, so that they could be deployed elsewhere.

Although things remained quiet for some time, there were reports of increased French activity. Wallmoden decided that the right of his line needed to be reinforced, as it was feared that the French would move against the mouths of the Rivers Weser and Elbe to cut off the army from all communication with England. It was considered that there were three main points where an attack might be expected: Leer, which was defended by the right wing of the British troops with around 3,500 infantry and 1,400 cavalry; towards Lingen, held by the left wing of the British, with nearly 3,500 infantry and 2,000 cavalry, and with the advance posts of these two corps held by around 600 infantry and 1,500 cavalry of the light troops; Rheine, held by the German troops under the overall command of *General-Lieutenant* von Dalwigk, with 6,000 infantry and 2,600 cavalry. Dalwigk was to send a detachment to Greven to link with the Austrians and was instructed that the post of Bentheim (now called Bad Bentheim), in front of Rheine, was of great importance and was to be held for as long as possible, to allow time for the Hanoverian and Austrian troops to assemble and march to its support. The commanders of these three corps were instructed to be in constant communication and to support each other without

1   Wallmoden to York 3 February 1795, TNA: WO 1/172, pp.219-26.
2   Harcourt to York 11 February 1795, TNA: WO 1/172, pp.237-44.

waiting for further orders and the troops were to begin their march to take up their positions on 25 February.[3]

The French attacks began in late February, with the British advance posts being pushed back on the 24th, and the posts on the left bank of the Ems under Major General Cathcart were forced to cross to the right bank on 3 March. In order to meet this growing threat, Wallmoden moved some British troops to cover the Ems and reinforced the garrison at Emden. He also concentrated the German troops at Lingen and Rheine, leaving the Austrians to defend the major part of Munster.

At this time, Wallmoden was reinforced by the Brunswick corps of about 2,000 men under *General-Major* Riedesel, which had at last been taken into British pay, and arrived in the area around Bentheim on 27 February. As usual, the arrangements to take on these additional troops had not been handled well. Wallmoden reported that they had marched through Osnabrück in a good state, but noted that the first he had heard of their march to join his army was from the Duke of Brunswick, asking where to send them. He complained that no provision had been made to supply or to pay them and he had found it necessary to provide them with ammunition. He also asked that the Duke of York to authorise someone to set up a small hospital for them.[4] The ammunition needed for the Brunswick troops included 256,000 musket cartridges, 1,800 round shot and 1,200 case shot for the 6-pounders and 360 round shot and 240 case shot for the 3-pounders.[5] It was also necessary to provide three British tumbrils with horses and drivers to transport the small arms ammunition and to send Hanoverian drivers to replace the English ones, who were to return to England.[6]

Wallmoden also wrote to inform the Duke that large numbers of Dutch troops were serving with the Hanoverians and that he had received a proposal to attach a body of Dutch gunners with their cannon to the Hanoverian artillery. This included much-needed 12-pounders, as well as 6-pounders to strengthen the horse artillery, ammunition wagons, horses and drivers. He urged the Duke to support this proposal. Accordingly, Henry Dundas asked the Duke to instruct Harcourt to make arrangements for them to be taken into British pay and the articles were signed on 29 March. Wallmoden was still chasing for the necessary funds to be sent at the end of April.[7]

Dalwigk established his own headquarters at Tecklenburg on 27 February, just over 20 kilometres south west of Wallmoden's headquarters at Osnabrück. This location was not ideal as it was six hours from Rheine and 10 hours from Bentheim.[8] His troops were organised as follows:

---

3   Wallmoden's dispositions dated 21 February 1795, TNA: WO 1/172, pp.529-33.
4   Wallmoden to York 6 March 1795, TNA: WO 1/172, pp.601-3.
5   Harcourt to York and enclosures, 6 April 1795, TNA: WO 1/172, pp.971-85.
6   Captain Trotter, Major of Brigade of the British artillery, to Don 8 April 1795, BL Add MS 46704, f. 175.
7   Wallmoden to York 23 February 1795, TNA: WO 1/172, pp.553-60, Dundas to York 3 March 1795, TNA: WO 6/12, pp.105-7 and Wallmoden to York 27 April 1795, TNA: WO 1/173, p.91.
8   Porbeck, *Kritische Geschichte*, Vol.2, pp.543-4.

- *General-Major* Riedesel was at Bentheim and the surrounding villages with the Brunswick corps and Hesse Cassel troops, consisting of four squadrons of dragoons, two battalions of grenadiers, the Jägers and Fusilier Battalion;
- *General-Major* von Scheither held Gronau, Ochtrup and the surrounding villages with a force of Hanoverian cavalry and infantry made up of a squadron of the 1st Leibregiment, the 7th Dragoons and 10th Light Dragoons, 4th Grenadier Battalion, 6th and 9th Infantry Regiments and the battalions of the 11th and 14th Infantry Regiments which had not been captured at Sluis, together with the two companies of Jägers;
- *General-Major* von Wurmb commanded the first line between Rheine and Emsdetten, just over half way between Rheine and Greven, with a mixed force of Hanoverian and Hesse Cassel cavalry and Hesse Cassel infantry;
- *General-Major* von Hanstein commanded the second line between Hopsten and Tecklenburg with the rest of the Hesse Cassel infantry;
- *General-Major* von Schmied was with the rest of the Hesse Cassel cavalry in the villages in front of Osnabrück and Tecklenburg;
- *General-Major* von Düring's Hesse Darmstadt brigade was around Greven.[9]

The enemy efforts intensified in early March and the advance posts around Bentheim were forced back by greatly superior numbers on the 3rd. Riedesel became concerned about the growing enemy strength on his right flank, which was uncovered when the British pulled back from Nordhorn, and decided to fall back. This, in turn, left the Hanoverians under Scheither on his left exposed, but he soon returned to his former positions. Wallmoden was convinced that the French intended to penetrate his weak cordon, and thought that it was only the almost impassable roads and flooding, caused by the heavy rain, that had prevented them from launching a major attack already.[10]

Wallmoden did not have to wait long, as the French sent four columns to attack the allied advance posts on 13 March. The strongest column was to march from Nordhorn through Engden and along the right bank of the Vechte, to take up a position behind Schüttorf and Ohne and cut off the line of retreat of Riedesel's corps. However, they got bogged down in the rough country around Engden and took no part in the battle. Wallmoden estimated the strength of the other three columns as 10-12,000 men, which was far too strong for the feeble forces he had been able to post along the line.[11] The right column pushed back Scheither's corps from its position at Gronau, and it retreated to Ochtrup with the loss of one dead, 13 wounded and 11 captured, leaving the left flank of Riedesel's corps exposed.[12] At this time, Scheither was absent due to illness and there are conflicting accounts as to who had taken over the temporary command his corps. Porbeck states that it was *Oberst* von Diepenbroick of the 14th Infantry Regiment, but Sichart gives the command to

---

9   Porbeck, *Kritische Geschichte*, Vol.2, pp.541-3.
10 Wallmoden to York 11 March 1795, TNA: WO 1/172, pp.677-80.
11 Note by Wallmoden dated 14 March 1795, TNA: WO 1/172, pp.713-7.
12 Sichart, *Geschichte der Königlich-Hannoverschen Armee*, Vol.4, p.589.

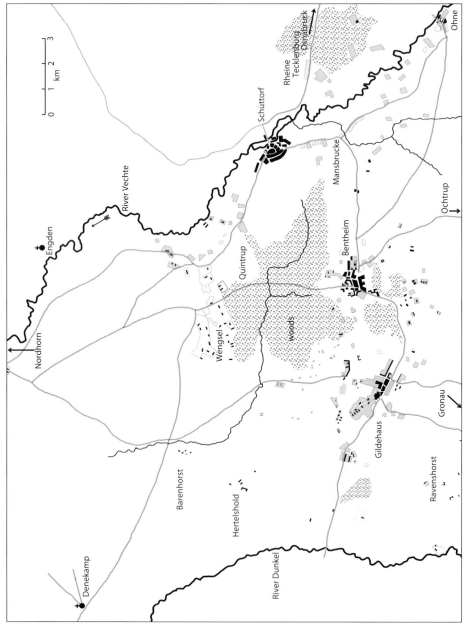

Map 10 Bentheim, March 1795. Based on map of the action at Bentheim in M. von Ditfurth, *Die Hessen in den Feldzügen von 1793, 1794 und 1795 in Flandern, Brabant, Holland und Westphalen*, Vol. 2)

Oberst von Düring of the 9th Infantry Regiment, who is the more likely as he was senior to Diepenbroick.[13]

The main attack was against Riedesel's corps, which was stationed as follows:

- The post at Gildehaus, a little under five kilometres west of Bentheim, was commanded by *Oberst* Philip von Wurmb, with the Fusilier Battalion, a company of Brunswick Jägers and the mounted Jäger company, a squadron each of the Hesse Cassel Leib and Prinz Friedrichs Dragoons, the 3rd Hanoverian Grenadier Battalion, and three guns of the Hanoverian horse artillery, with a squadron of the Hanoverian 5th Dragoons in reserve between Gildehaus and Bentheim;
- Riedesel was in Bentheim with the Brunswick Infantry Regiment Prinz Friedrich, the Hesse Cassel Grenadier Battalion Reuting (3rd, formerly von Wurmb), with their battalion guns, and three Brunswick 6-pounders and four Hanoverian cannon from the 2nd Heavy Division;
- The Brunswick *Oberst* von Hille was in command at Schüttorf, about 7½ kilometres north-east of Bentheim, with the Brunswick Infantry Regiment Riedesel, a company of Brunswick Jägers, and the Hesse Cassel Grenadier Battalion Lelong (1st, formerly von Germann), with their battalion guns and the other three Brunswick 6-pounders and a squadron each of the Hesse Cassel Leib and Prinz Friedrichs Dragoons;
- The Hesse Cassel Jägers under *Capitain* Ochs were around Wengsel, in front of the posts at Bentheim and Schüttorf and the rest of the Brunswick Jägers were in the advance posts.[14]

At the same time a French column pushed back the advance posts to Gildehaus, where they were attacked at all points. They held for a while, but the flanks of this position were uncovered and the French threatened their rear, so they had to fall back to Bentheim. In the course of the retreat, the French captured a number of the Brunswick Jägers and a gun from the Hanoverian horse artillery. Riedesel decided that he could not hold his position and began his retreat to Ohne and the bridge over the Vechte, leaving a force of two officers and 60 men drawn from the various infantry regiments in the castle, to gain time for the rest of the corps to retreat.

The final French column moved to attack Schüttorf. The town had high, thick walls and Hille had been warned of the approaching French column, but he kept most of his men in the market place and did not place enough men to guard the gates. The French got into the town and attacked the troops in the square, who retreated in disorder. The French were held back by a detachment of the Grenadier Battalion Lelong, but one of the battalion guns was captured.

---

13 Porbeck, *Kritische Geschichte*, Vol.2, p.581, Sichart, *Geschichte der Königlich-Hannoverschen Armee*, Vol.4, p.589 and Anon., *Königl. Gross-Britannisch- und Churfürstl. Braunschweig-Lüneburgscher Staats-Kalender* (Lauenburg: Joh. Georg Berenberg, 1793-5), p.105.
14 Porbeck, *Kritische Geschichte*, Vol.2, pp.527, 541 and 588-90 and Journal des Hauptmanns Ochs vom Feldjägerbataillon, HStAM 10 e, II/18, pp.367-8.

The whole of Riedesel's corps was now in retreat, with the French in pursuit, and the Hanoverian 5th Dragoon Regiment forming the rear guard was severely mauled. The total losses of Riedesel's corps on the 13th were three officers and 11 men killed, five officers and 70 men wounded, 10 officers and 119 men captured, with the Brunswick Jägers having the most severe losses, four killed, seven wounded and 63 captured.[15] The small garrison left in Bentheim castle under *Lieutenant* du Plat of the Hanoverian 11th Infantry Regiment, who was serving with the 3rd Grenadier Battalion, came under heavy French artillery fire. Du Plat refused to surrender as prisoners of war. His men were allowed to leave the castle on the morning of the 14th with their arms, and to return to the allied army to continue to serve against the French, who also agreed to provide two waggons to transport the garrison's wounded, sick and baggage.

After this defeat, the advance posts retreated to the right bank of the Ems. Wallmoden complained that, at this critical time for the army and for the protection of Hanover and Osnabrück, Harcourt had informed him of his orders to embark the British infantry and artillery immediately. He had argued that these orders must have been issued before the current situation was known and asked Harcourt to stay, at least until Prussia's intentions were known, but Harcourt had stated that he had clear orders and that he could not delay his departure. Wallmoden pointed out that he could not hold a line of 36 leagues (over 170 kilometres) with only 14-15,000 troops, of whom at least 6,000 had been ordered to return to England, but he would continue to do his duty and would do everything possible to protect the King's domains, until the total destruction of the army made that no longer possible.[16]

The British infantry and most of the artillery were evacuated in April to be sent back to be England for use on various expeditions, leaving the cavalry with a small detachment of artillery under the command of Lieutenant General David Dundas. A number of foreign regiments were also being raised on the Continent for service on these expeditions, causing difficulties with the local authorities, who did not want them on their territory. Bentheim would prove to be the last military action of the campaign and the focus turned to political issues.

The high hopes for the 1793 and 1794 campaigns had ended in disappointment and, in the spring of 1795, the political situation deteriorated rapidly. French military successes and the rivalry between Austria and Prussia, with the latter increasingly losing interest in the war with France and focusing its attention on Poland, were leading to the breakdown of the coalition. The British government also feared that the German princes with whom it had subsidy treaties wanted peace with France.

Wallmoden wrote to the Duke of York on 16 April 1795, notifying him of the peace treaty that had recently been concluded between France and Prussia. He had received a request from the Prussians to evacuate Ostfriesland and he requested clear instructions.[17] A little later, he reported that the Landgrave of Hesse Cassel and the Duke of Brunswick had been negotiating with the Prussian court for some time. Since the army had arrived in Germany, the necessary replacements had not

15   Sichart, *Geschichte der Königlich-Hannoverschen Armee*, Vol.4, p.596.
16   Wallmoden to York and note dated 14 March 1795, TNA: WO 1/172, pp.713-7 and 721-5.
17   Wallmoden to York 16 April 1795, TNA: WO 1/173, pp.21-8.

been sent and he suspected their ill will and desire for peace.[18] He considered that it was more than likely that the Hesse Cassel or Brunswick troops would receive orders to leave the army and that the Prussians had included the return home of the German troops as part of the peace negotiations with France. He went on to express his belief that the Prussians wanted to disarm the other states of the Empire, whilst maintaining their own forces so that they could control the situation, and suspected that the peace treaty had a secret clause for the destruction, partition, or dismemberment of the Empire. In another report sent on the same day, he enclosed a copy of a declaration from the French to the Prussian commander *Generalfeldmarschall* von Möllendorff, calling for the Prussians to take prompt measures to remove the Hanoverians from Cuxhaven and the fort of Rizebuttel in the territory of Hamburg, which they had occupied on the night of 11-12 April. He took this as evidence of France's intentions to interfere in the internal affairs of Germany, with the friendly support of Prussia.[19]

Henry Dundas directed the Duke of York to issue orders for the troops to withdraw from Ostfriesland in accordance with Möllendorff's request and to take up positions on the Weser, both to protect Hanover from any hostile action by Prussia and to control the navigation of the river.[20] He also informed the Duke that Wallmoden's belief that Hesse Cassel and Brunswick were taking measures to be included in the Prussian peace was corroborated by information from other sources. The Duke was to instruct Wallmoden to oppose any attempt by them to withdraw their troops and to use force if necessary to oblige them to honour their treaty obligations.[21]

Kutzleben had written to Grenville earlier in the year, denying the reports of the Landgrave's intentions but, on 12 June, he forwarded a translation of a letter from the Landgrave, stating openly that he had to consider peace with France to protect his dominions from further suffering, but he was still very far from doing anything against the treaty with Britain. He wrote again at the beginning of July that reports of a separate peace between Hesse Cassel and France were false and that the subsidy treaty would continue until its expiry date. However, it was confirmed that the Landgrave's minister, Baron von Waitz, had been at Basel and was intending to return there with the Prussian minister Hardenberg. He also noted that the peace treaty between Prussia and France seemed to be 'a very lame one', but that as a result of it, the Hessian prisoners of war in France had been released and some of them had already arrived at Cassel and in Westphalia.[22]

Doubts about Hesse Cassel's commitment to the subsidy treaty continued to grow. Wallmoden reported to the Duke of York that he had issued orders to the commanders of the troops in British pay, especially the Hessian generals, to make sure that everything was ready for them to begin the new campaign. However, to his great surprise, the Hesse Cassel commander, *General-Lieutenant* von Dalwigk had reported that he had barely enough tents for two regiments and that no arrangements

---

18 Wallmoden to York 27 April 1795, TNA: WO 1/173, p.91.
19 Wallmoden to York 27 April 1795, TNA: WO 1/173, pp.121-5.
20 Dundas to York 30 April 1795, TNA: WO 6/12, pp.207-12.
21 Dundas to York 15 May 1795, TNA: WO 6/12, pp.219-25.
22 Kutzleben to Grenville 4 February, 12 June and 5 July 1795, TNA: FO 31/7.

had been made to supply more. He did not blame Dalwigk for the situation, but the orders of the Landgrave. It had been clear for some time that the Landgrave had put his troops on a peacetime footing and that he was missing no opportunity to profit as much as possible from the British subsidy. He stated that the troops had received very modest amounts to live on, causing high levels of discontent, and they had often showed a spirit of mutiny. It was also known that large numbers of former prisoners of war from the garrison of Ypres had been allowed to return home and they should now re-join the army. If they had been released on parole, they could be exchanged for French prisoners.[23]

Wallmoden wrote again that he had sent an officer to investigate the situation at Cassel, who had returned and reported that the Landgrave had at first pretended not to know that the French had released the troops who had been taken prisoner. However, it became very clear that almost all of the three regiments taken at Ypres had returned, lacking at most 300 men and six officers. He went on that the Landgrave no longer seemed to consider these three regiments as part of the army, as they had been put on a peace footing since June and were serving in his own dominions. When pressed to equip and return them to the army, the Landgrave made the excuse that they were no longer fit to go on campaign and he refused to fix a time for their return, even though they were still in British pay. Wallmoden's opinion was that they would never return unless they were struck off the musters, and that the Landgrave would continue to pocket the majority of their pay. He asked for the government to make a strong complaint to the Landgrave, as he considered it unbelievable that a corps should not be ready to start a new campaign after five months rest.[24]

Henry Dundas replied to Wallmoden that his complaints about the state of the Hessian troops and the retention of the former prisoners returned from Ypres had been passed on to Lord Grenville, who would take the necessary steps to ensure strict compliance by the Landgrave with his treaty obligations.[25] Grenville in turn sent Wallmoden's two letters to Heathcote, the British representative at Mergentheim, expressing the King's great concern at these infringements of the subsidy treaties. He instructed Heathcote to make the strongest representations to the Landgrave's minister, to be passed on to the Landgrave without delay, stating in express terms that unless the latter gave immediate orders to have his obligations under the treaties fulfilled, 'it is not to be expected that the King should continue any longer to adhere to the pecuniary Engagements which He has contracted with the Landgrave'. Heathcote was to report back to Wallmoden and Grenville as soon as possible on the Landgrave's response. Grenville also sent copies of the correspondence to Kutzleben, stating his regret that these gave clear evidence of the failure of the Landgrave to meet his treaty obligations, and that the King awaited immediate and precise orders from the Landgrave to rectify the situation.[26]

---

23 Wallmoden to York 15 July 1795, TNA FO 31/7.
24 Wallmoden to York 11 August 1795, TNA FO 31/7.
25 Dundas to Wallmoden 26 August 1795, TNA: WO 6/12, pp.321-30.
26 Grenville to Heathcote 27 August 1795 and Grenville to Kutzleben (undated), TNA: FO 31/7.

Grenville also instructed Heathcote to give immediate notice to the Landgrave through his minister that, in accordance with the 9th Article of the treaty, the Landgrave's troops would be returned in three months from the date of the notice and that, in the meantime, Wallmoden had been instructed to order the Hessian commander to join the Austrian army and to obey Clerfayt's orders. He was to get an explicit answer from the Hessian minister whether this order would be obeyed. Heathcote replied that he had made the necessary representation to the minister and would report back as soon as possible, but that news had just been received that a separate peace treaty had been concluded between Hesse Cassel and France.[27]

Under the terms of the peace treaty with France signed at Basel on 28 August 1795, the Landgrave agreed not to prolong or renew the subsidy treaties with Britain and to observe the neutral zone agreed by the convention between France and Prussia. France would continue to occupy the fortress of Rheinfels, the town of Saint-Goar, and the part of the county of Catzenellenbogen on the left bank of the Rhine, pending a definitive resolution of matters on the conclusion of a general peace between France and the parts of Germany still at war with it. All prisoners of war were to be exchanged within two months, excluding the Hessian troops in British pay. There were also four secret articles, which provided that, as the three captured Hessian regiments (those taken at Ypres) had already been released without swearing not to fight against France, the Landgrave guaranteed that they would take no further part in the war, and that he would not provide the recruits for the corps in British pay that were due each spring under the terms of the subsidy treaties.[28] These secret articles explain the Landgrave's behaviour, which had led to Wallmoden's complaints.

British fears of possible Prussian aggression and the defection of Hanover, Hesse Cassel, and Brunswick rose during September. Wallmoden wrote to Henry Dundas that he believed the Prussians would abandon the line of demarcation, leaving his army exposed. He also enclosed correspondence between the Prussian ministry and Duke of Brunswick and from the latter to *General-Major* Riedesel, which stated that the need for self-preservation and the security of North Germany, including the Duke's dominions, made it essential that the neutral zone be observed strictly. This meant that the Brunswick troops could not be used in any demonstrations against France or Holland, which had also signed a peace treaty and formed an alliance with France on 16 May 1795, and the Prussians had warned of the consequences of even assembling troops behind the demarcation line.[29] Wallmoden wrote to the Duke of Brunswick and Riedesel to reassure them that the army had always complied with

---

27 Grenville to Heathcote 18 September 1795 and Heathcote to Grenville 22 September 1795, TNA: FO 31/7.

28 The text of the treaty, excluding the secret articles is in G.F. de Martens and Baron C. de Martens, *Recueil des Principaux Traités d'Alliance, de Paix, de Trêve, de Neutralité, de Commerce, de Limites, d'Echange etc. Conclus par les Puissances de l'Europe tant entre elles qu'avec les Puissances et Etats dans d'autres parties du Monde depuis 1761 jusqu'à Présent* (Gottingue: Librairie de Dieterich, 1818-29), Vol.VI 1795-1799, pp.130-135. The secret articles are in Baron Fain, *Manuscit de l'An Trois 1794-1795* (Paris: Delaunay, 1829), pp.424-5.

29 Wallmoden to Dundas 12 September 1795, TNA: WO 1/173, pp.445-57 and 515-32.

the need to maintain the cordon protecting the demarcation line, and had avoided any measures contrary to the stipulations of the treaty between France and Prussia.[30]

David Dundas also reported his fears that it was probable that Hanover, Brunswick, and Hesse Cassel would sue for immediate peace with France with Prussian mediation, and would recall their troops. He thought that Prussia might abandon the cordon and allow the French to take such measures as they thought fit, including the invasion of Hanover and blocking navigation of the Weser and Elbe. It was even rumoured that the King of Prussia was to receive Hanover as indemnity.[31] However, things soon calmed down and he wrote that he no longer believed that the Prussians would quit the demarcation line. He summed up his view of the value of maintaining the army in Germany quite bluntly as 'This Army certainly costs not under 2 Million per Annum, and from the Bunswic [sic] Instructions, the Hessian peace, and the Hannoverian Good Will, I don't think we are likely to afford You a good Pennyworth.'[32]

As the situation was becoming increasingly untenable, Henry Dundas wrote to the Duke of York to inform him that papers he had received from Baron von Steinberg, the head of the Hanoverian Chancery in London, confirmed that the Hanoverian Regency had indicated to the court of Berlin that they wished to take advantage of the neutrality offered under the Franco-Prussian peace treaty.[33] The British ministry had informed the King that, on this basis, it was not worth the expense of maintaining the army in British pay in the Electorate. Consequently, the Duke of York was to issue the necessary orders for the embarkation of the British cavalry and artillery and to begin the process of releasing the German troops. Notice was to be given that the service of the Hanoverian troops was no longer required, so they were at the disposal of the Electoral government, and that Britain would honour its obligations under the agreements. The situation of the other German contingents was more complicated and Dundas considered each in turn.

The complaints in Wallmoden's despatches about the state of the Hesse Cassel troops and the Landgrave's conduct amounted to failure to comply strictly with his treaty obligations and, as he had since made peace with France, he was even less likely to adhere to them in future. Further examination of the extent of his non-compliance was required to determine what future payments would be made to him, and the Duke was to instruct Wallmoden to report on this with the assistance of Lieutenant Colonel Gunn. As no reply had yet been received to the complaints made to the Landgrave, the Treasury had been instructed to suspend payments under the treaty until further notice. In the meantime, Wallmoden was to allow these troops to return home, as it was not intended to keep them in the pay of Britain.

30 Wallmoden to the Duke of Brunswick and Riedesel 12 September 1795, TNA WO 1/173, pp.459-65.
31 Private letters from David Dundas to Henry Dundas dated 13 and 15 September 1795, TNA: WO 1/173, pp.467-70 and 483-4.
32 David Dundas to Henry Dundas 21 and 24 September 1795, TNA: WO 1/173, pp.495-8 and 535-7.
33 Dundas to York 20 September 1795, TNA: WO 6/12, pp.369-94.

The Brunswick troops and Hesse Darmstadt infantry were intended to be sent to a British garrison in Europe, possibly Gibraltar or more probably Jersey and Guernsey. This was not expected to be opposed by the Landgrave and, although the Duke of Brunswick might be 'in a contrary disposition', Wallmoden was to make it clear to him that refusal would lead to the cancellation of the treaty. It was considered desirable for the Hesse Darmstadt cavalry to join Clerfayt's army on the Rhine, but, if the Landgrave objected to this, they would be allowed to return home.

Having received Wallmoden's dispatch of 12 September and taking into account the probable secession of the Hessian troops and the attitude of the Hanoverian Regency, Henry Dundas issued instructions to Wallmoden to use every endeavour to provide for the safety of 'His Majesty's Electoral Dominions', without provoking hostilities. He informed Wallmoden that he had instructed General Dundas to give him every assistance in his power and to support him in the defence of the Electorate. However, General Dundas was made aware of the need to preserve the British troops, who were not to be exposed in 'hazardous and desperate operations'.[34]

Henry Dundas wrote to the Duke of York again, only three days after sending the instructions on the return of the German contingents, stating that these plans needed to be revised in the light of dispatches received from Wallmoden.[35] He stated that correspondence between Wallmoden and the Duke of Brunswick indicated that the Brunswick troops did not seem to be at His Majesty's disposal in the manner stipulated in the treaty, so they were to be allowed to return home and all future payments would cease from the date Wallmoden notified their commander. In addition, the position of the French army had made it impossible for the Hesse Darmstadt troops to join Clerfayt's army, so they would also be allowed to return home.

Henry Dundas sent new instructions to the Duke on 10 October that 'every possible exertion' was to be made to expedite the evacuation of the British cavalry, and gave further directions for the release of the German troops.[36] The government of the Electorate were to be informed that the Hanoverian troops in British pay were no longer required and would be placed at their disposal as soon as possible. The Hesse Darmstadt, Hesse Cassel, and Brunswick troops were to return to their own territories, as soon as possible after the appropriate notifications had been served. The Landgrave of Hesse Darmstadt had met his obligations, so Britain would make the payments stipulated in the treaty, but this was not the case for the Landgrave of Hesse Cassel and the Duke of Brunswick, whose situation would have to be discussed separately. Wallmoden was authorised to keep the Hanoverian and Hesse Darmstadt troops for a short time, if it would facilitate the embarkation of the British cavalry or serve any other useful purpose. Dundas stated that this could be done under the treaty clauses, by which Britain continued to pay for the troops for three months from the date of notification of their return. The Hesse Cassel and Brunswick troops were to be sent back immediately.

---

34 Dundas to Wallmoden 23 September 1795, TNA: WO 6/7, pp.401-9.
35 Dundas to York 23 September 1795, TNA: WO 6/7, pp.397-9.
36 Dundas to York 10 October 1795, TNA: WO 6/7, pp.433-47.

Meanwhile, Heathcote informed Grenville that he had received a reply to his complaints from the Hesse Cassel minister, von Wittorff, which rejected Wallmoden's allegations. Wittorff had sent a translated copy of a letter that the Landgrave had received from Wallmoden at the beginning of September, in which Wallmoden thanked him for the measures he had taken to have his troops ready for campaign as soon as possible. The Landgrave pointed out the contradiction between this and the reports made to London and felt that he had done everything required of him under the subsidy treaties. He claimed that the small reduction made to the pay of the troops when they had returned to the territories of the Empire was quite normal, and had not in any way affected their enthusiasm. As far as the prisoners from Ypres were concerned, a large part of them had not been released, and those who had been were only returned on the condition that they would not serve against France for the remainder of the war. He concluded that Wallmoden's complaints were ill-founded and the Landgrave would complain against these false accusations through Kutzleben.[37]

Kutzleben duly wrote to Grenville, enclosing a letter from the Landgrave's private secretary with a postscript written by the Landgrave himself.[38] The letter expressed the Landgrave's surprise at Grenville's representations to Kutzleben, in which he had made the most unjust accusations based on Wallmoden's false reports. It reiterated the Landgrave's absolute commitment to abiding by the subsidy treaties and noted that the Landgrave had just discovered that the British Treasury had ordered the cessation of payments to him. He explained that he had been forced to make peace with France against his will and that all his territories were ruined, but that did not change anything with respect to the treaties with Britain.

As the slow process of winding up the treaties continued, Wallmoden sent a report to Henry Dundas that he had sent an officer to Cassel, who had received 'the most direct & positive assurances, that the Landgrave looked upon this Corps as entirely at His Majesty's Disposal, to every Service, excepting to force any offensive measure through the Line of Demarcation'. As for the Brunswick troops, he had not seen any further declaration that would limit their service in any other way than by respecting the demarcation line. This Corps was in a 'more serviceable state' than the Hesse Darmstadt troops, who were much reduced by the number of prisoners and were in a 'less military Situation' by the loss of many officers. He also noted that he had recently received a request from Clerfayt to send the Hessian troops to join his army, but he would inform him that this was not possible.[39]

Further clarification of the Landgrave of Hesse Cassel's position came in another letter from Wittorff, which Heathcote forwarded to Grenville, asking for understanding of the situation the Landgrave found himself in. He was facing the imminent danger of invasion by the French, accompanied by the ruin and total devastation of his subjects, and this had led him to reluctantly begin negotiations six months previously. Although the preliminary articles were agreed in the first three months, the Landgrave had delayed bringing the negotiations to a conclusion in the hope of

---

37 Heathcote to Grenville 10 October 1795, TNA: FO 31/7.
38 Kutzleben to Grenville 14 October 1795, TNA: FO 31/7.
39 Wallmoden to Dundas 22 October 1795, TNA: WO 1/173, pp.611-4.

a general peace being agreed. The final straw was the occupation by the French of a large part of the County of Hanau. In these circumstances, the Hessian corps could not be allowed to join Clerfayt's Austrian army. As for the three months' notice to return the Hessian troops, the Landgrave bowed to the will of the King, in spite of the sorrow it caused him. Kutzleben also wrote to Grenville, enclosing a letter from the Landgrave, which pointed out that the Regency in Hanover had issued a proclamation on 29 September, by order of the King and Elector, calling for the withdrawal of all foreign troops from Hanoverian territory as Hanover had agreed to acquiesce in the Franco-Prussian peace treaty of 5 April. In these circumstances, Kutzleben asked Grenville for payment of the amounts due under the treaties, which the Treasury had suspended.[40]

Henry Dundas sent yet another set of instructions to the Duke of York that, as Wallmoden's dispatches indicated that the Duke of Brunswick would not prevent his troops in British pay from being used on any service allowed under the subsidy treaty, provided it did not violate the Line of Demarcation, it had been decided to send them to Gibraltar. The Duke was to instruct Wallmoden to prepare them to embark as soon as transports could be provided. No similar plans existed for the Hesse Cassel and Hesse Darmstadt troops as the relevant treaties were to expire in a few months, and the previous instructions for their return were to proceed.[41]

Wallmoden informed David Dundas on 6 November that he had delayed as long as he could in sending to the Duke of Brunswick the official declaration that his troops were no longer required. He was going to visit the Duke to try to explain matters, so that the plan for them could be put into effect. He expected this to be very difficult, as there was a delay in getting transports and the Duke had already announced publicly that his troops would be returning home. He also wrote that the British government's declaration releasing the Hanoverian corps meant that he could no longer exercise the command of the army, as he saw himself as part of that corps, and any further arrangements would have to be made by David Dundas.[42] Accordingly, David Dundas reported to Henry Dundas that arrangements were made for the immediate march of the Hesse Cassel and Hesse Darmstadt troops to their own territories and, as it appeared that the Hanoverians were to be withdrawn to theirs, Wallmoden considered his command of the army to have ceased.[43]

In spite of this, Wallmoden continued to involve himself in the arrangements for the return of the German troops. He wrote to David Dundas again on 20 November, confirming that he had given up the command of the Hanoverian troops from the time they had returned to their quarters. The Hesse Cassel troops were all gone and the Hesse Darmstadt troops would leave in the next few days. There only remained the Brunswick troops, of which the cavalry and artillery would leave in two or three days. The departure of the infantry from the Weser depended on the decision

40 Heathcote to Grenville 24 October 1795 and Kutzleben to Grenville 4 November 1795, TNA: FO 31/7.
41 Dundas to York 22 October 1795, TNA: WO 6/12, pp.491-5.
42 Wallmoden to David Dundas 6 November 6 November 1795, copy marked 'private' and 7 November 1795, TNA: WO 1/173, pp 865-7 and 877-8.
43 David Dundas to Henry Dundas 9 Novembers 1795, TNA: WO 1/173, pp.861-3.

whether or not they would be sent to Gibraltar.[44] He also wrote to inform the Duke of York that the Hesse Cassel troops had marched and that the Hesse Darmstadt troops, although delayed by a few days in sorting out subsistence for their march, had left on 1, 3, and 5 December. Only the Brunswick infantry remained, as he had taken it upon himself to send back the heavy battery and the few mounted Jägers, as he was sure that cavalry and artillery would not be sent to Gibraltar In any event, he doubted that it would be practicable to send the infantry there so late in the season, because of the lack of transports.[45]

Finally, Henry Dundas informed Wallmoden that it appeared that the Duke of Brunswick did not wish his troops to be sent to Gibraltar, so it had been agreed that they could return home and Wallmoden was to notify the Duke of this and to make the necessary arrangements. Wallmoden replied that he had done so and they would be leaving in the course of that week.[46]

Lieutenant Colonel Gunn appears to have been forgotten in all this. He wrote to Henry Dundas from Hanover on 16 December, pointing out that all German troops in British pay were on their march home and the British had embarked, but that he was still there waiting for orders what he was to do next.[47] He finally returned to Britain on 30 May 1796, at which point his pay as commissary ceased.[48]

---

44 Wallmoden to David Dundas 20 November 1795, copy marked 'private', TNA: WO 1/173, pp.977-80.
45 Wallmoden to York 6 December 1795, TNA: WO 1/173, pp.1,055-7.
46 Henry Dundas to Wallmoden 8 December 1795 and Wallmoden to Henry Dundas 27 December 1795, TNA: WO 6/12, pp.543-4 and WO 1/173, pp.1,067-8.
47 TNA: WO 1/898, p.107.
48 Gunn to Dundas 16 December 1795, TNA: WO 1/898, p.107 and T 52/83, p.203.

8

Was it Worth it?

The expedition to the continent had ended in miserable failure and the subsidy treaties had been terminated. The British government had not even achieved its initial limited objective of protecting the United Provinces from French attack and had been unable to secure the services of German auxiliaries to pursue its plans in other parts of Europe and overseas.

From Britain's point of view, the hiring of German auxiliaries had been necessary to enable it to put sufficient troops into the field to meet its strategic objectives, although money and naval power would always be Britain's main contribution to the coalition. The total British and Irish military establishments were increased from 97,070 to 317,651 men between 1793 and 1795, although the figures for 1795 include over 105,000 British and Irish militia and fencibles who could not be used for foreign service.[1] Britain was not prepared to introduce the mass levies adopted by the French and was only able to increase the number of British troops by raising large numbers of new recruits, either directly for the old regiments or by raising independent companies or new regiments for rank, which led to a dramatic reduction in the quality of officers and men. Even this was not enough to meet the government's desire to wage war on several fronts and the only options available to it were to subsidise the other belligerent powers or to take foreign troops into British pay. Subsidies were a necessary, if expensive, means to keep Britain's allies in the war, but their outcome was uncertain, as shown most clearly by the failed Prussian treaty of 1794. This left hiring foreign auxiliaries as an essential means of providing the troops required for the war.

The estimate for 1794 of the cost of the foreign troops in British pay presented to the House of Commons on 29 January 1794 was £969,323.[2] The estimate for 1795, reflecting the artillery added to the Hesse Cassel contingent, the treaty with Brunswick, and the return of the Baden troops, was £997,226.[3] These were very substantial amounts in relation to the estimates for 1794 of the total cost of the British land forces in Great Britain, Guernsey and Jersey, in Flanders, with Lord

---

1   Fortescue, *A History of the British Army*, Vol.IV Part II, pp.938-40.
2   The total costs relating to the troops from Hanover, Hesse Cassel, Hesse Darmstadt and Baden, Anon., *Journals of the House of Commons*, Vol.49, p.67.
3   Estimate presented 14 January 1795, Anon., *Journals of the House of Commons*, Vol.50, p.68.

Moira, and on board the fleet of £1,492, 813.[4] They are equivalent to a present-day value of over £130 million per year.

The actual payments made were even higher. The historian J.M. Sherwig has pointed out the difficulties in calculating the subsidy payments made by Britain accurately, but has estimated the total paid to Hanover, Hesse Cassel Hesse Darmstadt, Baden and Brunswick between 1793 and 1807, the year in which Hesse Cassel's claims were finally settled, at £3.26 million.[5] After adjusting for the £68,851 paid to Hesse Cassel for expenses incurred in the American War of Independence and the £36,676 paid to Hesse Darmstadt relating to a later subsidy treaty signed in June 1796, the total paid under the subsidy treaties signed in 1793-4 was approximately £3.16 million, including pensions to Hanoverian veterans.[6] Again, this is a very significant sum, but represents much better value than the £1.2 million paid to Prussia under the treaty of 19 April 1794, before it became clear that Prussia would not honour its commitments.[7]

Grenville wrote to Malmesbury in response to Prussia's financial demands that 'The German Princes think England a pretty good milch cow', and there were regular complaints relating to the greed of the Landgrave of Hesse Cassel.[8] Yarmouth was asked by Pitt to give his views on how Britain could get the full advantages that were expected from the various subsidy treaties. He started by pointing out that 'from the moment of the signature the Party which hires & the party which furnishes troops have opposite & contradictory interests' and that, whereas the King wanted the regiments to be complete, the German princes had 'a double advantage' if they had only half their complement. He singled out the Landgrave of Hesse Cassel to illustrate this 'vicious principle'. The problem arose because the treaties provided that the number of troops to be paid for was established at a muster each spring and continued until the following year, whatever the actual numbers who were present in the intervening period. He noted the danger of abuse of this system and went so far as to suggest that the Landgrave of Hesse Cassel, of whom he seems to have formed a particularly low opinion, was failing to punish deserters from the regiments in British pay, who were then able to re-enlist in other regiments and thereby increase the payments he received. Although Yarmouth stated that he did not suspect any prince of countenancing such practices and could not say that this was definitely what had happened, he concluded 'I suspect it has much foundation'.[9]

Yarmouth's feelings about the Landgrave of Hesse Cassel are in marked contrast to his comment on the good faith of the Margrave of Baden, in providing replacements for deserters, and his belief that the Landgrave of Hesse Darmstadt would do the same. In fact all of the German contingents suffered from desertion and the problem was most acute with the Baden troops.

---

4   Anon., *Journals of the House of Commons*, Vol.49, pp.28-9.
5   J.M. Sherwig, *Guineas & Gunpowder, British Foreign Aid in the Wars with France, 1793-1815* (Cambridge, Massachusetts: Harvard University Press, 1969), pp.362-368.
6   TNA: T 52/82, p.272 and T52/83, pp.206, 327 and 449.
7   Sherwig, *Guineas & Gunpowder*, pp.40-53.
8   Grenville to Malmesbury 17 January 1794, in Historical Manuscripts Commission, *The Manuscripts of J.B. Fortescue*, Vol.2, pp.496-7.
9   Yarmouth to Grenville 6 December 1793, TNA: FO 29/3.

The British government was also quick to complain about perceived failures by the princes to fulfil their treaty obligations, for example in the proposed embarkation of troops to join Lord Moira's expedition, and in the second half of 1795. In these circumstances, Britain was prepared to resort to threats and ultimately to suspend payments, but was far from perfect in meeting its own obligations, most obviously in the question of payments to the princes.

Some of the problems arose from a lack of clarity in the wording of the treaties. Gunn pointed out that the rates of pay for the troops were not specified in the treaties, which merely referred to the rates applicable to the various places where they might be serving.[10] Lord Yarmouth wrote to the Treasury on several occasions to request this information, but without success. The official rates were lower than those paid to British troops, and the situation of the men was made worse by the practice of making payments to the rulers, who then decided how much they would actually pay to their troops. Gunn recognised that the Landgrave of Hesse Cassel, whose troops had been in British pay on numerous occasions, must have known the rates, but would not divulge the information, as it would then be clear how much he was withholding from the troops for his own benefit. The poor pay and misunderstandings about entitlements had caused regular problems, for example the disturbances among the Hanoverians in early 1793. Gunn was certain that the dissatisfaction among the troops on this point had been the cause of much desertion.[11]

There was also a long-running dispute relating to levy money due to the Landgrave of Hesse Darmstadt. The matter was first raised by the Landgrave's ministers in March 1794 and, when nothing happened, it was taken up again in July. In addition to the payments for each cavalryman and infantryman, as specified in the treaty, the Hessians claimed payment in respect of the officers, drivers and batmen, hospital, and commissariat staff, without whom the corps could not enter service, and the artillery reserve that had been added after the treaty had been concluded.[12] Jennison Walworth, Hesse Darmstadt's Minister in London, was finally informed that the Treasury had rejected this claim and wrote to Grenville explaining that, in the pressing circumstances of the time, the treaty had been concluded in haste and without detailed examination of each clause, but trusting to the loyalty and justice of the British King and his ministers.[13] This appeal had no effect, but the Landgrave was not prepared to let the matter drop and his representative in London raised it again in July 1795.[14]

The Comptrollers of Army Accounts stuck to the strict interpretation of the treaty, that levy money was only payable in respect of 'each horseman or dragoon properly armed and mounted' and 'each foot soldier'.[15] It was conceded that there

10 See Article VII of the Hesse Cassel treaty, which was copied in the subsequent treaties, in Appendix II.
11 Gunn to Don 22 September 1795, BL Add MS 46705, f. 107.
12 Jenison Walworth to Grenville 29 March 1794 and Barkhaus to Grenville 22 July 1794, TNA: FO 31/6. The relevant article in the treaty is identical to that in Article V of the Hesse Cassel treaty in Appendix II.
13 Jenison Walworth to Grenville 14 November 1794, TNA: FO 31/6.
14 Malcor to Grenville 6 July 1795, TNA: FO 31/7.
15 As set out in Article V of the Hesse Cassel Treaty in Appendix II.

might be a payment due for the additional artillery, but nothing could be done until they received confirmation that the augmentation had been agreed and a certificate of their state from Major Gunn.[16] Accordingly, Henry Dundas wrote to Gunn on 7 November, asking him to explain the additional Hesse Darmstadt artillerymen, in excess of the number specified in the treaty.[17] Gunn replied that it was not uncommon for the numbers actually mustered to differ from those specified in the treaty and that the extra men had indeed been offered by the Landgrave and accepted by Lord Yarmouth. He went on 'there was no time during the War that would admit of refusing 100 fine Men, which was the number of the Artillery in question'.[18]

Payments were often late, even when the amounts due were not in dispute. For example, the levy money for the Baden and Hesse Darmstadt troops was payable 15 days after the signature of the treaties, which had been on 21 September and 5 October 1793 respectively, but the warrants were only signed on 31 and 17 March 1794.[19] Some amounts due were not paid until the following decade, such as the payment for costs of the Hanoverian corps relating to the period from 1 November to 31 December 1795 which was only made in June 1803 and 'extraordinaries' of the Hesse Cassel troops were still being processed up to June 1807.[20] The government's inability to manage payments in accordance with the treaties resulted in delays in getting the troops to the front, even though they were always required urgently.

In addition to their financial interests, the German princes looked to Britain for the support promised in the subsidy treaties, which stated that there would be a 'a strict friendship, and a sincere, firm, and constant union, so that the one shall consider the interests of the other as his own' and that Britain would do as much as possible to ensure the safety of the German states and indemnification for losses suffered.[21] In practice, these promises counted for little. The concerns expressed by the Margrave of Baden were ignored and direct requests by the Landgraves of Hesse Cassel and Hesse Darmstadt for British guaranties of their possessions and indemnification for losses suffered were met with only vague assurances and a statement that the circumstances prevailing at the time of future peace negotiations could not be foreseen.[22]

Further evidence of the government's lack of interest in German security was given when Baron von Barkhaus, Director of the Hesse Darmstadt War Department, put forward a proposal on behalf of the Landgrave for Britain to provide subsidies and territorial guarantees to the small German states threatened by French advances, in order to persuade them to raise a force of 10-12,000 men for mutual defence.

---

16   Charles Long, Secretary of the Treasury, to George Aust, Under-Secretary of State at the Foreign Office, 27 October 1795, TNA: FO 31/7.
17   Dundas to Gunn 7 November 1795, TNA: WO 6/12, p.501.
18   Gunn to Dundas 30 November 1795, TNA: FO 31/7.
19   Entry books of Royal Warrants, TNA: T 52/81, pp.196 and188.
20   Entry books of Royal Warrants, TNA: T52/88-91.
21   Articles I and X of the treaty with Hesse Cassel in Appendix II.
22   Landgrave of Hesse Cassel to Kutzleben 22 August 1793 and Grenville's reply and again on 4 August 1794 in TNA: FO 31/5-6. Grenville to Jenison Walworth 4 April 1794 in TNA: FO 31/6.

Although he received some initial encouragement that the plan would be considered, nothing came of it.[23]

The Landgrave of Hesse Cassel also complained that his troops had borne more than their fair share of the hardships and risks of the campaign. Instead of embarking a mixed force for the Isle of Wight, the troops of Hanover, Baden, and the others had been left on the Continent and only his troops had been sent, which had led to the ruin of a large part of them. After their return, six battalions and a squadron of his troops had been put into garrison at Ypres, where they were subsequently taken prisoner when it surrendered, contrary to 'all the rules of war, treaties and equity', by which this danger should have been shared with others. He then made it clear that even these events had not diminished his enthusiasm for the British cause and he reiterated his absolute commitment to fulfilling the subsidy treaties.[24]

On balance, and whatever the complaints of the British, the German princes had done more to meet their treaty obligations than had the British government, even though French successes in Germany and pressure from Prussia had made it increasingly difficult for them to do so. The failure of the campaigns owed much to the lack of cohesion amongst the major powers in the coalition, made even worse by the British government's confused and unrealistic policies, and its inability to remain focused on the key objective at any time. As so often, the British and German troops had done their duty and had been badly let down by their political masters.

23 Barkhaus to Grenville 16 August 1794 and Barkhaus to Grenville 7 September 1794, TNA: FO 31/6.
24 Kutzleben to Grenville with enclosures 14 October 1795, TNA: FO 31/7.

Part II

The German Contingents

9

Hanover

Introduction

The Electorate of Brunswick-Lüneburg, more usually referred to as Hanover, had around 800,000 inhabitants.[1] It was by far the largest and most important state in the Lower Saxon Circle and the fifth largest in the Empire, although much smaller than Austria, Prussia, Bavaria, or Saxony. The Prince-Elector of Brunswick-Lüneburg was also the King of Great Britain and Ireland, as well as being a member of the Electoral College which had the right to choose the Holy Roman Emperor. The British Kings generally spent little time in the Electorate – indeed, George III never visited it – and in their absence it was governed by a Regency of Hanoverian ministers. The right to appoint the ruler of the Prince-Bishopric of Osnabrück alternated between the Protestant Elector of Brunswick-Lüneburg and the Catholic Archbishop of Cologne. The last Prince-Bishop was George III's second son Frederick, Duke of York and Albany, until the Prince-Bishopric was dissolved and given to Hanover in 1803 as part of the process of secularisation and reorganisation of Germany. Hanover's situation, lying between Brandenburg and Prussia's scattered provinces to the west, left it vulnerable to aggression from its powerful and ambitious neighbour.

At the end of 1791, Hanover's armed forces had a theoretical strength of around 4,200 cavalry and 11,000 infantry, excluding the militia regiments, as shown in Table 6. A new body of horse artillery was ordered to be raised in 1790. It was based on the Prussian model, with some of the gunners riding on the gun carriages and limbers and some mounted. The 14th and 15th Infantry Regiments had been sent to India in the pay of the British East India Company and returned in 1791-2. Half of the first company of engineers was made up of miners and the other half of sappers, and the second company was half pontoniers and half pioneers. There were also four garrison regiments and a small body of garrison artillery.

When they returned from India, the men of the old 14th Regiment were used to form the new 14th Light Infantry Regiment, together with men drawn from the regiments which were not to be sent on active service, and the 15th Regiment was disbanded. The former 14th Regiment also provided most of the officers and senior NCOs for the new regiment's two Jäger companies and the remainder were marksmen, recruited from the hunting and forestry services.

---

1   K.E.A. von Hoff, *Das Teutsche Reich vor der französischer Revolution und nach dem Frieden von Lunéville, Erster Theil* (Gotha: Justus Perthes, 1801), pp.66-7.

Table 6: The Hanoverian Army in 1791

	Squadrons	Battalions	Companies	Strength[a]
Cavalry				
Leibgarde	4		8	380
4 Cavalry Regiments (Nos. 1-4)	16		32	1,520
4 Dragoon Regiments (Nos. 5-8)	16		32	1,532
2 Light Dragoon Regiments (Nos. 9-10)	8		16	766
	44		88	4,198
Infantry				
Garde Regiment		2	12	787
13 Infantry Regiments[b, c]		26	156	10,231
		28	168	11,018
Artillery		2	10	668
Engineers			2	95
10 Land Regiments (militia)			50	5,500
	44	30	318	21,479

Sources:
C.G.C. von Wurmb, *Gegenwärtiger Be- und Zustand der Churhannövrischen Trouppen*, (Göttingen: Johann Georg Rosenbusch, 1791), p.4. Slightly different numbers are given in Sichart, *Geschichte der Königlich-Hannoverschen Armee*, Vol.4 pp.9-12.

Notes:
a   The strengths shown are the full establishments (*Sollstärke*).
b   Each regiment had two battalions, and each battalion one grenadier and five musketeer companies.
c   The 14th and 15th Regiments in the service of the British East India Company are not included above.

Hanover only maintained a small general staff in peacetime. At the end of 1792 it was made up of *Feldmarschall* von Reden who, at the age of 75, had resigned the supreme command of the forces in October 1792; *General der Cavallerie* von Freytag, who had replaced Reden as commander of all Hanover's armed forces; *General-Lieutenant* von Estorff, the Quartermaster-General and Inspector of Cavalry; *General-Lieutenant* von dem Bussche, the Inspector of Infantry; *Oberst-Lieutenant* von Spörken, the *Flügel-Adjudant*; *Oberst-Lieutenant* Kunze, the Assistant Quartermaster-General; two aides de camp, *Hauptmann* von Alten of the infantry and *Rittmeister* von Ende of the cavalry; and two secretaries.[2]

Orders were issued in December 1792 to mobilise Hanover's contingent to the *Reichsarmee*, which was being assembled to defend the Empire against French aggression.[3] This force was to be commanded by *General-Lieutenant* von dem

2   Anon., *Königl. Gross-Britannisch- und Churfürstl. Braunschweig-Lüneburgscher Staats-Kalender, 1793*, p.93.
3   Appendix IV contains a brief overview of the structure of the *Reichsarmee*.

Bussche and was to consist of the 1st and 4th Cavalry Regiments, the 9th and 10th Light Dragoons, the 4th and 10th Infantry Regiments, and a battery of horse artillery. The Duke of Brunswick asked for the contingent to be sent to join the Prussian forces commanded by *General-Lieutenant* von Knobelsdorf, but the British King expressed his view that the forces on the Rhine were already strong enough and stated that he would only allow his contingent to join the *Reichsarmee*. As this army had not been formed, he refused to send the contingent and an auxiliary corps was sent to serve with the British in the Low Countries instead.

Organisation and Strength of the Contingent

The contingent provided under the 'Preliminary Articles' dated 4 March 1793 was commanded by Freytag, who had been promoted to *Feldmarschall* on 26 February 1793. It was made up of four cavalry regiments, a brigade of three battalions of grenadiers, six infantry regiments, two divisions of heavy artillery and one of horse artillery, a detachment of pioneers, staff, and hospital.[4] Only two of the four squadrons from each cavalry regiment and eight of the 10 musketeer companies in each infantry regiment were taken to form the field regiments, while the others remained behind as depots for these regiments. The composition of the corps is shown in Table 7.

The King explained to Pitt that the infantry battalions had been made very strong with relatively few officers, in order to reduce cost.[5] The increase from the peacetime establishment, of 90 officers and men for a grenadier company and 60 for a musketeer company, required a major effort. Recruiting agents were sent to neighbouring territories and 60 grenadiers, 200 musketeers and six gunners were taken from each of the eight regiments left at home. These measures were insufficient to raise the number of men required, so orders were issued for 7,000 new recruits to be enlisted from the King's German territories. These recruits were to be between 16 and 40-50 years old, in good health and certain occupations, such as factory workers, were excluded. The augmentation of the field regiments was to be achieved by adding 40 men from the other regiments and 42 recruits to each grenadier company, and 33 men from the other regiments and 60 recruits to each musketeer company, so that 27 percent of the lance corporals and privates of a grenadier company was made up of men from the new levy and 43 percent for a musketeer company.[6] Obviously, the influx of untrained recruits and the promotion of a large number of officers and NCOs had a dramatic effect on the quality of the infantry.

A 'Return of his Majesty's Hanoverian Forces taken into British Pay' is annexed to the 'Preliminary Articles'. This gives a detailed breakdown of the composition of the corps and the figures given below are taken from this return, unless otherwise stated.

---

4   The text of the Articles is in Appendix I.
5   George III to Pitt 24 January 1793, in Aspinall (ed.), *Later Correspondence*, Vol.1, p.649.
6   Order dated 9 February 1793 and plan for the augmentation of the infantry regiments, Hann. 38 E Nr. 35, ff. 4-5 and 10-11.

Table 7: Hanoverian Troops taken into British Pay 22 February 1793

	Squadrons	Battalions	Strength[a]
Cavalry			
Leibgarde	2		
2nd Cavalry Regiment von Hammerstein	2		} 628
4th Cavalry Regiment von dem Bussche	2		
1st Leibregiment	2		} 628
5th Dragoon Regiment von Ramdohr	2		
7th Dragoon Regiment Graf von Oeyenhausen	2		} 628
9th Light Dragoon Regiment Königin	2		
10th Light Dragoon Regiment Prinz von Wallis	2		} 629
	16		2,513
Infantry			
Grenadier Brigade		3	2,187
Garde Regiment		2	1,306
4th Regiment von Bothmer[b]		2	1,306
5th Regiment von Hohorst[c]		2	1,306
6th Regiment von Hammerstein		2	1,306
10th Regiment von Diepenbroick		2	1,306
11th Regiment Graf Taube		2	1,306
		15	10,023
Artillery and Pioneers			
Artillery			599
Train and reserve			968
Pioneers			18
			1,585
Total excluding Staff and Hospital	16	15	14,121

Sources:
Return of the troops taken into British pay 22 February 1793 annexed to the 'Preliminary Articles', in Debrett (ed.), *A Collection of State Papers*, 1794, pp. 33-41; Anon., *Annalen der Braunschweig-Lüneburgischen Churlande* 1793, pp. 460-70; Sichart, *Geschichte der Königlich-Hannoverschen Armee*, pp. 32-3; reports in Hann. 38 E Nr. 144.

Notes:
a   The strengths shown are the full establishments shown in the Return and include regimental staff and men serving the battalion guns in the regimental totals. The totals for the cavalry are slightly lower in the *Annalen* and in Sichart.
b   The 4th Regiment is named von Lösecke in the returns for the early part of the 1793 campaign but is shown as von Bothmer by 1 December.
c   The 5th Regiment is named von Klinkowström in the returns for the early part of the 1793 campaign but is shown as von Hohorst by 1 December.

Each of the cavalry regiments allocated to the corps had four squadrons, formed by combining two squadrons from each of two regiments: the Leibgarde with the 2nd Cavalry Regiment; the 4th and 1st Cavalry Regiments; the 5th and 7th Dragoons; the 9th and 10th Light Dragoons. Although nominally forming these combined regiments, the detachments from the cavalry regiments often served as independent units. The staff of a combined regiment consisted of:

- 2 Colonels*
- 2 Lieutenant Colonels*
- 2 Majors*
- 2 Regimental Quartermasters and Paymasters*
- 2 Adjutants*
- 1 Regimental Riding Master
- 1 Chaplain
- 1 Judge Advocate
- 1 Regimental Surgeon
- 4 Squadron Surgeons
- 1 Regimental Farrier
- 2 Staff Trumpeters*
- 4 Squadron Trumpeters
- 1 Waggon Master
- 1 Saddler
- 1 Provost
  Total 28

The ranks marked * had one from each of the constituent regiments, although the *Annalen der Braunschweig-Lüneburgischen Churlande* only shows one of each for a combined regiment.[7] The staff of the combined regiment of light dragoons also included an armourer.

Each squadron had two companies and was made up of:

- 2 Captains
- 2 First Lieutenants
- 4 Second Lieutenants and Cornets
- 4 Sergeants
- 2 Quarter-Masters
- 2 Company Riding-Masters
- 8 Corporals
- 1 Farrier
- 2 Trumpeters
- 123 Privates
  Total 150

---

7   Anon., *Annalen* 1793, pp.461-2.

The grenadier brigade was formed by combining the two grenadier companies from the infantry regiments in the contingent into three battalions of four companies each. The 1st Grenadier Battalion was made up of the companies from the Garde and 10th Infantry Regiments, and was designated as a light grenadier battalion to cover the shortage of light troops. It was intended to join the 1st Grenadier Battalion with the light dragoons, with each company from the Garde Regiment paired with a squadron of the 9th Light Dragoons and those of the 10th Infantry Regiment with the 10th Light Dragoons.[8] The 2nd Grenadier Battalion was formed from the 5th and 6th Infantry Regiments and the 3rd Battalion from the 4th and 11th Infantry Regiments. In practice, the grenadier battalions generally served as independent battalions rather than as a brigade.

The brigade's staff comprised:

- 1 Regimental Quartermaster or Paymaster
- 1 Chaplain
- 1 Judge Advocate
- 1 Surgeon Major
- 1 Armourer
  Total 5

An officer and three NCOs from the Artillery Regiment were attached to the brigade and each battalion had two 3-pounder cannon, served by two corporals and 16 trained men from the infantry regiments, making 58 in total for the brigade's artillery.

Each battalion's staff had:

- 1 Major commanding the battalion
- 1 Adjutant
- 1 Quartermaster
- 1 Provost
  Total 4

And each company:

- 1 Captain
- 2 First Lieutenants
- 2 Second Lieutenants
- 1 Sergeant Major
- 2 Sergeants
- 1 *Gefreite-Corporal*
- 1 Quartermaster
- 6 Corporals
- 1 Company Surgeon

8   Memorandum dated 12 February 1793, Hann. 38 E Nr. 36, ff. 1-4.

- 2 Fifers
- 3 Drummers
- 16 Lance-Corporals
- 138 Privates
  Total 176

An infantry regiment had two battalions each with four musketeer companies. The regimental staff was made up of:

- 1 Colonel*
- 1 Lieutenant Colonel*
- 2 Majors*
- 1 Regimental Quartermaster and Paymaster
- 2 Adjutants
- 1 Chaplain
- 1 Judge Advocate
- 1 Regimental Surgeon
- 1 Drum-Major
- 8 Musicians
- 2 Provosts
- 1 Armourer
- 1 Waggon-Master
  Total 19, excluding the 4 officers marked * who nominally commanded companies

Each company had:

- 1 Captain
- 1 First Lieutenant
- 1 Second Lieutenant
- 1 Ensign
- 1 Sergeant Major
- 2 Sergeants
- 1 *Gefreite-Corporal*
- 1 Quartermaster
- 5 Corporals
- 1 Company Surgeon
- 3 Drummers
- 14 Lance-Corporals
- 124 Privates
  Total 156

Each battalion had two 3-pounder cannon manned by trained officers, NCOs, and men from the battalion. Each gun was served by a corporal and eight men, with an officer and two sergeants for the regiment.

The regulations specified the number of waggons and horses allowed to each rank of officer to transport his personal baggage, ranging from a colonel, who was allowed a carriage with four horses, a baggage waggon with four horses, three pack horses, two riding horses and a servant's horse, down to a lieutenant or ensign, who only had a pack horse, a riding horse and a servant's horse.[9]

The artillery was commanded by *General-Major* von Trew, the Colonel-in-Chief of the Artillery Regiment, and was made up of two divisions of heavy artillery, each with 10 6-pounder cannon, two 30-pounder howitzers, and four 7-pounder howitzers, and a division of horse artillery with four 3-pounder cannon and two 7-pounder howitzers. A heavy artillery division was further divided into two equal-sized batteries. Unlike the battalion guns, these divisions were made up entirely of officers and men from the Artillery Regiment.

The staff consisted of:

- 1 Commander (*General-Major* von Trew)
- 2 Majors
- 2 Regimental Adjutants
- 1 Paymaster
- 1 Chaplain
- 1 Judge Advocate
- 1 Secretary
- 1 Surgeon Major
- 4 Surgeons Mates
- 1 Drum Major
- 1 Storekeeper
- 4 Clerks of Deliveries
- 4 Assistant Clerks
- 1 Armourer
- 2 Assistants
- 1 Master Cooper
- 1 Journeyman
- 1 Provost
  Total 30

And for the divisions:

- 4 Captains
- 3 Captain-Lieutenants
- 4 Lieutenants
- 15 Second Lieutenants and Ensigns
- 16 Master Fireworkers
- 60 Fireworkers
- 7 Quartermasters

---

9   Anon., *Haushalts-Reglement für die Chur-Braunschweig-Lüneburgische Infanterie; in Friedens-auch Krieges-Zeiten* (Hannover: G.C. Schlüter, 1786), pp.93-5.

- 14 Assistants
- 14 Drummers
- 432 Bombardiers and Gunners
  Total 569

The heavy artillery divisions were each commanded by a major and the horse artillery by a captain. Major Gunn's muster return shows one of the musicians as a bugle horn player, presumably for the horse artillery. The men shown above as quartermasters are described as 'Fouriers', i.e. quartermasters, on the muster return and in the copy of the return from the 'Preliminary Articles' included with Major Gunn's instructions, but as farriers in the copy in Debret's collection of state papers.[10]

The artillery train, including the transport of the reserve ammunition for the infantry and cavalry, was commanded by a major and had a total of 968 men including officers, NCOs, surgeons, farriers, craftsmen and drivers, and 2,274 horses. The pioneer detachment was made up of a sergeant, corporal, drummer and 15 pioneers with two portable bridges. There were eight horses and two drivers to transport the bridges and a two horse waggon with a driver for their tents and other equipment.

The details of the staff of the corps are shown in Table 8 and the hospital consisted of the physician general and aide, surgeon general, steward, chaplain, 14 surgeons, three clerks, four purveyors and assistants, a cook, and 60 attendants and nurses. They were supported by a captain, two sergeants, six corporals, a train corporal, and 14 drivers, with 50 horses for the hospital waggons.[11]

The British Commissary, Major Gunn, mustered the Hanoverian troops during their march to join the Duke's army on various dates between the beginning of April and 4 June. He reported that the total strength of the corps was 14,660 men, including 306 bread waggon drivers and batmen, and 5,529 horses. Gunn sent the muster returns to Henry Dundas, together with his report that 'The troops are in general very fine, as likewise the horses, & not one amongst the whole that I could think unserviceable'. He found their clothing and equipment to be good, and finished by praising the artillery which 'exceeds everything of the kind I have ever seen for neatness & convenience'; although he noted that the reserve artillery had not yet joined the army. More worrying was the fact that the return showed that155 recruits had not yet arrived, when he had mustered the 4th Infantry Regiment on 16 May. He did not think it necessary to comment on this, or on the large number of new recruits in the other regiments.[12]

The 'Preliminary Articles' also specified that a number of Hanoverian officers would be attached to the personal staff of the Duke of York and those of his two younger brothers, who were serving with their Hanoverian regiments. Prince Ernest was colonel of the 9th Light Dragoons and transferred to the 2nd Cavalry Regiment towards the end of 1793, and Prince Adolphus was colonel in the Garde

---

10 Muster return of the artillery dated 4 June 1793, TNA: WO 1/166, p.351, Instructions dated 2 March 1793, TNA: HO 51/147, p.48, Debrett (ed.), *A Collection of State Papers*, 1794, p.36.

11 Anon., *Annalen* 1793, pp.468-9 and muster return 4 June 1793, TNA: WO 1/166, p.355.

12 Gunn to Dundas 4 June 1793 and enclosures, TNA: WO 1/166, pp.341-55.

Table 8: Staff of the Hanoverian Auxiliary Corps 4 June 1793

Position	Name	Regiment
Commanding General	*Feldmarschall* von Freytag	
Adjutant General	*Oberst* von Spörken	
Aide-de-camp to Spörken	*Fähndrich* Sothen	
Flügel-Adjudant to Freytag	*Major* von Wenkstern	
Aide-de-camp to Freytag	*Hauptmann* von Alten	
Aide-de-camp to Freytag	*Rittmeister* von Ende	
Lt. General of Cavalry	*General der Cavallerie* von Wallmoden-Gimborn	
Aide-de-camp	*Lieutenant* von Vinck	Leibgarde
Aide-de-camp	*Lieutenant* von Behr	5th Infantry
Lt. General of Infantry	*General-Lieutenant* G.W.D. von dem Bussche	
Aide-de-camp	*Lieutenant* von dem Bussche	7th Infantry
Aide-de-camp	*Lieutenant* von Töbing	8th Dragoons
Major General of Cavalry	*General-Major* von Minnigerode	
Aide-de-camp	*Lieutenant* von Jonquieres	2nd Cavalry
Major General of Cavalry	*General-Major* J.F. von dem Bussche	
Aide-de-camp	*Fähndrich* von dem Bussche	4th Cavalry
Major General of Infantry	*General-Major* von Diepenbroick	
Aide-de-camp	*Lieutenant* von Grote	Garde
Major General of Infantry	*General-Major* von Hammerstein	
Aide-de-camp	*Lieutenant* du Plat	11th Infantry
Major General of Artillery	*General-Major* von Trew	
Aide-de-camp	*Tit. Hauptmann* Symbher	Artillery
Major of Brigade Cavalry	*Major* Pflug	8th Dragoons
Brigade Adjutant Cavalry	*Fähndrich* Scriba	8th Dragoons
Major of Brigade Infantry	*Hauptmann* Schuster	7th Infantry
Brigade Adjutant Infantry	*Fähndrich* Bethe	7th Infantry
Quartermaster General	*Oberst-Lieutenant* Kunze	
Assistant	*Seconde-Lieutenant* Kunze	7th Infantry
Six engineer officers		
Six guides		
Staff secretary and clerk	Nörlinger	
Auditor and clerk	Mövius	
Chaplain and clerk	Ritscher	
Physician	Guckenberger	
Surgeon	Taberger	
Waggon Master General	*Capitain* Harten	5th Cavalry
Staff Quartermaster	*Fähndrich* Schäffer	7th Infantry
Field Postmaster	Bremer (later Wolf)	

Sources:
Return of the troops taken into British pay 22 February 1793 annexed to the 'Preliminary Articles', in Debrett (ed.), *A Collection of State Papers*, 1794, pp. 33-41; Anon., *Annalen* 1793, pp. 466-8 and 490-1; List of the staff dated 14 March 1793 and signed by Freytag, Hann. 38 E Nr. 73 ff. 14-15; Return of the Staff of the Hanoverian Troops in the service of Great Britain, mustered by Major Gunn 4 June 1793, TNA: WO 1/166 pp. 353-5.

Notes:
General-Major von Mutio of the infantry died on the march to join the Duke of York's army. Gunn shows his aide-de-camp *Lieutenant* von Hedemann of the 4th Infantry Regiment on Freytag's personal staff.
General-Majors von Oeynhausen, von Dachenhausen, von Maydell and von Wangenheim were also present with their regiments.

Regiment. The officers appointed to the Duke's staff were *Flügel-Adjudant, Oberst-Lieutenant* von Hake of the 6th Infantry Regiment, *Major* Hogrewe of the engineers, and *Hauptmann* von Alten of the 8th Dragoon Regiment and *Hauptmann* von Marschalck of the Garde Regiment as aides de camp. Prince Ernest had *Rittmeister* von Linsingen of the 1st Cavalry Regiment and *Lieutenant* von Ramdohr of the 10th Light Dragoons as aides de camp, and Prince Adolphus had *Hauptmann* von Uslar of the 10th Infantry Regiment and *Lieutenant* Wangenheim of the 7th Infantry Regiment.

The Duke had to replace two of these officers early in the campaign when Hake was injured in a fall with his horse around the end of June 1793, and had to return to Hanover to recover, and Marschalck was killed at Hondschoote on 8 September. Hake was replaced by *Hauptmann* von Löw of the Garde Regiment, who was promoted to major, and whose appointment as 'Deputy Adjutant General to H.R.H the Duke of York' was noted in general orders on 17 August 1793.[13] *Major* von Hardenberg of the 10th Light Dragoons took over from Marschalck.

Prince Adolphus also lost both his aides de camp in early September 1793, as Uslar was killed on the 5th and Wangenheim was badly wounded when Adolphus was captured at Rexpoëde on the 6th. Princes Ernest and Adolphus were both promoted to the rank of *General-Major* on 18 and 26 August 1794 respectively, and each had one aide-de-camp, *Lieutenant* von Ramdohr for Ernest and *Hauptmann* von Hedemann for Adolphus.

The Duke of York wrote to the King that it was essential for Freytag to have an English aide-de-camp attached to his staff. He recommended Ensign John Murray of the 3rd Foot Guards, the brother of his Adjutant General Sir James Murray, as he spoke both French and German. The appointment was approved and Murray was promoted to lieutenant and ordered abroad immediately.[14] Murray later became an aide-de-camp to the Duke.

Hanover was also called upon to provide a field bakery for the army as the British government had made no such provision. The Duke of York had to ask the Hanoverian Chancery of War to make their bakery available to Brook Watson, his Commissary General, and to upgrade it to be sufficient for 20,000 troops. He confirmed that Watson would pay the costs of it immediately, if the King approved the proposal. The King's approval was forthcoming and the bakery was sent to join the army with the men required to work and transport it.[15] This bakery was of considerable size, at its peak being served by about 170 bakers in addition to the labourers, artificers, and a waggon train, with the whole under the command of a commissary, with its own chaplain, surgeon, clerks, and a military guard. Its 24 ovens weighed 1,400 pounds and needed 10 waggons to transport it, with further

13 Orderly book in the papers of Major General Charles Barnett, 3rd Foot Guards, 1786-1803, NAM 1985-12-15.

14 York to the King 19 April 1793, in Aspinall (ed.), *The Later Correspondence*, Vol.2, p.29 and Sir George Yonge, Secretary at War, to York 25 April 1793, TNA: WO 4/291, p.46.

15 York to the King 22, 25 and 31 March 1793, in Aspinall (ed.), *The Later Correspondence*, Vol.2, pp.23-5.

waggons needed for the tents and implements. It was left on the continent when the army returned at the end of 1795.[16]

In addition to the bakery for the troops, the catering for the Duke of York and the headquarters staff, known as his family, was provided by 'His Majesty's Hanoverian kitchen'. Harry Calvert, one of the Duke's aides de camp, wrote to his sister of their arrival with 'an amazing retinue of cooks and laced footmen' and the anonymous 'officer of the guards' recorded that the family was fed by means of 'a set of Hanoverian sumpter mules, employed to carry, on a march, cold meats, the service of plate, rich wines, and other necessary articles of refreshment', while the Hanoverian cooks and servants preceded the mules in large covered waggons with the larger kitchen utensils.[17]

The corps was increased in January 1794 under a further 'Article of Agreement'.[18] The additional force was made up of the 1st and 9th Infantry Regiments, with a grenadier battalion formed from their grenadier companies, the 14th Light Infantry Regiment, an additional division of horse artillery, and a detachment of engineers with a pontoon train. The staff consisted of a major general, his aide-de-camp, a major of brigade, and a brigade adjutant. It was also decided to increase the number of officers in each infantry regiment by a *Titulair Capitain*, a lieutenant and two ensigns, to make up for the shortage of officers which had been experienced in the 1793 campaign, and to send a reinforcement of two lance corporals and 52 privates for each of the 9th and 10th Light Dragoons. The strength of the additional force is shown in Table 9.

The 1st and 9th Infantry Regiments were organised in the same way as the regiments in the original corps, with the additional officers noted above. The 14th Light Infantry Regiment had two battalions of four companies each and two companies of Jägers, who usually served separately. As the 'State of the additional Body of Hanoverian Troops taken into the pay of Great Britain' annexed to the 'Article of Agreement' does not give a detailed breakdown of the organisation of the regiment, the following figures are taken from Major Gunn's muster return, a report by *Oberst* Thies on the formation of the Jäger companies dated 14 June 1793, with annotations by Freytag, and Sichart.[19]

---

16   G. Spiller, *Observations on Certain Branches of the Commissariat System, Particularly connected with the present military State of the Country* (London: T. Bensley, 1806), pp.15-16.

17   Calvert to his sister 4 June 1793, in Verney (ed.), *The Journals and Correspondence of General Sir Harry Calvert*, p.80 and Anon., *An Accurate and Impartial Narrative of the War, by an Officer of the Guards* (London: Cadell and Davies, 1796), Vol.1, p.98.

18   Debrett (ed.), *A Collection of State Papers 1794*, pp.42-3.

19   Muster return for the 14th Regiment on 19 and 21 April 1794 TNA: WO 1/170, p.149, report by Oberst Thies dated 14 June 1793 in Hann. 38 E Nr. 37, ff. 68-78 and Sichart, *Geschichte der Königlich-Hannoverschen Armee*, Vol.4, pp.42-4.

Table 9: Hanoverian Troops taken into British Pay 22 January 1794

	Battalions	Strength
Cavalry		
Additional Light Dragoons		108
		108
Infantry		
4th Grenadier Battalion	1	728
1st Regiment von Stockhausen	2	1,310
9th Regiment von Wangenheim	2	1,310
14th Light Infantry Regiment	2	1,662
4 additional officers for each regiment already in British pay		24
	7	5,034
Artillery and Pioneers		
Artillery		71
Pioneers		82
		153
Total excluding Staff	7	5,295

Source:
State of the additional troops taken into British pay 22 January 1794 annexed to the 'Article of Agreement', in Debrett (ed.), *A Collection of State Papers*, 1794, pp. 42-3.

Note:
The strengths shown are the full establishments shown in the State and include regimental staff and men serving the battalion guns in the regimental totals.

The regimental staff consisted of:

- 1 Colonel*
- 1 Lieutenant Colonel*
- 2 Majors*
- 1 Regimental Quartermaster and Paymaster
- 2 Adjutants
- 1 Chaplain
- 1 Auditor
- 1 Regimental Surgeon
- 1 Drum-Major
- 2 Provosts
- 1 Armourer
- 1 Waggon-Master
  Total 11 excluding the 4 officers marked * who nominally commanded companies

The battalion companies were organised in the same way as grenadier companies, with each having the following theoretical strength according to Sichart, although the muster return shows the regiment as having six captains, nine first lieutenants, and 21 ensigns in total.

- 1 Captain
- 2 First Lieutenants
- 2 Ensigns
- 1 Sergeant Major
- 4 NCOs
- 6 Corporals
- 1 Surgeon's Mate
- 2 Fifers
- 3 Drummers
- 16 Lance-Corporals
- 138 Privates
  Total 176

Each Jäger company had:

- 1 Captain
- 1 First Lieutenant
- 2 Ensigns
- 1 Sergeant Major
- 2 Sergeants
- 1 Armourer
- 1 Quartermaster
- 4 Corporals
- 1 Company Surgeon
- 2 Horn Players
- 85 Riflemen
  Total 101, although Thies's report does not show the company surgeon, who is also not included in the total in the 'State' annexed to the 'Article of Agreement'.

The regiment had six 1-pounder amusettes instead of the usual 3-pounder battalion guns, which were allocated two to each battalion and one to each Jäger company. The 'State' only records that they were served by 43 officers and men, but the muster return shows one second lieutenant, two bombardiers, and 41 gunners and matrosses, the latter a grade lower than fully-trained artillery men, making 44 in total. Gunn also recorded one ammunition waggon for each gun.

The 'State' includes 71 men for the horse artillery and 82 for the pontoon detachment, which is described as 'additional pioneers', but does not show any further details. The horse artillery division had four 3-pounder cannon and two 7-pounder howitzers.

As usual, Gunn's repot on the whole corps was glowing, with the men of both cavalry and infantry being described as 'very fine, & as compleat as possible in every article they should have', while the artillery 'excelled every thing of the kind' and their horses were 'the admiration of the whole Army'.[20]

The pontoon detachment and train only left Hanover on 6 June 1794 and reached Brussels on 5 July. They were mustered by Gunn, recently promoted to lieutenant colonel, on 5 September, at which point the pontoon company was made up of:

- 1 Captain
- 1 Lieutenant
- 1 Pontoon Master
- 1 Sergeant
- 2 Corporals
- 1 Surgeon's Mate
- 1 Drummer
- 50 Privates
  Total 58

And the Train:

- 1 Lieutenant
- 2 Sergeants
- 6 Corporals
- 1 Harness Master
- 1 Surgeon's Mate
- 1 Farrier
- 1 Assistant to the Farrier
- 3 Copper Smiths
- 2 Saddlers
- 3 Blacksmiths
- 2 Wheelwrights
- 80 Drivers
  Total 103

They had 242 horses, 42 waggons, and 24 copper pontoons. As usual, the men were reported to be 'remarkably fine', the pontoons, carriages and waggons 'of the best kind' and the horses as good as those of the artillery.[21]

The Hanoverian corps lost over 15,000 men in the campaigns of 1793-5. The summary in Table 10 shows that the great majority were not battlefield casualties, but were either prisoners of war or those incapacitated by sickness, deserters, missing etc., classified as 'other'. They also lost a significant amount of ordnance during the 1793 and 1794 campaigns. The return for the heavy artillery for 1 December 1794 shows that the two 30-pounder howitzers of the 2nd division, which had been lost at Menin, had been replaced by three 7-pounders and that the heavy artillery was short

---

20 Gunn to Dundas 5 August 1794, TNA: WO 1/170, p.143.
21 Gunn to Dundas with enclosure 5 September 1794, TNA: WO 1/170, pp.361-5.

of three 6-pounder cannon.[22] Scharnhorst also recorded that three battalions of infantry were using captured French 4-pounders and ammunition waggons during 1794 to replace their original equipment.[23]

Table 10: Losses of the Hanoverian Corps 1793-5

	Dead	Wounded	POWs	Other	Total
Infantry					
Officers	35	138	162		335
NCOs and men	456	2,887	5,258	4,990	13,591
Total	491	3,025	5,420	4,990	13,926
Artillery					
Officers	4	5	8		17
NCOs and men	16	119	76	112	323
Total	20	124	84	112	340
Cavalry					
Officers	11	32	12		55
NCOs and men	77	269	131	586	1,063
Total	88	301	143	586	1,118
Total					
Officers	50	175	182		407
NCOs and men	549	3,275	5,465	5,688	14,977
Grand Total	599	3,450	5,647	5,688	15,384

Source: Anon., 'Verlust-Liste des Churbraunschweig-Lüneburgischen Corps in den Feldzügen 1793, 1794 und 1795 bis zum 5ten December', *Neues Militairisches Magazin*, 1805, vol. 3, no. 8 p. 62.

Assessment of Their Quality

In contrast with Gunn's repeated praise for the Hanoverian troops, the letters and memoirs of British officers were often very critical of the performance of the infantry under fire. A typical example is in the journal of Captain Atherley of the Coldstream Guards for 13 May 1794, which recorded that 'The Hanoverians behaved very ill on this as on every other Occasion'.[24] Lord Malmesbury's diary for 7 December 1793 records details of a conversation with Lord Herbert, Lieutenant Colonel of the 2nd Dragoon Guards, during which Herbert 'praised the Hanoverians for *fighting*, but not their *activity*' and described Freytag as 'an old woman'.[25] The Duke of York also complained of their indiscipline and sickliness. On the other side, Lieutenant von

---

22 Report 1 December 1794, Hann. 38 E Nr. 213, p.41.
23 G. von Scharnhorst, *Handbuch der Artillerie* (Hannover: Helwingschen Hofbuchhandlung, 1804-14), Vol.1, p.30.
24 Manuscript Journal of Captain Atherley, Coldstream Guards, NAM 1997-10-131.
25 Malmesbury (ed.), *Diaries and Correspondence of James Harris*, Vol.3, p.19.

Ompteda of the Hanoverian Garde Regiment noted the coolness and indifference, characteristic of the English.[26]

A more measured assessment was given by Sir Herbert Taylor, who had served on the staff of the Duke of York's army when he was a young man. He recorded that Freytag was 'not young, and had become slow and inactive', while Wallmoden 'had been employed chiefly in diplomacy, was a clever, well-informed man, but as a soldier slow and undecided and a bad horseman'. He commented that the major generals were mostly old men, although he recognised that some, particularly Hammerstein, did good service. Apart from Freytag, who was born in 1720, and G.W.D. von dem Bussche, born in 1726, the generals were generally born in the 1730s, making them in their late 50s or early 60s during the campaigns. For example, Hammerstein was born in 1735.[27] Taylor also noted that there were some good Hanoverian staff officers and that many of the cavalry and infantry regiments were well-commanded. He praised the artillery, but thought that their calibre was too small, and the cavalry, especially the Leibgarde and the light dragoons, but the infantry 'were, in general, of low standard', with a large proportion of young recruits, although the grenadiers were select. He also commented that the Hanoverians 'were great plunderers', as were the British, especially the new levies and the women who accompanied the army.[28]

Uniforms and Equipment

(Plates A 1-4, C 1-4, E - H)

The uniforms worn by Hanoverian troops were very similar to those of the British and they were often mistaken for them by the French. Apart from differences of detail, the most obvious distinguishing feature was the yellow sash worn by Hanoverian officers, whereas the British wore crimson. The cut of uniforms took on a more modern appearance through the 1790s, with the collars of coats becoming taller and lapels shorter. The lapels also changed from being open from about half way down showing the waistcoat, to being closed to the waist. The anonymous manuscript in the British Royal Collection, dated 1795 in the catalogue, and Huck's engravings of the Hanoverian troops on campaign, which were published in 1799-1801, show the infantry coats with closed lapels, although the *Album de Berlin* still shows open lapels in 1795. It is likely that the change occurred a little after the contingent returned home, in line with the British practice, and Schirmer illustrates a uniform in this style in the Zeughaus in Berlin, which is dated 1797.[29]

---

26 Ompteda, 'Hannoversche leichte Grenadiere im Feldzuge von 1793', p.329.

27 B. von Poten, 'Die Generale der Königlich Hannoverschen Armee und ihrer Stammtruppen', *Beiheft zum Militär-Wochenblatt*, especially pp.273, 281 and 284-5.

28 E. Taylor (ed.), *The Taylor Papers* (London: Longmans, Green, and Co., 1913), pp.29-30.

29 A.E. Haswell Miller and N.P. Dawnay, *Military Drawings and Paintings in the Collection of Her Majesty the Queen* (London: Phaidon, 1969 and 1970), Vol.2 nos. 354/1-38; F. Schirmer, 'Die Uniformierung der kurhannoverschen Infanterie 1740-1803' part 10, *Zeitschrift für Heereskunde*, 1972, pp.71-3.

Like the British troops, the Hanoverians suffered from the lack of adequate warm clothing during the winter of 1793-4 and the response was similar, with patriotic donations to provide flannel waistcoats. 7,090 waistcoats arrived in late February and were distributed to the cavalry, infantry, artillery and pioneers by mid-March.[30] The Hanoverians were luckier than the British, as arrangements were also made to purchase over 14,000 greatcoats for the infantry, artillery, pioneers and pontoniers, this time including the additional troops engaged in January 1794.[31]

Muskets and pistols were manufactured by the Herzberg factory and three new models of muskets were introduced for the infantry, dragoons, and grenadiers in 1786. The calibre of all three was smaller than the previous models at 16.5-16.6 mm, and they featured the latest innovations; a conical touch hole, flash guard (*Feurschirm*), and screwless lock (*Stiftschloss*). The grenadier muskets were shorter than the infantry model and the dragoon musket even shorter. The cavalry also received new pistols of the new calibre in 1790.[32] The 14th Light Infantry Regiment had short light infantry muskets, while the Jäger companies, including NCOs and horn players, carried a short rifle and a *Hirschfänger*. Musket slings were generally white, but the 14th Light Infantry Regiment is sometimes shown with red, which was also authorised for the 1st Grenadier Battalion.[33]

Generals wore black cocked hats edged with gold lace, yellow and silver cords, and a black silk cockade, held in place by gold lace and a button. Some contemporary portraits show a white over yellow plume. They had scarlet coats with a dark blue turned over collar, round cuffs and lapels, and white turnbacks, which Ronnenberg shows closed with a patch of white cloth and a button. The buttons were gilt and, from contemporary portraits, appear to have been like those of British generals, with a crossed sabre and baton in the centre and a laurel wreath around the edge. The collar, cuffs and lapels had gold lace edging and the button holes were decorated with gold lace, with one on each side of the collar, a pair on the cuffs and on the lapels. Schirmer states that the buttons and lace on the lapels were in four pairs on each side, apparently based on Ronnenberg.[34] However, Merker shows 10 evenly spaced laced buttons (Plate E 1), and portraits of Freytag and Hammerstein also show them evenly spaced. The horizontal pocket on each coat tail was edged in gold and also had two buttons and lace. Epaulettes had red straps with gold lace and fringes and are usually shown on both shoulders, although an engraving of Hammerstein, drawn from life by Huck, only shows one on the right shoulder. A yellow waist sash was worn under the coat around 1790-1, but is shown worn over the coat in later portraits. The *Degen* had a silver hilt with a gold grip and a silver and yellow strap. It was carried in a black scabbard with silver fittings, worn from a waist belt. The shirt, waistcoat, and breeches were white, worn with high black boots.

---

30 Report dated 14 March 1794 and receipts from the various regiments, Hann. 38 E Nr. 418, ff. 2-23.

31 Records of purchase and allocation of greatcoats, Hann. 38 E Nr. 419.

32 U. Vollmer, *Deutsche Militär-Handfeuerwaffen*, (Privately Published, 2003-2007), No.8, pp.54, 98.

33 Memorandum dated 12 February 1793, Hann. 38 E Nr. 36, ff. 1-4.

34 F. Schirmer, *Nec Aspera Terrent: eine Heereskunde der Hannoverschen Armee* (Hannover, Helwingsche Verlagsbuchhandlung, 1929), p.143.

An order was issued on 12 March 1793 that cavalry generals should wear blue uniforms in the field, rather than the usual red, to match the blue uniforms of the cavalry regiments.[35]

Flügeladjutanten and aides de camp of the general staff had the same hats as generals. Their scarlet coats had a stand-up collar with blue tabs at the front, blue round cuffs, no lapels, and white turnbacks. There was a button and strip of gold lace on the collar tab and 10 strips on the buttons on each side of the coat front. There were also four buttons and gold lace chevrons with the points downwards on each sleeve, one on the cuff and the other three evenly spaced to the elbow, and another four on the coat tails. The other details were the same as generals. This is the uniform described by Wurmb and shown by Merker, although Ronnenberg's version does not have the blue collar tabs or cuffs.[36]

The uniforms of all cavalry regiments were in the same style, distinguished by the colour of the coat, facings and button colour, as shown in Table 11.

Table 11: Hanover Cavalry Uniforms

	Coat	Facings	Buttons /Lace
Leibgarde	Red	Blue	Gold
1st Cavalry	Blue	Red	Gold
2nd Cavalry	Blue	White	Gold
4th Cavalry	Blue	White	Silver
5th Dragoons	Blue	White	Silver
7th Dragoons	Blue	Lemon Yellow	Silver
9th Light Dragoons	Blue	Red	Gold
10th Light Dragoons	Blue	Red	Silver

Source:
Anon., *Königl. Gross-Britannisch- und Churfürstl. Braunschweig-Lüneburgscher Staats-Kalender*, 1795.

Notes:
The facing colour appears on the collar, lapels and cuffs for the Leibgarde and cavalry regiments, but only on the lapels and cuffs for dragoons and light dragoons.
All regiments had white waistcoats and breeches.

The Leibgarde, cavalry and dragoon regiments wore cocked hats with a black cockade, held in place by a gold or silver loop and button, depending on the button colour. The hats of the Leibgarde were edged in gold lace and the other regiments either laced in the button colour or plain. The hat cords ended in silver and yellow tassels for officers. The ends of the cords for privates are not shown clearly, but appear to be gold with a red centre for the Leibgarde and white for the other regiments, sometimes with a blue centre. Some sources show the hats without plumes,

---

35 Note to the King from Freytag and order dated 12 March, Hann. 38 E Nr. 25, ff. 17-18.
36 Wurmb, *Gegenwärtiger Be- und Zustand der Churhannövrischen Trouppen*, p.7.

but others have white or white and yellow plumes and the Merker set in the British Library shows oak leaves worn in the hats. The records of uniforms and equipment lost on campaign include *Casquets* for all regiments, presumably the metal skull caps which were commonly worn by cavalry under their hats as protection against sword cuts.[37]

The light dragoons wore leather helmets with a crest in yellow or white metal, depending on the button colour, and a red mane hanging down from it. The front plate was edged in yellow or white metal and had a silver leaping horse emblem. Most sources do not show plumes, although the *Gmundener Prachtwerk* and Merker show oak leaves on the left side.

The Leibgarde and cavalry regiments had a turned over collar in the facing colour, generally shown attached to the top button on the lapels. The dragoons and light dragoons had a low blue collar, on which the *Gmundener Prachtwerk* shows a patch in the facing colour with a button on each side. This is only shown for officers by Ronnenberg and only for the light dragoons by Merker. All regiments had white turnbacks, which were closed by a button and patch of cloth. Schirmer shows these patches as blue edged in the button colour, except for the light dragoons, where the patch was red edged in the button colour. Ronnenberg shows it as plain white for all regiments except the Leibgarde and light dragoons, and the anonymous set from around 1790 only shows it for the light dragoons.

A coat belonging to a Leibgarde private dated 1788, which was in the Zeughaus in Berlin, has five pairs of buttons on each lapel, two on the round cuffs, two on the pockets and two in the small of the back.[38] Ronnenberg shows shorter lapels with four pairs of lace and an additional button at the top on each side, except for the light dragoons who have the fourth pair set below the lapels. Merker has the same arrangement for the dragoons and light dragoons, but shows five pairs for the cavalry regiments. This may reflect changes in style, as the lapels became shorter with fewer buttons. The button holes were laced in the button colour for the Leibgarde and light dragoons but not for the other regiments. The light dragoons also had a button and three chevrons of lace pointing downwards on each sleeve, one on the cuff and two above it, and three on each coat tail.

Officers had epaulettes in the button colour, which are shown on both shoulders for all regiments by Ronnenberg, but only on the right for regiments other than the Leibgarde and light dragoons by Merker. Privates of the Leibgarde and cavalry regiments had a blue strap on the left shoulder to keep the belts for the ammunition pouch and musket in place. This was laced gold for the Leibgarde and replaced by a single white fringed epaulette for the dragoons. The light dragoons had two epaulettes mixed red and the button colour. Merker also shows officers wearing yellow waist sashes under their coats.

---

37 Lists of uniforms and equipment lost in the campaigns of 1793 and 1794, Hann. 38 E Nr. 542-3.
38 F. Schirmer, 'Eine Bekleidungsvorschrift des hannoverschen Leib-Garde-Regiments aus dem Jahre 1788', *Zeitschrift für Heereskunde*, 1943, pp.22-9.

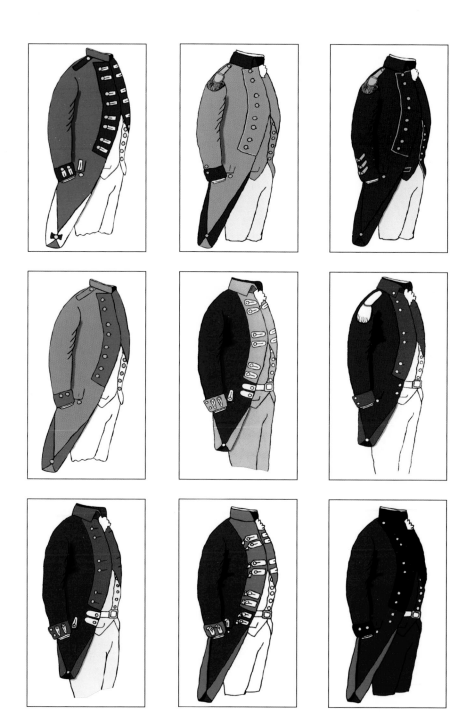

Plate A – Uniform Coats: Hannover, Hesse Cassel, and Baden
A1: Hanover 6th Infantry Regiment. A2: Hanover 14th Light Infantry Regiment.
A3: Hanover Jäger Company 14th Light Infantry Regiment. A4: Hanover Artillery Regiment.
A5: Hesse Cassel Leib-Regiment. A6: Hesse Cassel Jäger Battalion. A7: Hesse Cassel Artillery
Regiment. A8: Baden Leibinfanterie Regiment. A9: Baden Artillery Company.

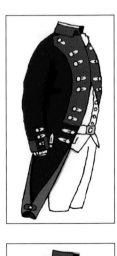  

Plate B – Uniform Coats: Hesse Darmstadt and Brunswick
B1: Hesse Darmstadt 1st Leibgrenadier Battalion. B2: Hesse Darmstadt Regiment Landgraf.
B3: Hesse Darmstadt Light Infantry Battalion. B4: Hesse Darmstadt Feldjäger-Corps.
B5: Hesse Darmstadt Artillery. B6: Brunswick Regiment Prinz Friedrich.
B7: Brunswick Regiment von Riedesel. B8: Brunswick Jäger Battalion. B9: Brunswick Artillery.

Plate C – *Album de Berlin*: Hanover, Hesse Cassel, and Hesse Darmstadt
C1: Hanover 1st Cavalry Regiment or Leibregiment. C2: Hanover Garde Regiment.
C3: Hanover 14th Light Infantry Regiment. C4: Hanover Jäger Company 14th Light Infantry
Regiment. C5: Hesse Cassel Garde-Grenadier-Regiment. C6: Hesse Cassel Fusilier Battalion.
C7: Hesse Darmstadt 1st Leibgrenadier Battalion.

Plate D – *Album de Berlin*: Hesse Darmstadt and Brunswick
D1: Hesse Darmstadt Chevauxlegers. D2: Hesse Darmstadt Regiment Landgraf.
D3: Hesse Darmstadt Feldjäger-Corps. D4: Hesse Darmstadt Artillery.
D5: Brunswick Regiment von Riedesel. D6: Brunswick Jäger Battalion.
D7: Brunswick Artillery.

Plate E – Hanover: Staff and Cavalry

E1: General in service uniform.
E2: Officer of the general staff
E3: Officer and private of the Leibgarde.
E4: Officer and private of the 5th Dragoon Regiment.

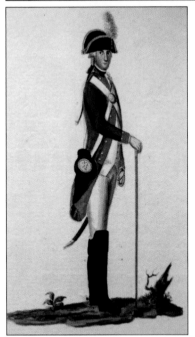

Plate F – Hanover: Infantry, Artillery, and Engineers
F1: Officer and private of the Garde Regiment.
F2: Officer and private of the 1st Infantry Regiment.
F3: NCO of the horse artillery.
F4: Private of the second company of the engineer corps.

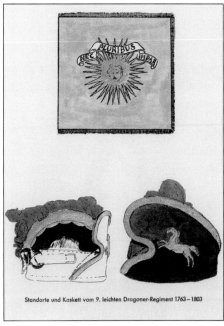

Standarte und Kaskett vom 9. leichten Dragoner-Regiment 1763–1803

Plate G – Hanover: Train and Light Dragoons
G1: Officer of the artillery train and an NCO.
G2: Drivers.
G3: On the left a harness master and on the right a wheelwright.
G4: Standard and helmet of the 9th Light Dragoon Regiment.

Plate H – Hanover: Cavalry and Infantry c.1790
H1: 7th Dragoon Regiment.
H2: 9th Light Dragoon Regiment.
H3: 6th Infantry Regiment wearing the Gibraltar cuff band.
H4: Jäger Company 14th Light Infantry Regiment.

Plate I – Hanover: Infantry Flags issued in the 1780s

I1: One of the four identical flags carried by the Garde Regiment.

I2: The centre of a *Gibraltarfahne*.

I3: 3rd Flag of the 10th Regiment.

I4: 2nd Flag of the 11th Regiment.

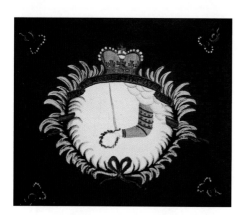

Plate J – Hanover: Infantry Flags 1756 Designs
J1: 2nd flag of the 1st Regiment. J2: 3rd flag of the 1st Regiment.
J3: 2nd flag of the 4th Regiment. J4: 4th flag of the 5th Regiment.
J5: 4th flag of the 6th Regiment. J6: 4th flag of the 9th Regiment.

Plate K – Hesse Cassel infantry 1780s
K1: Regiment Erb-Prinz
K2: Jäger Corps.

Plate L – Hesse Cassel Troops 1789
L1: Officer and private of the Carabinier-Regiment.
L2: Officer and private of the Garde-Grenadier-Regiment.
L3: Officer and private Regiment Prinz Carl.
L4: NCO and private of the Light Infantry Battalion.

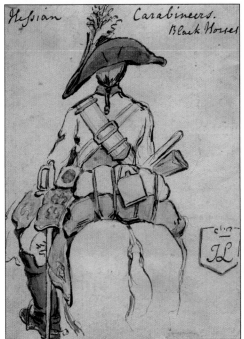

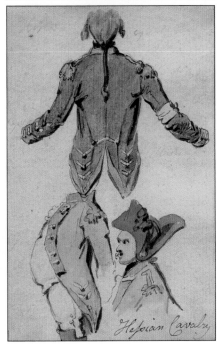

Plate M – Hesse Cassel Cavalry
M1 and M2: Gens d'Armes.
M3: A private of the Carabinier-Regiment.
M4: A private of the Prinz Friedrichs Dragoon Regiment.

In Uniform   Im Fraque   Regiments-Chirurgus   Feldscherer   Sergeant

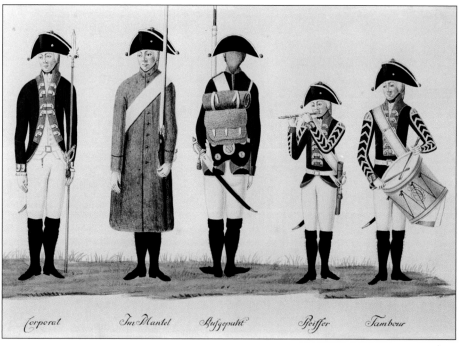

Corporal   Im Mantel   Aufgepakt   Pfeiffer   Tambour

Plate N – Baden Leibinfanterie Regiment

Plate O – Hesse Darmstadt Cavalry and Infantry
O1: Jan Rynhard Gerhard van Reede in the uniform of an officer of the Chevauxlegers.
O2: Musketeer of the 4th company of Regiment Landgraf.
O3: The flags of the Regiment Landgraf.
O4: Light Infantry Battalion.

Plate P – Brunswick Infantry and Artillery
P1: Grenadier of the Regiment Prinz Friedrich.
P2: Grenadier of the Regiment von Riedesel.
P3: Jäger.
P4: Artilleryman.

All regiments wore white gauntlets, waistcoats, and breeches with high cuffed boots. For the campaigns in the Low Countries, the light dragoons were issued with white overalls made of kersey, a coarse woollen cloth, trimmed with leather.[39]

The 1795 set in the British Royal Collection shows the summer dress for all cavalry regiments except the light dragoons. This was a white single breasted shell jacket with coloured collar, cuffs and shoulder straps, and was worn with a plain hat. The facing colours are scarlet for the Leibgarde and 1st Cavalry Regiment, blue for the 2nd and 4th Cavalry Regiments and 5th Dragoons, and yellow for the 7th Dragoons.

Cavalry and dragoons carried a *Pallasch* and the light dragoons a curved sabre, both with a three-barred yellow metal hilt. They were worn in a black scabbard with yellow metal fittings from a white waist belt with a silver plate engraved 'GR' for officers and yellow metal for privates. Ronnenberg shows officers with brown scabbards. Officers' sword knots had silver and yellow straps and fringes. Merker shows them as brown for privates, except in the Leibgarde who had red and gold fringes. Ronnenberg shows the straps as black for the regiments other than the Leibgarde, and with fringes mixed red and the button colour for the light dragoons. All were armed with two pistols, carried in the saddle holsters, and a short musket in a bucket on the right side of the saddle or from a swivel on the shoulder belt. The ammunition pouch had a white flap and was worn on a white belt over the left shoulder.

Saddle cloths and holster covers were red for the Leibgarde and light dragoons and dark blue for the other regiments, edged in lace of the button colour. The Leibgarde had the monogram 'GR' surrounded by the garter and topped by a crown in the rear corner and the crowned 'GR' on the holster covers. The cavalry and dragoon regiments had the white horse on a red background surrounded by a laurel wreath and surmounted by a crown in the corner and on the holster covers, although the *Gmundener Prachtwerk* shows the 'GR' monogram within a silver band instead of the horse for the 4th Cavalry Regiment. It also shows the 9th Light Dragoons with the crowned 'GR' monogram, surrounded by a gold laurel wreath on the saddle cloth, but plain on the holster covers, and the 10th Light Dragoons with the 'GR' within the blue garter and topped by the Prince of Wales's feathers on the saddle cloth and the feathers alone on the holster covers. The use of expensive gold and silver laced saddle cloths on campaign is confirmed by the records of horse furniture lost in 1793-4.[40]

The portmanteau was carried behind the saddle, and was red and white for the Leibgarde and blue and white for the other regiments. The Leibgarde uniform in the Zeughaus in Berlin includes a dark blue cloak with white lining, and Ompteda described them wearing blue '*Capottes*' over their red uniforms at Famars.[41]

The infantry received new hats and uniforms in May every two years, although the men had to provide their own shirts, breeches, and shoes and officers were

39 Diary of Capitain von Stoltzenberg of the 9th Light Dragoons, in Sichart, *Geschichte der Königlich-Hannoverschen Armee*, Vol.4, p.152.
40 Lists of uniforms and equipment lost in the campaigns of 1793 and 1794, Hann. 38 E Nr. 542-3.
41 Ompteda, 'Hannoversche leichte Grenadiere im Feldzuge von 1793', p.324.

responsible for providing their own spontoons, gorgets, swords, and sashes.[42] Uniforms for the infantry, artillery and engineers were very similar, and were distinguished by the colour of the coat, facings and buttons, as shown in Table 12.

Table 12: Hanover Infantry, Artillery, and Engineer Uniforms

	Coat	Lapels/Cuffs	Shoulder Straps	Buttons /Lace
Garde Regiment	Red	Dark Blue	Red	Gold
1st Regiment	Red	Dark Green	Green	Silver
4th Regiment	Red	Light Blue	Blue	Silver
5th Regiment	Red	Lemon Yellow	Red	Silver
6th Regiment	Red	Dark Green	Green	Silver
9th Regiment	Red	White	White	Silver
10th Regiment	Red	Dark Green	Red	Silver
11th Regiment	Red	Black	Red	Silver
14th Regiment	Grey	Dark Green	Green	Gold
Jäger Companies	Green	Green	Green	Gold
Artillery Regiment	Light Blue	Red	Light Blue	Gold
Engineers	Dark Blue	Red	Dark Blue	Gold

Source:
Anon., *Königl. Gross-Britannisch- und Churfürstl. Braunschweig-Lüneburgscher Staats-Kalender*, 1795.

Notes:
Waistcoats were white for all regiments except for the 14th, including the Jäger companies, where they were green.
The buttons had the regiment's number on them for both officers and men.

Musketeer officers wore cocked hats with silver and yellow cords and tassels, lace edging, and a black silk cockade, held in place by a loop of lace and button in gold for the Garde Regiment and silver for the line regiments. NCOs' hats were like those of the officers, but the cockade was made of horsehair and their cords were mixed silver and the facing colour. The men's hats were edged in yellow for the Garde Regiment and white for the line regiments, with a yellow or white loop and button respectively. They had a large pompom over the loop and smaller ones at the ends of the cords at the sides of the hat. The pompoms for the Garde Regiment were yellow with a blue centre, and generally white with a centre in the facing colour for the line regiments. Ronnenberg shows an additional red band around the light blue centre for the 4th Regiment, white with a yellow ring around the red centre for the 5th, white with a red centre for the 9th, and white with a black ring round the red centre for the 11th.

---

42 Anon., *Haushalts-Reglement für die Chur-Braunschweig-Lüneburgische Infanterie*, pp.19, 48, 67.

Grenadiers wore black bearskin caps, similar to the British pattern, with a metal plate on the front. The first battalions of the 3rd, 5th and 6th Regiments had served in the defence of Gibraltar during the great siege and were distinguished by a plate with the word 'Gibraltar' on the front of their bearskins. The 1st Grenadier Battalion had been designated as light grenadiers in 1793 and wore the so-called *Corsenhut*, with the brim turned up on the left side and edged in white, and with a white and yellow plume for officers or white for privates. Unlike musketeers, grenadiers are generally depicted wearing moustaches and side whiskers. Huck's engraving of the breakout from Menin shows the company officers and men of the 1st Grenadier Battalion in this way.

Officers of all infantry regiments except the 14th had scarlet coats, which had a small tab of cloth in the facing colour with a button on each side of the small upright collar. The buttons were spaced evenly on the lapels, two on each cuff, and two on each pocket in the coat tails, with a button on a patch of cloth closing the white turnbacks. According to Ronnenberg, the cloth patches were gold for the Garde Regiment and in the facing colour for the other regiments. Officers of the Garde Regiment had gold lace on their button holes, but line officers were specifically forbidden to add lace to their coats, waistcoats, or button holes.[43] Garde and line officers wore two fringed epaulettes in the button colour and a yellow silk sash and gilt gorget when on duty. Gloves, waistcoat and breeches were white, worn with black half-gaiters which were replaced by boots when off duty or in bad weather. In bad weather, they also wore a dark blue coat (*Rebenrock*) over the waistcoat with a hat, without lace but with the cords, cockade, loop, and button. This coat had white lining and the collar and cuffs were in the facing colour, except for regiments with green facings, when it was blue. They also had a dark blue overcoat (*Oberrock*) with white lining and large regimental buttons.[44] The overcoats were to be red for officers of the 1st Grenadier Battalion. [45]

Privates' red coats were of poorer quality than those of the officers and did not have the tabs on the collar, but had four pairs of buttons with lace on each lapel, two on each cuff and two on the horizontal pockets in the coat tails. The 'Gibraltar battalions' also wore a blue band above the right cuff, with white edges at top and bottom with a yellow zig zag pattern, and the yellow word 'Gibraltar' in the middle. NCOs' coats were distinguished from those of the men by a narrow band of lace round the cuffs, in silver for the line regiments and probably gold for the Garde Regiment. They also carried a cane. Waistcoats and breeches were white, worn with black half-gaiters.

The drum major's and band musicians' uniforms cost the same as those of sergeants and NCOs and were the same cut and colour as the rest of the regiment. They had gold or silver lace interwoven with silk, and swallows nests in the facing colour, also lined with lace, and the drum major's bandolier was laced in gold or silver. Drummers' and fifers' uniforms cost the same as for the privates, with

43 Anon., *Haushalts-Reglement für die Chur-Braunschweig-Lüneburgische Infanterie*, pp.64-5.
44 Anon., *Haushalts-Reglement für die Chur-Braunschweig-Lüneburgische Infanterie*, Appendix XI, pp.89-90.
45 Memorandum dated 12 February 1793, Hann. 38 E Nr. 36, ff. 1-4.

distinctions like the musicians but with the lace made of camelhair or wool.[46] A surviving drum from the grenadier company of the 1st Infantry Regiment has a brass shell, decorated with a cartouche showing the leaping Hanoverian horse under a scroll with the motto 'NEC ASPERA TERRENT' and topped by the British Royal crown. At the bottom it has 'REG.E' on the left and 'GRD COMP' on the right.[47]

The uniforms of the 14th Light Infantry Regiment and its Jäger companies are described in a memorandum dated 5 March and a report dated 14 June 1793 by *Oberst* Thies, the regiment's colonel-in-chief.[48] The regiment wore the *Corsenhut* with a green plume. The battalion companies had grey coats with grey lapels, and green turned over collar, round cuffs, and turnbacks. All ranks wore yellow epaulettes and yellow buttons with the number 14. Officers' gold epaulettes were of better quality than those of NCOs, which in turn were better than the privates. Officers' lapels had gold edging and they wore a yellow sash, but no gorget. All ranks wore grey waistcoats and leather breeches and the belts were black leather. The Jägers wore the same hats, but their coats, lapels, collar, cuffs, and turnbacks were all green. Officers and NCOs had the same gold epaulettes and edging as the battalion companies, but the privates' coats were plain and had only a little gold interwoven into their epaulettes. They wore green waistcoats, yellow leather breeches and grey cloth gaiters.

Schirmer describes some differences and additional details shown in contemporary illustrations. These include narrow yellow edging on the lapels of coats for privates in the battalion companies and yellow edging to the brims of the hats and a leather band around the crowns, which was laced in silver or white and yellow for officers or white and yellow for sergeants.[49] The *Album de Berlin* shows yellow laced button holes on the lapels, and chevrons on the sleeves for both the battalion and Jäger companies (Plate C 3 and 4), and the anonymous manuscript from around 1790 has a Jäger with yellow edging to the collar, lapels, and waistcoat, and chevrons on the sleeves (Plate H 4).

Musketeer officers carried a *Degen*, with a silver hilt and a gold grip. It had a silver and yellow sword knot, and was carried in a black (Merker) or brown (Ronnenberg) scabbard with yellow metal fittings. When on duty, the belt was worn from a white belt over the right shoulder, with an oval silver plate mounted on red cloth backing. They should also have had spontoons, but an investigation of the officers' private effects lost on campaign shows not a single one listed amongst all the gorgets, sashes, swords, pairs of pistols, and so forth.[50] Grenadier officers normally carried a sabre and a musket and bayonet, although the officers of the 1st Light Grenadier Battalion were ordered to carry the *Degen* but no musket. However, this order does not appear to have been followed as the records of equipment lost by the battalion

---

46 Anon., *Haushalts-Reglement für die Chur-Braunschweig-Lüneburgische Infanterie*; p.22 and Appendix X p.85.

47 The drum is described and illustrated in H. Ritgen, 'Eine kurhannoversche Trommel in Holland', *Zeitschrift für Heereskunde*, 1964, pp.4-11.

48 Papers relating to the formation of the regiment, Hann. 38 E Nr. 37, ff. 10-12 and 68-78.

49 Schirmer, 'Die Uniformierung der kurhannoverschen Infanterie 1740-1803' Part 9, 1972, p.27.

50 Lists of uniforms and equipment lost in the campaigns of 1793 and 1794, Hann. 38 E Nr. 542-3.

include officers' muskets.[51] Huck's engraving of the breakout from Menin also shows *Capitaines* von Alten and von Hugo leading their men with a musket in hand.

Musketeer NCOs were armed with a *Kurzgewehr* and sabre, while grenadier NCOs and those in the 14th Light Infantry Regiment had a musket, bayonet and sabre. Infantrymen wore white leather cross belts, held in place by shoulder straps in the colours shown in Table 12, and with an oval brass plate, The belt over the right shoulder was for the short sword, which had a brass handle and was carried in a black scabbard with brass fittings, and the belt over the left shoulder was for the black leather cartridge pouch, which was plain for musketeers, but with a large grenade badge in the middle for grenadiers. NCOs had silver sword knots, while privates had none.

Artillery uniforms were very similar those of the infantry, with the distinction shown in Table 12, red turnbacks, and white waistcoats and breeches, which were worn with black half-gaiters. Officers wore gold-laced hats, gold epaulettes and yellow waist sashes, but not gorgets. Unlike the infantry, other ranks' coats did not have lace on the button holes. Merker shows an NCO of the horse artillery, wearing a gold-laced hat with a yellow-over-white plume and high black boots. Otherwise, the uniform is the same as for the foot artillery. Over his right shoulder, he has a white belt with what appears to be a black pistol holster with a round yellow metal plate instead of an ammunition pouch (Plate F 3).

Infantrymen serving the battalion guns wore the normal regimental uniform with two epaulettes, which were gold or silver for NCOs and presumably yellow or white for privates. The NCOs and men were armed with an artillery-pattern musket.[52]

Engineer uniforms were also in the same style, with white turnbacks, which were closed with a patch of red cloth and a button, white waistcoats and breeches, and black half-gaiters. Officers wore gold-laced hats, gold epaulettes and yellow waist sashes, but not gorgets, and Merker shows an officer in high black boots. Other ranks in the pioneer and pontonier company wore hats with the brim turned up at the back and edged in yellow, with a yellow band around the crown. They had a yellow metal crowned 'GR' on the front and a black plume, which is shown as yellow over red in the anonymous set from around 1790. The only difference between them was the yellow metal badge on the back of the hat, which was a crossed axe and pick, with a spade in the middle, for the pioneers, and crossed anchors for the pontoniers. Their coats did not have lace on the button holes and had vertical pockets with three buttons on the tails. They wore mixed red and yellow epaulettes on both shoulders and their ammunition pouches had white flaps.

Train officers wore a plain black hat with a black cockade, held in place by gold lace and button, and with silver and yellow cords and tassels. The dark blue coat was single breasted with a row of nine gold buttons down the front, worn open to show the top of the shirt and the waistcoat. It had a red turned over collar and turnbacks and round blue cuffs, closed by two buttons. The waistcoat, gloves and breeches were

---

51   Memorandum dated 12 February 1793, Hann. 38 E Nr. 36, ff. 1-4 and lists of uniforms and
      equipment lost in the campaigns of 1793 and 1794, Hann. 38 E Nr. 542-3.
52   Anon., *Haushalts-Reglement für die Chur-Braunschweig-Lüneburgische Infanterie;* pp.20, 25
      and Appendix X p.85.

light buff and high black boots were worn. A yellow waist sash was worn under the coat and Merker shows gold cords on the right shoulder (Plate G 1), while the set showing the pontoon train has cords on both shoulders. The sabre had a silver hilt, with a yellow and silver sword knot, and was carried in a black scabbard with silver fittings, worn on a light buff or white leather shoulder belt with an oval gilded plate.

The uniform of NCOs was similar, but with the hat cords ending in red and gold or yellow tassels and the waistcoat and turnbacks were dark blue. For train corporals, the hat cords were wool and the shoulder cords yellow camel hair. The sabre hilt and scabbard fittings were yellow metal and the belt plate was brass with the crowned 'GR' monogram. They did not have the officer's rank distinctions of sash or sword knot, although both carried canes.

Drivers wore a wide-brimmed plain black hat and a short red jacket, which was closed with two rows of yellow metal buttons and had a dark blue turned over collar and round cuffs. They had a wide red waist band, closed with two or three pairs of yellow metal buttons on the front, and red breeches with buff leather inserts were worn with high back boots. A blue armband on the upper left arm had the monogram 'GR' in yellow, or 'P.T.' for the pontoon train. In bad weather, a long red coat, closed by yellow metal buttons down the front and with a red cape was worn with red gloves.

The harness master and craftsmen wore a similar uniform, but the jacket and coat are generally shown as dark blue and the breeches light buff, worn with white stockings and short black gaiters. The set showing the train around 1780 gives the craftsmen light blue jackets. They did not have the waist band or arm band, and the lower part of the jacket was closed by a single row of two or three yellow metal buttons. Their round cuffs were dark blue and their trade was indicated by the colour of the collar and cape, which were red for the harness master, buff for the wheelwright, black for the smith, dark blue for the saddler, and red for the pontoon train's copper smith. Black or brown leather aprons were worn tied round the waist.

The Hanoverian artillery had been improved and made lighter after the Seven Years War and the 3-pounders of the horse artillery were given a flintlock firing mechanism, based on those used on British naval cannon.[53] As for the calibre of the artillery, Scharnhorst wrote that the Hanoverians had no 12-pounders in the campaigns of 1793-5, having to make do with their 6-pounders. He pointed out that 12 pounders had been found to be prone to damage quite quickly when carrying out rapid fire.[54] The gun carriages were painted red with black metal fittings.

Flags and Standards

(Plates G 4, I and J)

Up to 1803, each cavalry and dragoon regiment had a standard for each squadron of the same design as those used in the Seven Years War. The regiments which were paired for service in the Auxiliary Corps carried only two standards each, selected

---

53   Scharnhorst, *Handbuch der Artillerie*, Vol.1, p.86 and plate XI.
54   Scharnhorst, *Handbuch der Artillerie*, Vol.2, pp.533-4.

according to the condition of the cloth, but it has proved impossible to confirm which particular standards were retained.

The Leibgarde carried the standards from the former Garde du Corps. These were white with heavy silver embroidery and fringes. The central emblem was the same on both sides and consisted of the British Royal coat of arms in the centre, supported by a lion on the left and a unicorn on the right, and surrounded by the order of the garter with the motto 'HONI SOIT QUI MAL Y PENSE'. It was surmounted by the Royal crown and a scroll with the motto 'DIEU ET MON DROIT' beneath.

The 1st or Leibregiment received new standards in 1781 which were lighter than the old ones, but kept the same designs. The *Leibstandarte* was white with gold fringes and embroidery and the design of the obverse was the same as for the Leibgarde with the double-looped monogram 'GR' on the reverse. The second standard was also white with a gold fringe and a round orange center with the white horse on it, surrounded by the garter. The centre panel sat on an ermine cloak, surmounted by a helmet, with the motto 'NEC ASPERA TERRENT' on a scroll below. The reverse had silver and gold column inscribed 'GR' supporting gold scales, with an unsheathed sword on it, and the motto 'PRO LEGE ET GREGE'. The third standard was white with silver embroidery and the British coat of arms on both sides. The fourth was yellow with gold embroidery and with the British arms on the obverse. The reverse had a silver column with laurel leaves round it, topped by a gold crown and with the motto 'MEREAMUR' above and a trophy of arms around the base of the column.

The 2nd Cavalry Regiment's *Leibstandarte* was white. The obverse had the monogram 'GR' surrounded by the garter, with a lion on the left and a unicorn on the right, a crown above and the motto 'DIEU ET MON DROIT' below. The reverse showed Saint George on horseback fighting a dragon and a scroll above with the motto 'VIRTUS ANIMI SUPERAT OMNIA'. The second standard was green with the obverse showing the monogram 'GR' surrounded by the garter with the motto 'NEC ASPERA TERRENT' below and on the reverse the mythological Fama with the motto 'ARMA VIROSQUE CANO'. The third and fourth standards were both white with the same emblems. The obverse had the white horse on a red ground, surrounded by the garter and the motto 'DIEU ET MON DROIT' below, and the reverse had a column with hanging gold scales, a drawn sword, trophies around the base of the column and the motto 'PRO LEGE ET GREGE' below.

The 4th Cavalry Regiment had a white *Leibstandarte* with the white horse on a red ground surrounded by the garter on the obverse and, on the reverse, a column surmounted by a crown with the motto 'MUORO DOVE M'ATTACCO' above. The second standard was blue with the gold monogram 'GR' surrounded by the garter on the obverse and the reverse showing the same emblem and motto as the *Leibstandarte*. The third standard was white with the white horse on a red ground surrounded by the garter on the obverse and the gold monogram 'GR' within the garter on the reverse, in each case with the motto 'NEC ASPERA TERRENT' below. The fourth standard was probably blue with the obverse like the third standard and the reverse showing an upright gold lion holding a sword and the motto 'IN PACE AD BELLUM PARATUS' above.

The 5th Dragoon Regiment's *Leibstandarte* was white with the British Royal coat of arms with the garter, lion and unicorn, and the usual mottos on both sides. The other standards were crimson with the obverse of each bearing the white horse on a red ground surrounded by the garter and the motto 'DIEU ET MON DROIT' beneath. The reverse of these standards showed a different emblem in each case: that of the second had an upright tournament lance with a small silver flag also bearing the lance. Around the middle of the lance lay a bundle of arrows and above it the motto 'VIRTUS UNIONE INVICTA'; the third had a recumbent lion with its front paws on a pair of kettle drums and other trophies and the motto 'PARCERE SUBJECTIS' above; the fourth had Saint George stabbing a dragon in the throat with his lance and the motto 'VIRTUS ANIMI SUPERAT OMNIA' above.

The 7th Dragoon Regiment had a white *Leibstandarte* with the white horse on a red ground surrounded by the garter and topped by a crown, with the motto 'NEC ASPERA TERRENT' below and the 'GR' monogram in the corners on the obverse. The reverse had the two-faced god Janus in an open helmet with trophies on each side and the motto 'DECET ET ORNATE' above. The other three standards were blue with different emblems on each side. The obverse of the second standard had Mars sitting on a pile of trophies, holding a sword in one hand and a laurel branch in the other, with the motto 'POST BELLUM NOMEN' below and the revere had Saint George killing a dragon and the motto 'VIRTUS ANIMI SUPERAT OMNIA' above. The third standard had the monogram 'GR' with a crown, lion and unicorn and the motto 'DIEU ET MON DROIT' below on the obverse. The reverse showed the 'Bülow bird' (golden oriole) with a ring in its beak and the motto 'FELICI AUSPICIO' below. The obverse of the fourth standard had an eagle followed by a youngster flying towards the sun with the motto below, given as 'PROSPOROS FAVET' by Wissel, but with variations in other sources. The reverse had a shield bearing four crowns, a lion with a sword and the monogram 'GR' in the corners.

The two light dragoon regiments each carried a standard of the French Rougrave Cuirassier Regiment, which had been captured by Freytag's Jäger-Corps during the Seven Years War. The standard of the 9th Regiment was light red, almost flesh colour, with a gold embroidered sun in the centre under the motto 'NEC PLURIBUS IMPAR' and although the design of the 10th Regiment's standard is not known according to Wissel, it was probably the same as that of the 9th (Plate G 4).[55]

Each infantry regiment had four flags, with the first flag of the first battalion being the white *Leibfahne*. Wissel states that all regiments had the same design of *Leibfahne*, with the British Royal coat of arms in the centre. However, he gives the *Leibfahne* of the 4th Regiment as having the coat of arms replaced by the white horse of Lüneburg on a red ground surrounded by the garter, with the lion, unicorn, and crown, but with the motto 'NEC ASPERA TERRENT' on the scroll below. He also describes the new *Leibfahne* issued to the 11th Regiment in 1785 as being the same as the 1st Regiment, but with the coat of arms replaced by the monogram 'GR'.[56]

---

55 F. von Wissel, continued by G. von Wissel, *Geschichte der Errichtung sämmtlicher Chur-Braunschweig-Lüneburgischen Truppen* (Zelle: Johann Dieterich Schultze, 1786), pp.292 and 295 and F.Schirmer, 'Althannoversche Feldzeichen (1620-1803)', *Niedersächsisches Jahrbuch für Landesgeschichte*, pp.204-6.

56 Wissel, *Geschichte der Errichtung sämmtlicher Chur-Braunschweig-Lüneburgischen Truppen*, pp.331, 446 and.

Hanoverian 11th Infantry Regiment, Centre of the *Leibfahne* 1790. From F. Schirmer, *Neue Beiträge zur Heereskunde der niedersächsischen Kontingente.* (Historischer Bilderdienst)

Schirmer describes the *Leibfahne* of the 11th Regiment, based on the actual flag saved from the dissolution of the Hanoverian army following the French occupation in 1803. It is identical to that given by Wissel for the 4th Regiment with the crowned monogram 'GR' in the corners.[57]

All four flags of the Garde Regiment were white, with the centre design showing the British Royal coat of arms as described above and with the crowned badges of the Orders of the Garter, the Thistle, the Bath, and Saint Patrick in the corners (Plate I 1). The second, third, and fourth flags of the other infantry regiments were in different colours, with a painted emblem in the centre, a gold motto and the gold crowned monogram 'GR' in the corners. Of the regiments serving with the British, the 4th, 10th, and 11th received new flags in 1783-5, but many of the flags remained the same as those dating from 1756. The battalions which had taken part in the

---

57 Schirmer, 'Althannoversche Feldzeichen (1620-1803)', p.197.

defence of Gibraltar during the great siege were also awarded special *Gibraltarfahne* by the King in 1785 (Plate I 2).

The 2nd flag of the 1st Regiment was dark green with clouds round a central white oval panel with a scimitar and shield on the left and a lion on the right, all surrounded by palm branches, and a scroll above with the motto 'TU NE CEDE MALIS' (Plate J 1). Its 3rd flag was red with a lion lying down, surrounded by green palm branches and with a white scroll above with the motto 'VIGILANTIA VINCIT' (Plate J 2). The colour and design of the 4th flag are not known.

The 2nd, 3rd and 4th flags of the 4th Regiment were light blue. The 2nd flag had a white centre surrounded by palm branches, with a crown on top and a blue scroll, with an armoured arm holding a sword and laurel wreath coming from the clouds, and with the motto 'DULCE ET DECORUM EST PRO PATRIA MORI' (Plate J 3). The 3rd flag had Mars sitting on a pile of trophies in the centre, with the motto 'PRO FIDE, REGE ET LEGE', and the 4th had a standing armoured man holding a lance in his left hand and pointing with his right toward a pillar with a laurel wreath on it and the motto 'BELLICAE VIRTUTIS PRAEMIUM'.

The 2nd flag of the 5th Regiment was the special *Gibraltarfahne* in yellow. It showed the Rock of Gibraltar and floating batteries with a blue scroll above, surrounded by a laurel wreath with a white scroll below tied with a red ribbon,. The motto on the upper scroll was 'MIT ELIOTT RUHM UND SIEG' and below 'DEN 14TEN SEPT. IM JAHR 1782'. Its 3rd flag was white and was like the *Leibfahne* of the 1st Regiment. The 4th was yellow with a man in Roman armour holding up a sword between two marble pillars, which were joined by a chain with two crowns and three laurel wreaths hanging from it, and with the motto 'ANTIQUAE AVIDUS GLORIAE' (Plate J 4).

The 2nd flag of the 6th Regiment was a dark green *Gibraltarfahne*, decorated like that of the 5th Regiment. Its white 3rd flag was like the *Leibfahne* of the 1st Regiment and its 4th was yellow with Mars sitting on a pile of trophies with a flying figure above him and the motto 'NULLI SINE MARTE TRIUMPHI' (Plate J 5).[58]

The 2nd flag of the 9th Regiment was green with a lion standing upright holding a sword and the motto 'PRO FIDE, REGE ET LEGE'. The white 3rd flag was again like the *Leibfahne* of the 1st Regiment and the 4th was dark green, showing clouds surrounded by trophies with a central piece of paper bearing the word 'Jehovah' in Hebrew and a white scroll underneath and the motto 'QUIS CONTRA NOS' (Plate J 6).

The 2nd, 3rd, and 4th flags of the 10th Regiment were dark green. The 2nd flag had a white centre panel surrounded by a thick laurel wreath, with an armoured arm holding a sword coming from the clouds, and a blue scroll with the motto 'CUI VULT'. The 3rd had a laurel wreath round a white centre panel, containing a red banner with gold lace and fringes bearing the crowned monogram 'GR', surrounded by trophies and a blue scroll with the motto 'BEI DIESEN NAHMEN ÜBERWINDEN ODER STERBEN' (Plate I 3). The 4th had a laurel wreath round a

---

58   Wissel gives 'MORTE' but Schirmer states that it should be 'MARTE' as on the old flag of the former Regiment von Zandré, which the 6th Regiment carried.

white centre panel, showing a memorial surrounded by trophies and a blue scroll with the motto 'DER TAPFERKEIT BELOHNUNG'.

The 2nd flag of the 11th Regiment was yellow with a white centre panel surrounded by a laurel wreath with a gold lion facing left, supported by a tree stump and holding a sword, and a blue scroll with the motto 'WER DARF MIR ES NEHMEN' (Plate I 4). The 3rd flag was white with a laurel wreath round a white ermine next to a cave, and a blue scroll with the motto 'LIEBER STERBEN ALS BEFLECKT SEIN'. The 4th flag was like the 3rd, but with the central device surrounded by trophies and with two chained slaves below.

The 14th Light Infantry Regiment did not carry any flags.

10

Hesse Cassel

Introduction

The Landgraviate of Hesse Cassel was the largest state of the Upper Rhenish Circle of the Empire and had around 450,000 inhabitants.[1] Wilhelm IX, who was a cousin of George III and already Count of Hanau, succeeded his father Friedrich II as Landgrave on 31 October 1785. He subsequently achieved his ambition of being elevated to the status of Elector in 1803, at which time he assumed the title as Wilhelm I, but was forced into exile from 1806 to 1813 when Hesse Cassel was invaded by the French and subsequently absorbed into the new Kingdom of Westphalia.

His father had been a leading player in the 'soldier trade' and he inherited a substantial and well-disciplined army. Wilhelm started the reorganisation of his army as soon as he became Landgrave, incorporating the Hanau forces and amalgamating or disbanding the old regiments, to form the basic structure that would be in place through the early campaigns against Revolutionary France. The uniforms, equipment and drill all followed the Prussian style and, as in Prussia, the troops took part in large-scale annual exercises.

At the end of 1792 Hesse Cassel's armed forces had a full strength of over 14,000 men, and consisted of a small staff, six regiments of cavalry, eight regiments of infantry, the Feld-Jäger-Corps, Light Infantry Battalion Lentz, and the Artillery Regiment. There were also two depot battalions, each with four companies, to provide trained replacements for the infantry regiments, a cadet corps, and an invalid battalion. Squadrons of the Garde du Corps, Gens d'Armes, and Carabinier-Regiment had two companies each, but only one in the dragoons and hussars. An infantry regiment had two battalions, each with a grenadier and five musketeer companies. The grenadier companies were combined to form four independent grenadier battalions of four companies each, which were known by the names of their commander. Table 13 shows the strength and composition of the army.

---

1   M.C. Curtius, *Geschichte und Statistik von Hessen*, p.298 and K.E.A. von Hoff, *Das Teutsche Reich vor der französischer Revolution und nach dem Frieden von Lunéville, Erster Theil*, pp.66-7.

Table 13: Hesse Cassel's Army in 1792

	Squadrons	Battalions	Companies	Strength
Cavalry				
Garde du Corps	1		2	120
Regiment Gens d'Armes	3		6	359
Carabinier-Regiment	3		6	359
Leib Dragoon Regiment	5		5	584
Prinz Friedrichs Dragoon Regiment	5		5	584
Hussar Regiment	3		3	352
	20		27	2,358
Infantry and Artillery				
Regiment Garde		2	12	1,326
Garde-Grenadier-Regiment		2	12	1,326
Leib-Regiment		2	12	1,326
Regiment Erb-Prinz		2	12	1,326
Regiment Prinz Carl		2	12	1,326
Regiment von Lossberg		2	12	1,326
Regiment von Kospoth		2	12	1,326
Regiment von Hanstein		2	12	1,326
Artillery Regiment			3	694
Feld-Jäger-Corps		1	2	341
Light Infantry Battalion Lentz		1	2	346
		18	103	11,989
	20	18	130	14,347

Sources:
C. Renouard, *Geschichte des französischen Revolutionskrieges im Jahre 1792* (Cassel: Theodor Fischer, 1865), p. 489 and Anon., *Landgräfl. Hessen-Casselischer Staats- und Adress-Kalender* (Cassel: Verlag des Armen-Waisenhauses, 1793-6), 1793, pp. XV-XLIII.

Note:
The strengths shown are the full establishments (*Sollstärke*) for officers, NCOs, company and squadron surgeons, musicians, and privates. They do not include the middle and lower staff, drivers, and servants.

The Hesse Cassel infantry enjoyed a very high reputation. The Prussian General von Valentini, who served in the campaigns of 1792-4 as a young officer wrote that 'of all the peoples who took the field against France, those of Hessen-Kassel had the greatest military spirit [*Soldatensinn*]'. He went on that the practical experience they had gained in America had left the Hessian officers better than the Prussians at taking appropriate security measures when close to the enemy, instructing patrols, and making quick decisions to deal with unexpected circumstances.[2] The cavalry

---

2   G.W. von Valentini, *Erinnerungen eines alten preussischen Offiziers aus den Feldzügen von 1792, 1793 und 1794 in Frankreich und am Rhein Rhein* (Glogau and Leipzig: Carl Heymann,

were not so well-regarded. They had not seen action since the Seven Years War and had suffered from economy measures and were not fully mounted.

An agreement between the Landgrave and the King of Prussia was signed at Koblenz in July 1792, under which the Landgrave was to provide a corps of 6,000 men at his own expense to serve under the Duke of Brunswick for the duration of the war against France. In return, the King agreed to support the Landgrave's ambition to be elevated to the status of Elector. This corps was brought up to strength by drafts of men and horses from the regiments left in Hesse, including almost all of the horses from the Gens d'Armes and Prince Friedrichs Dragoons. It served in the invasion of France in 1792 and the recapture of Frankfurt.

In the first half of 1793 there were two bodies of Hesse Cassel troops serving on the Rhine. A corps under *General-Lieutenant* von Biesenrodt was with the Prussians at the siege of Mainz, comprising the Leib Dragoon Regiment, Garde-Grenadier-Regiment, Leib-Regiment, and a grenadier battalion commanded by *Oberstlieutenant* von Dincklage, which was made up from their grenadier companies. Dincklage retired during the siege of Mainz and was replaced by *Oberstlieutenant* von Germann. In addition, a body of light troops under *Oberst* Schreiber, consisting of the Hussar Regiment, Feld-Jäger-Corps, and Light Infantry Battalion, was attached to the Prussian army and later to the Austrians.

Organisation and Strength of the Contingent

The troops taken into British pay in April 1793 were commanded by *General-Lieutenant* von Buttlar and comprised two regiments of heavy cavalry, a regiment of dragoons, two grenadier battalions, four infantry regiments, a new Jäger Battalion, a detachment from the Artillery Regiment to serve the battalion guns, and the staff, hospital, and commissariat. The composition and strength of this force are shown in Table 14.

Arrangements began to prepare the corps for service as soon as the treaty was signed. An order was issued on 11 April that the two heavy cavalry regiments were to be augmented by 10 men per company and by 20 men per company for the dragoons.[3] In addition, large numbers of horses had to be purchased. Between 13 April and 30 May, 292 horses were acquired for the Prinz Friedrichs Dragoons and 266 for the artillery. According to Ditfurth a total of 1,863 horses were purchased.[4] The infantry regiments were also brought up to strength by transferring men from the depot battalions.

The *Tableau* annexed to the treaty set out the theoretical strength of each regiment, including officers' servants and clerks, and included two drivers and eight horses for the two waggons attached to the staff of each regiment. The actual strength of the corps was recorded when Major Gunn mustered the troops in June and July, and the

---

1833), pp.17-8.
3   Order in HStAM 4 h 4461 part 1, f. 3.
4   Lists in HStAM 4 h 4461 part 1, ff. 78-96 and Ditfurth, *Die Hessen*, Vol.1, p.50.

Table 14: Hesse Cassel Troops Taken into British Pay 10 April 1793

	Officers	NCOs	Surgeons	Musicians	Privates	Total
Cavalry						
Regiment Gens d'Armes	18	48	6	8	360	440
Carabinier-Regiment	18	48	3	8	360	437
Prinz Friedrichs Dragoons	20	60	4	10	600	694
	56	156	13	26	1,320	1,571
Infantry and Artillery						
1st Grenadier Battalion	16	44	4	20	360	444
3rd Grenadier Battalion	16	44	4	20	360	444
Regiment Erb-Prinz	40	120	8	37	900	1,105
Regiment Prinz Carl	40	120	8	37	900	1,105
Regiment von Lossberg	40	120	8	37	900	1,105
Regiment von Kospoth	40	120	8	37	900	1,105
Jäger Battalion	8	20	2	6	150	186
Artillery detachment	6	20			200	226
	206	608	42	194	4,670	5,720
Total	262	764	55	220	5,990	7,291

Source:
Report dated 21 July 1793, HStAM 4 h 3358 ff. 16-17.

Note:
The strengths shown are the full establishments (*Sollstärke*) for officers, NCOs, company and squadron surgeons, musicians, and privates. They do not include the middle and junior staff, drivers, and servants.

following figures are taken from the *Tableau*, excluding the servants, drivers, and clerks, and noting the main differences shown at the muster.[5]

The staff of a cavalry regiment was to be made up of:

- 1 Colonel*
- 1 Lieutenant Colonel*
- 1 Major*
- 1 Adjutant
- 1 Quartermaster
- 1 Surgeon
- 1 Auditor
- 1 Chaplain
- 1 Riding Master
- 1 Waggon Master

---

5   *Tableau d'un Corps Hessoises de 8,000 Hommes*, TNA: FO 26/20 and Gunn to Dundas 18 July 1793 and enclosures, copy in TNA: WO 6/7, pp.195-201.

- 1 Armourer
- 2 Smiths and Farriers
- 1 Kettle Drummer
- 1 Staff Trumpeter
- 2 Saddlers
- 1 Provost
  Total 15

The 3 officers marked * nominally commanded companies and are not included in the total above.

A company in the Gens d'Armes and Carabinier-Regiment should have had:

- 1 Captain or one of the staff officers marked *
- 1 Lieutenant
- 1 Cornet
- 1 Sergeant Major
- 1 Sergeant
- 6 Corporals
- 1 Surgeon
- 1 Trumpeter
- 60 Privates
  Total 73

And a squadron in the Prinz-Friedrichs Dragoons:

- 1 Captain or one of the staff officers marked *
- 1 First Lieutenant
- 1 Second Lieutenant
- 1 Ensign
- 1 Sergeant Major
- 1 Sergeant
- 10 Corporals
- 1 Surgeon
- 2 Trumpeters
- 120 Privates
  Total 139

The three regiments were almost complete at the muster, with only five men sick and seven on command, although the number of officers was slightly different. The Carabinier-Regiment had four extra first lieutenants, but was four cornets short, and the Prinz-Friedrichs Dragoons had three extra captains but two fewer ensigns. There were also 22 waggon drivers and batmen with each regiment of heavy cavalry and 19 with the dragoons.

The grenadier battalions were renumbered in 1793 and the former 2nd battalion now became the 1st and vice versa. The newly numbered 1st Grenadier Battalion was commanded by *Oberstlieutenant* von Eschwege of the Regiment Garde, and was made up of the grenadier companies of the Regiments Erb-Prinz and Kospoth. The 3rd Grenadier Battalion was commanded by *Oberstlieutenant* Philip von Wurmb of the Regiment Prinz Carl, who was promoted to *Oberst* later in the year, and was formed from the grenadier companies of the Regiments Prinz Carl and Lossberg.

The staff of a grenadier battalion was supposed to have:

- 1 Colonel*
- 1 Lieutenant Colonel*
- 1 Major*
- 1 Adjutant
- 1 Quartermaster
- 1 Surgeon
- 1 Drum Major
- 1 Waggon Master
- 1 Armourer
- 1 Provost
  Total 7, excluding the 3 officers marked * who nominally commanded companies

And a company:

- 1 Captain or one of the staff officers marked *
- 1 First Lieutenant
- 2 Second Lieutenants
- 1 Sergeant Major
- 3 Sergeants
- 1 Quartermaster
- 6 Corporals
- 1 Surgeon
- 2 Fifers
- 3 Drummers
- 18 Lance corporals
- 72 Privates
  Total 111

Both battalions were almost complete at the muster, with only nine men sick between them. The number of officers was again slightly different, with the 1st Battalion having three extra captains but one first lieutenant short and the 3rd Battalion an extra captain. They also had an auditor and a chaplain each and a total of 28 waggon drivers and batmen.

The staff of an infantry battalion was to have:

- 1 Colonel*
- 1 Lieutenant Colonel*
- 1 Major*
- 1 Adjutant
- 1 Quartermaster

- 1 Auditor
- 1 Chaplain
- 1 Surgeon
- 1 Drum Major
- 8 Musicians
- 1 Waggon Master
- 1 Armourer
- 1 Provost
  Total 17, excluding the 3 officers marked * who nominally commanded companies

And a company:

- 1 Captain or one of the staff officers marked *
- 1 First Lieutenant
- 1 Second Lieutenant
- 1 Ensign
- 1 Sergeant Major
- 3 Sergeants
- 1 Quartermaster
- 7 Corporals
- 1 Surgeon
- 3 Drummers
- 18 Lance corporals
- 72 Privates
  Total 110

The muster return shows a total of 30 men sick and 60 on command, including 57 men on command from Regiment Erb-Prinz. Each regiment was missing at least one member of its staff and, as usual, the number of company officers differed from the *Tableau*. Regiment Erb-Prinz was unusual in having four additional captains, offset by being short of four first lieutenants, and a number of the officers had been appointed to staff positions in the corps. Regiments Erb-Prinz and Kosposth were also short of NCOs, the difference being made up by additional corporals. Each battalion also had between 16 and 19 waggon drivers and batmen, making 139 in total.

The Jäger Battalion was raised in 1793, drawing men from the Feldjäger-Corps and good shots from the infantry regiments Erb-Prinz, Prinz Carl, Lossberg, Kosposth, and the depot battalions. It had two companies and a small staff, which should have been made up of:

- 1 Lieutenant Colonel*
- 1 Major*
- 1 Adjutant
- 1 Quartermaster
- 1 Surgeon

- 1 Waggon Master
- 1 Armourer
- 1 Provost
   Total 6, excluding the 2 officers marked * who nominally commanded companies

And each company:

1 Captain or one of the staff officers marked *
- 1 First Lieutenant
- 2 Second Lieutenants
- 1 Sergeant Major
- 3 Sergeants
- 1 Quartermaster
- 10 Corporals
- 1 Surgeon
- 3 Horn players
- 15 Lance corporals
- 60 Privates
   Total 98

They are shown on the muster return as having an auditor but no quartermaster on the staff and with seven sick and one man on command. They also had two captains commanding the companies, in addition to the two staff officers, and eight waggon drivers and batmen.
   The artillery detachment was to have:

- 1 Major
- 1 Captain-Lieutenant
- 1 First Lieutenant
- 2 Second Lieutenants
- 1 Quartermaster
- 20 Bombardiers
- 100 Gunners
- 100 Matrosses
   Total 226 and the train

Each battalion of grenadiers and musketeers had two 3-pounder cannon, making 20 in total. Each gun was served by a bombardier and 10 gunners or matrosses, and the muster return shows four captains and six second lieutenants, with one of these officers attached to each battalion. The Jäger Battalion did not have battalion guns. There was also a reserve train including a quartermaster, master smith, wheelwright, saddler, labourers, and drivers, with two spare gun carriages and various ammunition and support waggons.
   The details of the staff of the corps are shown in Table 15. The commissariat and supply staff had 11 personnel, including four drivers with eight horses for the commissariat and pay chest waggons. The hospital consisted of the director,

a physician general, a surgeon general, six surgeons, a chaplain, an administrator and clerk, an apothecary and assistant, a cook and assistant, with 14 drivers and 28 horses for the hospital waggons.

Table 15: Staff of the Hesse Cassel Corps 12 July 1793

Position	Name	Comments
Commanding General	*General-Lieutenant* von Buttlar	
Aide-de-camp	*Capitain* von Bassewitz	
Aide-de-camp	*Lieutenant* von Buttlar	
Secretary	Wippnicht	
Lt. General of Infantry	*General-Lieutenant* Friedrich von Wurmb	
Aide-de-camp	*Lieutenant* Kross	
Major General of Cavalry	*General-Major* von Dalwigk	
Aide-de-camp	*Cornet* von Dalwigk	
Major General of Cavalry	*General-Major* von Schmied	
Aide-de-camp	*Lieutenant* Kördel	
Major General of Infantry	*General-Major* von Borck	
Aide-de-camp	*Capitain* Bödicker	Later called von Porbeck
Major General of Infantry	*General-Major* von Cochenhausen	
Aide-de-camp	*Lieutenant* von Motz	
Quarter Master General	*Capitain* Engelhard	Artillery Regiment
Assistant	*Staabs-Capitain* Vollmar	Artillery Regiment
Major of Brigade Cavalry	*Rittmeister* Casselmann	
Brigade Adjutant	*Lieutenant* Scheffer	
Major of Brigade Infantry	*Capitain* Rüffer	
Brigade Adjutant	*Premier Lieutenant* von Trott	
Auditor General	Ries	
2 Chaplains	Huppeden and Schwartz	1 Reformed Church and 1 Lutheran
Physician	Pideret	
Surgeon General	Ammelung	
Waggon Master General	Wiess	
Grand Prevot	Lieutenant Krug	
Serjeant de Police	Walter	

Sources:
Major Gunn's muster return dated 12 July 1793, TNA: WO 6/7 pp. 196-7 and Ditfurth, *Die Hessen*, Vol.1 pp.55-9 and the Table facing p.55.

The squadrons and companies were short of officers, even before they suffered losses through combat or disease. This was the result of senior officers, who were nominally commanding squadrons or companies, in fact performing their other roles, and of company officers who were serving as aides de camp or on other duties.

Major Gunn mustered the troops between 29 June and 12 July 1793 and sent his report to Henry Dundas with the muster returns, showing a total of 7,875 men and 2,634 horses, including 238 waggon drivers and batmen with the cavalry and infantry regiments. He stated that 'The Men in General both Cavalry and Infantry are very good, but the appearance of many of the horses is not so', which he attributed to their being very young and having suffered from a long and severe march. He also commented that some of the regiments had indifferent clothing, although he had been assured that new was being made and would be sent forward as soon as it was finished.[6] The reason for the poor quality of their clothing was that the NCOs and men had been ordered to send their new uniforms to the arsenal in Cassel before setting off on campaign.[7]

The additional body of troops taken into British pay under the treaty of 23 August 1793 was commanded by *General-Major* von Hanstein and was made up of the Leib Dragoon Regiment, a grenadier battalion, two infantry regiments, a new Fusilier Battalion and an artillery detachment to serve the battalion guns, with a small staff and hospital. Table 16 shows the make-up of this force.

Table 16: Hesse Cassel troops taken into British Pay 23 August 1793

	Officers	NCOs	Surgeons	Musicians	Privates	Total
Cavalry						
Leib Dragoon Regiment	21	60	5	11	500	597
Infantry and Artillery						
2nd Grenadier Battalion	16	44	3	20	360	443
Garde-Grenadier-Regiment	41	120	8	37	900	1,106
Leib-Regiment	41	120	8	37	900	1,106
Fusilier Battalion	9	24	2	9	180	224
Artillery detachment	4	11			100	115
	111	319	21	103	2,440	2,994
Total	132	379	26	114	2,940	3,591

Source:
Report of the auxiliary corps in Flanders for 6-10 December 1793, HStAM 4 h 3358 f.112.

Note:
The strengths shown are the full establishments (*Sollstärke*) for officers, NCOs, company and squadron surgeons, musicians, and privates. They do not include the middle and junior staff, drivers, and servants.

The strength and organisation of the regiments was broadly the same as for the previous contingent, except that the Leib Dragoon Regiment was not augmented and had only 100 privates per squadron. The 2nd Grenadier Battalion was commanded by *Oberstlieutenant* von Germann of the Garde-Grenadier-Regiment and was made

---

6   Gunn to Dundas 18 July 1793 and enclosures, copy in TNA: WO 6/7, pp.195-201.
7   *Journal des Regiments Prinz Carl*, 8 June 1793, HStAM 10e II/8.

up from the grenadier companies of the Garde-Grenadier-Regiment and the Leib-Regiment. The numbering of the grenadier battalions was changed again in 1794 and this became the 1st Grenadier Battalion, while the former 1st battalion became the 2nd. The Fusilier Battalion of two companies was raised in 1793, drawing men from the infantry regiments and the depot battalions.

Major Gunn wrote to Yarmouth that he had mustered the Hessians at Hanau on the 14 and 15 October and that, after deducting those that were not accepted, the total was 3,991 men, 72 less than in the *Tableau*, and 936 horses. His sent his report to Dundas with the muster returns, noting that the men and their clothing were good and the dragoons' horses were much better than those of the first contingent, but that the horse accoutrements were 'but indifferent' and the Landgrave had promised to send better.[8]

The muster return shows the staff of the Fusilier Battalion as:

- 1 Lieutenant Colonel*
- 1 Major*
- 1 Adjutant
- 1 Quartermaster
- 1 Auditor
- 1 Chaplain
- 1 Surgeon
- 1 Drum Major
- 1 Waggon Master
- 1 Armourer
- 1 Provost
  Total 9 excluding the 2 officers marked * who nominally commanded companies

And each company:

- 2 Captains or First Lieutenants (total three captains and one first lieutenant)
- 2 Second Lieutenants
- 1 Sergeant Major
- 4 Sergeants and NCOs
- 7 Corporals
- 1 Surgeon
- 5 Musicians
- 18 Lance corporals
- 72 Privates
  Total 112

Each grenadier and musketeer battalion had two 3-pounder cannon, making 10 in total, and each gun was served by a bombardier and 10 gunners or matrosses. The muster return shows one captain and two second lieutenants, with an officer

---

8   Gunn to Yarmouth 27 October 1793, TNA: FO 29/3 and Gunn to Dundas 5 November 1793 with enclosures, TNA: WO 1/167, pp.597-607.

attached to the grenadier battalion and to the first battalion of each infantry regiment. The Fusilier Battalion did not have battalion guns.

The staff of the additional body of troops is set out in Table 17 and the hospital was made up of a physician, four surgeons, an apothecary and seven waggon drivers and attendants.

Table 17: Staff of the Additional Hesse Cassel Troops 14 October 1793

Position	Name
Commanding General	*General-Major* von Hanstein
Aide-de-camp	*Capitain* Marquard
Aide-de-camp	*Lieutenant* Bodecker
Secretary	Bodecker
Major General	*General-Major* von Lengercke
Aide-de-camp	*Fähnrich* Wilmowsky
Major General	Prince Friedrich von Hessen[a]
Aide-de-camp	*Lieutenant* Count Bernsdorff
Brigadier	*Oberst* L.J.A. von Wurmb[b]
Aide-de-camp	*Lieutenant* von Langenschwarz
Major of Brigade	*Lieutenant* von Blome
Brigade Adjutant	Kleinhaus
Deputy Quarter Master General	*Hauptmann* Wiederhold
Auditor General	Baur
Surgeon General	Ahlhaus
Waggon Master	
Provost	

Sources:
Major Gunn's muster return dated 14 October 1793, TNA: WO 1/167 p. 607 and Anon., *Landgräfl. Hessen-Casselischer Staats- und Adress-Kalender*, 1793-4.

Notes:
a   Son of the Landgrave's brother, Prince Carl, and a general in the Danish service. He was serving with the Hesse Cassel troops as a volunteer.
b   Aide-de-camp to the Landgrave.

The final element of the Hesse Cassel cops was the brigade of artillery, added by the *Article separé* signed on 23rd March 1794, consisting of two batteries, each of two 13-pounder howitzers, and four 12-pounder and four 6-pounder cannon.[9] As usual, the *Tableau* annexed to the *Article separé* includes officers' servants, but these are not included in the figures set out below. It also shows a driver and four horses for the waggon attached to the staff. The guns were manned by two companies, of whom the officers, NCOs, and 20 gunners per company were from the Artillery

---

9   Signed copy in TNA: WO 1/168, pp 577-586.

Regiment, and the other gunners were trained men from the two depot battalions.[10] The following figures show the theoretical strength of the two batteries from the *Tableau*.

The staff of the artillery brigade, including the drivers had:

- 1 Colonel*
- 1 Major*
- 1 Adjutant
- 1 Auditor and Quartermaster
- 1 Surgeon
- 1 Artillery Commissary
- 1 Drum Major
- 1 Provost
- 231 Drivers
  Total 237 excluding the 2 officers marked * who nominally commanded companies

And each company:

- 1 Captain, including the staff officers marked *
- 1 Captain Lieutenant
- 1 First Lieutenant
- 1 Second Lieutenant
- 12 Bombardiers
- 2 Surgeons
- 3 Drummers
- 53 Gunners
- 52 Matrosses
  Total 126

The artillery train had:

- 1 Commissary
- 2 Waggon Masters
- 6 Conductors
- 3 Artificers: master iron-worker, wheelwright and saddler
- 8 Assistants or Mates
- 6 Smiths
  Total 26

The total according to the *Tableau* was 535 men and 723 horses, including the staff waggon, but when Gunn mustered them on 6 July, he recorded a slightly different

10 Dr W. Has, *Geschichte des I. Kurhessischen Feldartillerie-Regiments Nr. 11 und seiner Stammtruppen* (Marburg: N.G. Elwertsche Universitäts- und Verlagsbuchhandlung, 1913), p.295.

breakdown and only 511 men and 716 horses. The muster return shows five spare gun carriages, six forges and carts, and 79 ammunition and other waggons. Gunn noted in his report that the men were very good and most of the horses were also good. He explained that he had not insisted on replacing the few that he did not like to avoid further delay, although he had written to complain to the Landgrave about them.[11]

The condition of the Hessian horses continued to cause concern and the Duke of York complained to Henry Dundas that the remount horses were 'exceedingly bad'. He enclosed a report by Major General Mansel and Colonel Vyse, who had been sent to inspect them, which showed that out of 298 horses, 132 were very old (many appeared to be over 20 years old) and the whole were in general in bad condition, including many with sore backs, some lame or broken winded, and some mares in foal. The horses for the Prinz Friedrichs Dragoons were particularly bad, with 103 out of 138 recorded as very old.[12] Gunn's letter to Dundas was more favourable, reporting that the cavalry horses were much better than in the previous year, the worst cases having died or broken down and been replaced by better ones. The horse accoutrements, which had also complained about after the previous year's muster, when 'many of the saddles appeared to be older than the Men that rode upon them', were also better, although many more new accoutrements were still required. The infantry were 'as usual, good, & rather better Clothed than they were last year', with their arms and accoutrements 'in very serviceable condition'.[13]

Assessment of Their Quality

Sir Herbert Taylor' assessment of the Hesse Cassel troops, who he had seen while serving on the Duke of York's staff, was that the Hessian commanders Buttlar and Wurmb were 'both old men, as were most of the other General officers'. He went on to say:

> The artillery and cavalry were few, ill-horsed and indifferent, but the infantry were excellent and useful troops, especially the Grenadier battalions, though not composed of very tall men, as they were selected on account of good conduct. Nevertheless, they were great plunderers, and systematically so, as I often saw them out by detachments under a noncommissioned officer, or even a subaltern, with sacks.[14]

Buttlar, who was born in 1727, and Wurmb, born in 1732, must indeed have seemed old men to the young Herbert Taylor. Buttlar became ill during the siege of Dunkirk and was sent to Bruges, where he died at the end of September 1793 and Wurmb took over the command of the corps. However, Wurmb incurred the anger of the

11 Gunn to Dundas and enclosures 5 August 1794, TNA: WO 1/898, pp 11-15.
12 York to Dundas with enclosures 26 March 1794, TNA: WO 1/168, pp.573-4 and 587-9.
13 Gunn to Dundas 5 August 1794, TNA: WO 1/898, pp.11-12.
14 Taylor (ed.), *The Taylor Papers*, p.30.

Landgrave by allowing his corps to be split up, in particular the three regiments sent to garrison Ypres and the dispersal of the Hessian corps between the various columns at Tourcoing. He was recalled to Cassel in June 1794, leaving *General-Lieutenant* von Dalwigk in command.

The Hessians' fondness for plunder was noted by many British observers, and was commented on by Fortescue, even though he concluded that 'on the whole, the Hessians seem to have been the most valuable fighting men in the army'. He also believed that the Hessian corps was 'the more effective since it was equipped with regimental transport upon a lavish scale, and was therefore mobile and self-dependent'.[15] The extent of the transport encumbering the army is described by Ditfurth, who noted that each infantry regiment of around 1,100 fighting men was accompanied by at least 116 drivers and servants with 231 draught and pack horses, including two four-horse waggons for the staff, two two-horse waggons for the pay chest and medical supplies, and a four-horse waggon for each company. However, in comparison with the other contingents, especially the Hanoverians, he still considered them to be a 'model of military mobility'.[16]

From the other side, the Hessian *Fähnrich* von Lossberg of the Garde-Grenadier-Regiment noted that it was very difficult to establish friendly relations with the British officers, partly as a result of the difference in language, but mainly because of their unsociable attitude to foreigners, which was often expressed in a very conceited manner. He also complained of the excesses committed by the British, which were often perpetrated by the women with the army.[17]

Uniforms and Equipment

(Plates A 5-7, C 5-6, K-M)

Generals did not have a special uniform and are generally depicted in contemporary portraits wearing the uniform of the regiment of which they were colonel-in-chief or commander. The generals serving in the Low Countries and the relevant regiments are set out in Table 18.

Müller's *Hochfürstlich Hessisches Corps* shows an officer of the general staff but, unfortunately, does not give any further details of his position. He is wearing a plain black cocked hat with a black cockade held in place by silver lace and a button, silver cords, and a white over red plume. His coat is dark blue with crimson turned over collar, lapels, and round cuffs, and white turnbacks. The coat has silver lace and buttons, one on each side of the collar and three pairs on the lapels, with three silver chevrons and a button above each cuff and three on the coat tails. He has a silver fringed epaulette on each shoulder, white waistcoat and breeches and is wearing

15 Fortescue, *A History of the British Army*, Vol.4, pp.94-5
16 Ditfurth, *Die Hessen*, Vol.1, p.40.
17 F.W. von Lossberg, 'Erinnerungen von Lossberg', *Zeitschrift für Kunst, Wissenschaft und Geschichte des Krieges*, Vol.73, pp.133-4.

Table 18: Hesse Cassel Regiments Commanded by the Generals in British Pay

Name	Regiment	Comments
General-Lieutenant von Buttlar	Leib Dragoon Regiment[b]	
General-Lieutenant F.W. von Wurmb	Leib-Regiment[b]	
General-Major von Dalwigk[d]	Carabinier-Regiment[b]	
General-Major von Schmied	Prinz Friedrichs Dragoon Regiment[b]	
General-Major von Borck	Regiment Prinz Carl[b]	
General-Major von Cochenhausen	Regiment Erb-Prinz[b]	
General-Major von Hanstein	Regiment von Hanstein[a]	1793-4
	Regiment Prinz Carl[b]	1795
General-Major von Lengercke	Regiment von Lossberg[c]	
Oberst L.J.A. von Wurmb[e]	Garde-Grenadier Regiment[c]	1793-4
	Leib-Regiment[b]	1795

Source:
Anon., *Landgräfl. Hessen-Casselischer Staats- und Adress-Kalender*, 1793-5.

Notes:
a   Colonel-in-Chief
b   Commander
c   Colonel 1st Battalion
d   Promoted to *General-Lieutenant* October 1793
e   Promoted to *General-Major* 1794

high black riding boots. He is armed with a sword with a gilded hilt and sword knot in a black scabbard and carries a cane.

The Gens d'Armes and Carabiniers received new uniforms every four years, with the last issue having been on 1 April 1791.[18] They were dressed very much like Prussian *Kürassier* regiments and had previously worn blackened breastplates. However, like the Prussians, they no longer wore their breastplates on campaign and these are not shown by Müller or the contemporary paintings of the regiments in the Low Countries. Officers and trumpeters were clean-shaven, whilst NCOs and privates wore moustaches.

Both regiments wore a cocked hat with a black cockade held in place by a loop of lace and button, which were gold or yellow for the Gens d'Armes and silver or white for the Carabiniers. The ends of the cords showing at the sides of the hat were silver with a red centre for officers and white with a red centre for other ranks. Plumes were white over red and had a red tip for NCOs and trumpeters.

They wore a *Collet* of pale buff kersey, fastened down the front with hooks and eyes, with a red turned over collar and cuffs for the Gens d'Armes and light blue for the Carabiniers. The front edges of the *Collet* and the cuffs were edged with lace and the short pale buff turnbacks were edged in a broad band in the facing colour for

---

18 *Montierungssachen 1791-9*, HStAM 4 h, 4208 f. 4.

officers or regimental lace for other ranks. The lace for the Gens d'Armes was gold for officers and NCOs and yellow with crimson edging and centre stripe for trumpeters and privates. The Carabiniers' lace was silver for officers and NCOs and white with light blue edging and centre stripe for trumpeters and privates. A short waist-coat or *Chemiset* in the facing colour was worn under the *Collet*, and was edged with the same lace. Officers wore a silver waist sash interwoven with crimson and other ranks had a sash in the facing colour. Other ranks had shoulder straps in the facing colour and trumpeters had false sleeves decorated with regimental lace hanging at the back. Trumpeters also had swallows' nests, decorated with regimental lace on the edges and with three vertical bands, and lace chevrons pointing downwards on their sleeves. The trumpet cords were mixed yellow and red for the Gens d'Armes and white and blue for the Carabiniers.

White breeches were worn with high black boots and white or light buff gloves with gauntlets. A wide white cross belt was worn over the left shoulder for the carbine and a narrower belt over the right shoulder for the cartridge pouch. The belts were edged in regimental lace for the Gens d'Armes, whose pouch flap was red and edged in regimental lace, with the yellow 'WL' monogram in the centre. The belts and pouch flap for the Carabiniers were plain white. The *Pallasch* had a gilded or brass hilt bearing the Hessian lion and was worn from a waist belt, in a brown scabbard for officers and trumpeters and black with steel fittings for NCOs and privates. Sword knots were silver and crimson for officers, brown leather with a white and red tassel for NCOs and trumpeters, and brown leather with a white tassel for privates. NCOs and privates wore a *sabretache* in the facing colour, with the crowned 'WL' monogram, yellow for the Gens d'Armes and white for the Carabiniers, in the centre and edged in regimental lace. A contemporary watercolour, probably by Gillray, shows a Carabinier's *sabretache*, which is still bearing the 'FL' monogram of Wilhelm's father (Plate M 3). This is quite possible, as Major Gunn reported that old equipment was still in use. Carl and Müller do not show *sabretaches* being worn by trumpeters, although the *Darmstädter Handschrift* shows them using the same pattern as NCOs, with lace of gold or silver as appropriate.

The full dress saddle cloths and holster covers were in the facing colour, edged with lace in the same way as the *Collets* and with the crowned Hessian lion within an olive wreath on the holster covers and rear corners of the saddle cloth. The Gillray watercolours show a plainer version with a simple lace design on the holster covers and saddle cloth. They also show a white cloak with cape in the facing colour, which was rolled behind the saddle, when not in use (Plates M 1 and 3).

The Dragoons received new uniforms every three years, having received the last issue on 1 April 1791.[19] In around 1789, a new light cavalry uniform had been adopted, with lace trim on the coats, metal helmets, and light hussar-style boots, as illustrated in both contemporary series for 1789 and by Knötel.[20] However, by 1793 the cocked hat and boots reaching above the knee, as worn by the heavy cavalry, were back in use and are shown in the paintings by Gillray and Gregorius and in

19 *Montierungssachen 1791-9*, HStAM 4 h, 4208 f. 5.
20 R. Knötel, continued by H. Knötel d. J., *Uniformenkunde* (Rathenow, Max Babenzien, 1890-1921), Band I No. 20.

the *Album de Berlin*, although the laced coat continued to be worn. As in the heavy cavalry, moustaches were worn by NCOs and privates and the hats and plumes were the same as those described for the Gens d'Armes and Carabiniers.

The coats were light blue with a turned over collar, lapels open from half way down showing the waistcoat, round cuffs, and long tails. The collar, lapels, cuffs, and turnbacks were in the facing colour, red for the Leib Dragoon Regiment and yellow for Prinz Friedrichs Regiment. There was a button on each side fastening the collar to the top of the lapels, three laced pairs on each lapel, and three buttons with chevrons pointing downwards on each sleeve, one on the cuff and two above it, three on the coat tails, and two in the small of the back. The lace and buttons are described as gold for the Leib Dragoon Regiment and silver for Prinz Friedrichs Regiment in the *Staats- und Adress-Kalender*, but Müller shows silver lace with tassels for the officers of both regiments and plain white for the privates. Müller also shows silver fringed epaulettes on both shoulders for officers and white for privates, but Gillray's painting of a dragoon of Prinz Friedrichs Regiment shows yellow epaulettes and four chevrons on the sleeves (Plate M 4). Officers wore silver and crimson waist sashes. The waistcoats were light buff for the Leib Dragoon Regiment and white for Prinz Friedrichs Regiment. Trumpeters are shown in the set by Carl and Müller and in the *Darmstädter Handschrift*, both dating from before the introduction of the light cavalry uniform, wearing the same coats as the men with lace edging to the lapels and with swallows nests and chevrons on the sleeves. The lace is yellow and red for the Leib Dragoon Regiment and white and yellow for Prinz Friedrichs Regiment, with the trumpet cords in the same colours.

White breeches were worn with high black boots by both regiments. Carl and Müller show a wide white cross belt, worn over the left shoulder for the carbine, as does the anonymous set from 1789. Both sets from 1789 show the straight sword worn from a white belt over the right shoulder with an oval silver plate bearing the 'WL' monogram. Müller also shows the monogram 'WL' on the hilt and both officers and privates with brown scabbards with steel fittings. Sword knots were the same as in the heavy cavalry.

The saddle cloths and holster covers were in the facing colour, edged with gold or yellow and red for the Leib Dragoon Regiment and silver or white and yellow for Prinz Friedrichs Regiment. Carl and Müller also show light blue cloaks rolled behind the saddle.

By 1789, the reorganisation of the infantry had been completed and the new uniforms are shown in J.C. Müller's *Hochfürstlich Hessisches Corps*, which was published in that year. The infantry and artillery received new uniforms every three years, with the last issue having been on 1 April 1793.[21] Although they had received new uniforms shortly before being taken into British pay, the campaign journal for the Regiment Prinz Carl records that the NCOs and men were ordered to send their new uniforms to the arsenal in Cassel before going on campaign.[22] Uniforms for the infantry and artillery were in the same style, distinguished by the colour of the facings, buttons, waistcoats and breeches, as shown in Table 19.

---

21 *Montierungssachen 1791-9*, HStAM 4 h, 4208 ff. 7-9.
22 *Journal des Regiments Prinz Carl*, 8 June 1793, HStAM 10e II/8.

Table 19: Hesse Cassel Infantry and Artillery Uniforms

	Collar/Lapels/Cuffs	Waistcoat/Breeches	Buttons/Lace
Garde-Grenadier-Regiment	Red	Yellow	Silver
Leib-Regiment	Yellow	Yellow	Silver
Regiment Erb-Prinz	Crimson velvet	White	Silver
Regiment Prinz Carl	Red	White	Gold
Regiment von Lossberg	Orange	White	Gold
Regiment von Kospoth	Light buff	Light buff	Silver
Regiment von Hanstein	Yellow	White	Silver
Jäger Battalion	Crimson	White	Silver
Fusilier Battalion	Red	White	Silver
Artillery	Crimson	Light buff	Gold

Source:
Anon., *Landgräfl. Hessen-Casselischer Staats- und Adress-Kalender*, 1794.

Note:
Although Regiment von Hanstein did not serve with the corps in British pay, *General-Major* von Hanstein did and probably wore its uniform as he was its colonel-in-chief.

Grenadiers wore bearskin caps and musketeers and artillerymen had cocked hats, whose main constituent was strong sized cardboard, and which quickly lost their shape in prolonged wet weather.[23] The Garde-Grenadier-Regiment had all worn bearskin caps but, according to von Dalwigk, these were given up in the spring of 1793 and replaced by hats with plumes.[24] This is confirmed by two notes signed by *Hauptmann* Wiederhold, *Quartiermeister Lieutenant* on the Hesse Cassel general staff, which state that the regiment was to give up its bearskin caps and send them to the Grenadier Battalion von Dinklage, later renamed von Germann and subsequently Lelong, and made up from the grenadier companies of the Garde-Grenadier and Leib regiments.[25] However, it seems that the grenadier companies kept their bearskins, as the report of uniforms and equipment lost in 1794 for the Grenadier Battalion Lelong includes 52 bearskins lacking and 241 worn out, but no hats.[26]

Infantry and artillery officers wore cocked hats, edged with gold or silver scalloped lace, depending on the button colour, with a black cockade held in place by a button and lace loop, and with silver cords with a red centre showing at the sides. Officers in the Leib-Regiment also had a white over red plume above the cockade. NCOs' hats were edged with a narrow strip of gold or silver lace, which was yellow or white for drummers and privates. Müller shows a black cockade held by a button

---

23 Ditfurth, *Die Hessen,* Vol.1, p.38.

24 Freiherr von Dalwigk zu Lichtenfells, *Geschichte der waldeckischen und kurhessischen Stammtruppen des Infanterie-Regiments v. Wittich (3. Kurhess.) Nr. 83. 1681-1866* (Oldenburg: Ad. Littmann, 1909), p.414.

25 Notes by von Wiederhold dated 23 and 24 May 1793, HStAM 4 h 3482, f. 32.

26 Report dated 27 November 1794, HStAM 4 h 4369, p.22

and loop of white lace, while the earlier sets show a button but no cockade or lace. The ends of the hat cords were white with a red centre.

Grenadier caps had a front plate of yellow or white metal, which was gilded or silver for officers. Two surviving examples in Schloss Friedrichstein, both of white metal, have varying designs, featuring the crowned lion, flaming grenades, and trophies of arms, and one has the arms of Hesse Cassel and the 'WL' monogram. They had a white plume with a red tip on the left side and a bag at the back in the facing colour, edged in white lace and ending with a tassel on the right.

The dark blue coats had a turned over collar, with lapels open from half way down showing the waistcoat and round cuffs. Officers' coats had long tails which were not turned back, but lined in the facing colour, except for the Garde-Grenadier-Regiment who had turnbacks. The coat tails for other ranks were much shorter, with turnbacks in the facing colour, except for the Regiment von Hanstein, where they were red. There were three pairs of buttons on each lapel, two buttons below the lapel on the right side, two on each cuff, and two on the pockets in the coat tails. Officers had silver lace with tassels on their button holes in the Garde-Grenadier, Leib, Erb Prinz, and Prinz Carl Regiments. The lace for NCOs in these regiments was silver without tassels for NCOs and white without tassels for privates, except for the Garde-Grenadier-Regiment, where the lace had tassels. The other infantry regiments had lace on the cuffs, below the lapels, and on the pockets, but not on the buttonholes on the lapels. Officers and NCOs of the Garde-Grenadier-Regiment also had silver epaulettes, which were white for privates. Drummers' coats had blue swallows' nests and lace chevrons with the points downwards on the sleeves. The lace was red and either yellow or white, depending on the button colour, and also decorated the swallows' nests, and edged the lapels and button holes for the Garde-Grenadier and Leib Regiments. All ranks wore black gaiters, reaching above the knee.

Officers also wore silver and crimson waist sashes and infantry officers wore gorgets, although these are not shown in the Müller set. They carried a *Degen* with a gilded hilt and a silver and crimson sword knot, in a brown scabbard from a white waist belt, except for officers in the Garde-Grenadier-Regiment and possibly other grenadier officers, who had sabres, and carried canes. Captains and subalterns also had spontoons, but they were ordered to leave them in the arsenal at Cassel, before going on campaign.[27] NCOs had a short sword with a brass hilt and a white and red sword knot, worn in a brown scabbard from a white waist belt. The records of equipment lost on campaign in 1794 confirm that musketeer NCOs carried the *Kurzgewehr*, while grenadier NCOs had muskets.[28] Privates also had a short sword with a brass hilt, worn in a brown scabbard from a white waist belt. The sword had a white strap with the knot and fringes in the company colour. The company colours had been set out in the 1767 regulations and were as follows: in the first battalion the fringes were black for the grenadier company, white for the *Leib-Compagnie*, light red for the colonel's, light blue for the first major's, orange for the second captain's, and green for the fourth captain's company; in the second battalion, the upper

27 *Journal des Regiments Prinz Carl*, 8 June 1793, HStAM 10e II/8.
28 Various reports in HStAM 4 h 4369.

part of the knot was black for the grenadier company, light red for the Lieutenant Colonel's company, light blue for the second major's, orange for the senior captain's, green for the third captain's, and dark blue for the fifth captain's company.[29]

Infantry muskets were manufactured by Pistor at Schmalkalden and had red leather slings. The black cartridge pouch was worn on a wide white belt over the left shoulder, held in place by a narrow shoulder strap in the facing colour. Drummers had short swords like the privates and the drums, which had brass shells decorated with the Hessian lion and trophies and painted hoops, were carried on a white belt edged in the regimental lace over the right shoulder.

New regulations were issued in late 1793, which introduced red turnbacks and white waistcoats and breeches for all regiments. They also specified that while officers would keep the lace with tassels on their button holes, NCOs would only have two strips of gold or silver lace on their cuffs and privates' coats would be plain.[30] It is not clear when, or even if, these new regulations were implemented in full. The first reference in the *Staats- und Adress-Kalender* to white waistcoats and breeches for those regiments that had previously had yellow or light buff is in 1796. The *Album de Berlin* shows infantry in both laced and plain coats and with yellow waistcoats and breeches in 1795 (Plate C 5), and a series of paintings by Kobold dated 1803 also show privates of the infantry in laced coats as before.[31]

The Jäger Battalion had the same uniform as the Feld-Jäger-Corps. The hats for Jäger officers and men did not have lace edging, but had a green cockade held in place by a button and loop of white lace, or silver for officers and NCOs, with cords like the infantry and white over green plumes, with a green tip for NCOs. Their green coats were cut like those of the infantry, without lace on the button holes, but with an extra button on each side of the collar, and officers had turnbacks. Officers and NCOs had silver epaulettes, which were white for privates, and horn players had green swallows' nests decorated with silver and red lace. Officers also had a silver and crimson waist sash, but no gorget, and wore high cuffed riding boots, while the other ranks had long black gaiters. Officers carried a sabre, with a gilded hilt and silver and crimson sword knot, in a brown scabbard worn from a waist belt. NCOs, horn players, and privates were all armed with a short rifle, with a red sling, and a *Hirschfänger* with a brass grip in a brown scabbard, worn from a white waist belt, instead of the usual infantry sword. NCOs and privates had brown leather pouch belts over the left shoulder. The brass horns had mixed silver, crimson, and green cords and tassels.

The Fusilier Battalion had the same uniform as the Light Infantry Battalion. They wore black helmets with a crest, from which a white mane hung down in ringlets, and a white over crimson plume on the left side, with a crimson tip for NCOs. It had a wide black band running all round with the 'WL' monogram in white metal on the front. The monogram was silver for officers and NCOs, who also had silver edging to the top of the band. The green coats were cut like those of the infantry, but had lace

---

29 Anon., *Reglement vor die Hessische Infanterie* (Cassel: 1767), pp.670-1.

30 Regulation dated 5 November 1793, HStAM 4 h 4208 ff. 24-33.

31 G. Ortenburg, 'Uniformen in Hessen-Kassel 1789 bis 1806', *Zeitschrift für Heereskunde*, 1997, pp.41-5.

chevrons in silver for officers and NCOs and white for privates, one on each cuff and three above it and three or four on the coat tails. The anonymous set from 1789 and the *Album de Berlin* also show lace on the buttonholes (Plates C 6 and L 4). Officers and NCOs had silver epaulettes, which were white for privates. The earlier set by Carl and Müller shows drummers' coats with green swallows nests, decorated with white and red lace. Officers had a sabre with a gilt hilt and silver and crimson sword knot in a brown scabbard, worn on a white belt with an oval silver plate over the right shoulder. NCOs and privates were armed with muskets with red slings, and the Carl and Müller set also shows the officers of the Light Infantry Battalion carrying muskets, which may have also been done in the Fusilier Battalion . Other ranks wore their short swords from a white belt over the right shoulder with a rectangular brass belt plate. NCOs had a black ammunition pouch on a white waist belt, while privates wore their pouch on a white belt over the left shoulder. All ranks wore short black gaiters.

Auditors, regimental quartermasters, and regimental surgeons all had the same uniform. The hats were like those of infantry officers with scalloped silver lace and cords and a black cockade, held in place by a loop of silver lace and a button. The dark blue coat did not have lapels and was worn open, showing the waistcoat. It had a dark blue collar and cuffs and the coat tails were lined red but not turned back. There were three pairs of silver buttons on each side of the coat front and two buttons on the right hip and on the cuffs. The dark blue waistcoat and its pockets were edged with wide silver lace. Dark blue breeches were worn with high black riding boots, and they had white gloves. They were armed with the *Degen*, with a gold hilt in a brown scabbard, and carried a cane. The uniform of company surgeons was similar, but with narrow lace on the hat, and lacking the lace on the waistcoat, but with a narrow lace edging on the cuff and flap. They wore black gaiters and were armed as above.

Artillery drivers wore a plain hat with a yellow metal button on the front and cords with white ends with a red centre. The plain dark blue coat had a row of yellow metal buttons down the front, but was worn open to show the waistcoat, and had blue cuffs and red turnbacks. The waistcoat was dark blue and the pale buff breeches were worn with high black riding boots.

Regimental saddlers had the same uniform, but with dark blue breeches, and carried a cane. Provosts wore the same hat and a grey coat, cut in the same style, with green cuffs and turnbacks, green buttons and piping on the button holes, grey waistcoat and breeches with black gaiters, a sword with a brass hilt worn from a white waist belt, and a cane.

Flags and Standards

There is a considerable amount of information on the flags and standards carried by the army of Friedrich II, but virtually nothing covering the early part of Wilhelm IX's reign. It is not known if new colours were issued or the old ones remained in use, reallocated where necessary to reflect the new organisation of the army. This is certainly a possibility, given Wilhelm's aversion to unnecessary expense. According to Ditfurth, each infantry company except the grenadiers and light infantry had a flag, making five for each battalion, which were carried by a *Gefreite-Corporal* and formed a colour party in the middle of the battalion.[32] The cavalry probably carried one standard for each squadron. These figures are consistent with the colours lost when Ypres surrendered, stated by Ditfurth to be 30 infantry flags, for the three regiments of two battalions each, and one cavalry standard for the *Leib-Escadron* of the Gens d'Armes.[33]

There is a surviving example of a *Leibfahne* in the museum at Schloss Friedrichstein, which is very tattered and faded, and the regiment to which it belonged is not known. This flag is illustrated by 'Otto von Pivka' and is white silk with a central design of a central cartouche with a coat of arms, supported by two gold lions, topped by a crown and with flags and trophies underneath. The crowned 'WL' monogram surrounded by a laurel wreath is in each corner.[34] This may be a flag issued to Wilhelm's newly reorganised army, but it is also quite similar to the design and inscriptions of the *Leibfahne* of the Hesse Hanau regiments.[35] It may have belonged to one of these regiments, which were incorporated into the army of Hesse Cassel when Wilhelm, already ruler of Hesse Hanau, became Landgrave of Hesse Cassel.

32 Ditfurth, *Die Hessen*, Vol.1 p.41.

33 Ditfurth, *Die Hessen*, Vol.2 p.501.

34 O. von Pivka, *Napoleon's German Allies (5): Hessen-Darmstadt & Hessen-Kassel* (London: Osprey, 1982), p.31.

35 G.Ortenburg, *das Militär der Landgrafschaft Hessen-Kassel zwischen 1783 und 1789* (Potsdam, Deutsche Gesellschaft für Heereskunde e. V., 1999), pp.61-2.

11

Baden

Introduction

The Margraviate of Baden, with 194,000 inhabitants, was the second largest state in the Swabian Circle of the Empire after Württemberg.[1] It also included part of the County of Sponheim in the Upper Rhenish Circle. Although the Margrave Carl Friedrich had united Baden-Durlach with Baden-Baden on the death of the Margrave of the latter in 1771, his lands were still fragmented and widely dispersed along the Upper Rhine and were extremely vulnerable to attack by the French.

Baden's armed forces at the end of 1792 consisted of the Leibinfanterie Regiment, the Fusilier Battalions Erbprinz and Rastatt, an artillery company, and two companies of Garde du Corps. There was also a small detachment of hussars, who acted as a police force, and a garrison company of invalids, making a little over 2,000 men in total. The contingent assigned to the Swabian Circle's forces was drawn from the fusilier battalions, the balance of which formed a depot battalion, and the Garde du Corps, leaving only the Leibinfanterie Regiment and part of the artillery company available for independent field service.

Organisation and Strength of the Contingent

The Leibinfanterie Regiment had two battalions, the first grenadier battalion and the second musketeer battalion, each of four companies. The battalion taken into British pay was commanded by *Obrist* von Freistedt, an illegitimate son of the Margrave, and was made up of the first company of the grenadier battalion and the whole of the musketeer battalion. It had two 3-pounder cannon served by men drawn approximately equally from the artillery company and the infantry, with two ammunition waggons. Major Gunn mustered the battalion at Carlsruhe on 28 October 1793. He sent his report and the muster returns to Henry Dundas, showing a total of 760 men and 69 horses and described them as 'fine men, good clothing & appointments' and noted that not a single man was absent from the muster, which he considered 'very

---

1   Hoff, *Das Teutsche Reich*, pp.66-7.

singular'.[2] The following figures are taken from the muster return and a report on the Baden infantry, artillery and train at Ypres dated 20 December 1793.[3]

The battalion's staff was made up of:

- 1 Colonel*
- 2 Majors*
- 2 Chaplains
- 1 Auditor
- 1 Quartermaster and Paymaster
- 1 Surgeon
- 1 Drum Major
- 8 Musicians in the Regimental Band
- 1 Waggon Master
- 1 Provost
- 1 Assistant to the Provost
  Total 20

The three officers marked * nominally commanded companies, but these were commanded by a captain-lieutenant in practice.

The five companies had 18 officers between them:

- 1 Captain
- 4 Captain-Lieutenants
- 5 First Lieutenants
- 6 Second Lieutenants
- 2 Ensigns

And each company had:

- 1 Sergeant Major
- 3 Sergeants and NCOs
- 5 Corporals
- 1 Surgeon's Mate
- 3 Musicians
- 7 *Schützen*
- 90 Privates for the grenadier company or 112 for a musketeer company
  Total 110 for the grenadier company and 132 for a musketeer company

The battalion's guns were commanded by *Feldwebel* Mössmer of the artillery company, with a corporal and 19 privates. The train consisted of the waggon master, waggon maker and wheelwright, smith, saddler, and eight drivers. In addition to the battalion's own surgeon and surgeon's mates, there was also a small hospital, made

---

2   Gunn's report to Dundas 5 November 1793 and enclosures, TNA: WO 1/167 pp.597-8 and 619-20
3   Report dated 20 December 1793, NLA HA Hann. 38 E Nr. 144, p.114.

up of a physician, apothecary, surgeon, clerk, two attendants. and two drivers. The battalion also had 42 waggon drivers, batmen and servants.

Service and Assessment of their Quality

In spite of its fine appearance, the battalion was not to play a significant part in front-line operations. After being sent to join the garrison at Ypres on its arrival with the army, it received orders on 3 February 1794 to march to Menin, leaving behind the numerous sick caused by doing outpost duty in bad weather.[4] The grenadier company was in action when the French attacked the allied advance post at Zandvoorde on 19 February. The allied force was commanded by Captain Behm of the Hanoverian 4th Infantry Regiment, and included the Baden grenadiers and a detachment of the York Rangers, a foreign rifle corps in British service. According to the report of *General-Major* von Linsingen, the total losses in this action were three officers and 98 men, including an officer and 34 men of the Baden grenadiers taken prisoner.[5]

Apart from some minor skirmishes in the following days, this was the battalion's last engagement, as it received orders on 7 March to relieve the British 14th Foot at Oudenaarde and take over guarding the French prisoners of war there. For the rest of the campaign it was behind the lines performing this duty. Freistedt became ill at the end of February and *Major* von Eck took over the command of the battalion. On 15 March, Freistedt's ill health forced him to return to Carlsruhe, where he died on 20 December 1795 aged 46.[6]

The troops did not find their service, so far from home, to be attractive. 63 deserters wrote to the Margrave in June 1794, asking to be pardoned and allowed to return home, and refusing to return to the Low Countries to be treated as slaves. A similar petition with 80 signatures was sent to *Major* von Rabenau in the following days.[7] When Major Gunn inspected the battalion again on 6 June, the number of privates and lance corporals present and fit for duty had fallen to 184, with a further 58 on command and 34 sick, in total just under half the original establishment. He reported to Dundas that 'the only fault to be found with [the battalion] is the smallness of its numbers'.[8]

There was also considerable tension between Eck and Lieutenant Colonel Durell, the British Commissary of Prisoners. Durell complained that Eck had been asked repeatedly to provide a return of the number of effectives present guarding the prisoners, but had refused to comply without an order signed by the Duke of York.[9] Their relationship continued to deteriorate. Durell wrote to Colonel Don, who had been appointed Deputy Adjutant General in November 1794, to inform him that

---

4   The report for 26 January 1794 shows 51 sick: NLA HA Hann. 38 E Nr. 144, p.110.
5   Sichart, *Geschichte der Königlich-Hannoverschen Armee*, Vol.4, pp.341-2
6   Anon., *Aus dem Leben des Freiherrn Ludwig Christian Heinrich Gayling von Altheim*, pp.37-41.
7   Badische Historische Commission, *Politische Correspondenz*, Vol.2 pp.80-81.
8   Gunn to Dundas 5 August 1794 and enclosures, TNA: WO 1/898, pp.11-12 and 23.
9   Durell to Craig 16 June 1794, TNA: AO 16/146, p.235.

Eck had refused to provide a detachment to escort the French prisoners who were
to be exchanged, and again to complain about mistreatment of the prisoners and
asking for the Baden battalion to be replaced.[10] He also wrote to Brook Watson, the
Commissary General, stating that he was nearly certain that the returns supplied by
Eck did not record the actual number of men present, for who bread and forage was
being drawn. He concluded that he did not know how to obtain an accurate return
unless a formal muster was held.[11]

Meanwhile, the Margrave had become increasingly concerned by French successes
on the Rhine and the threat they posed to his territories. As early as February 1794,
he had written to the King to ask for his troops to be sent back to join the forces on
the Upper Rhine.[12] When this request was rejected, he wrote to the Duke of York
that he wished to cancel the subsidy treaty with Britain if the Baden corps could
not be returned to defend the Rhine. The Duke forwarded this letter to Dundas
and added the comment that the high level of desertion in the battalion had obliged
him to send it to the rear to guard French prisoners.[13] The Duke went further in a
later letter in response to another request for the cancellation of the treaty, where he
stated that the battalion had served so badly and lost so many men from desertion
during their short period of active service, that 'I do not think it can be any object to
His Majesty to keep it any longer in His pay', but that it should not be released until
alternative arrangements had been made for guarding the prisoners of war.[14]

After much delay, Grenville wrote in November to Heathcote, the British representative at Mergentheim, instructing him to inform the Margrave that the King
had agreed to the cancellation of the subsidy treaty and the release of the Baden
troops, and that the Duke of York had been directed to allow their return. The Duke
acknowledged receipt of this order, but stated that he did not know what to do with
the prisoners, as no town was prepared to receive them.[15] Unfortunately, this was
not communicated to Wallmoden, who asked the Duke of York for instructions
when he was informed by Freistedt of the cancellation of the treaty. As he did not
hear anything, Wallmoden wrote to the Margrave that he had not received instructions to release the Baden contingent and that they should continue to serve.[16]

After the Margrave had written again to request the return of his troops, which
he said were needed to augment his contingent to the Empire's forces, Eck was
finally able to report at the beginning of May 1795, that he had received the order

---

10 Durell to Don 27 and 31 March 1795, BL Add MS 46706, ff. 20-1.
11 Durell to Watson 2 April 1795, TNA: AO 16/147.
12 Margrave of Baden to George III 4 February 1794, Badische Historische Commission,
    Politische Correspondenz, p.75.
13 York to Dundas 17 June 1794, forwarding the Margrave's letter of 18 May 1794, TNA: WO
    1/169, pp.451-60.
14 York to Dundas 23 October 1794, TNA WO 1/170, pp.813-4.
15 Grenville to Heathcote 7 November 1794, Heathcote to the Margrave 19 November, TNA: FO
    31/6 and York to Dundas 7 November 1794, TNA: WO 1/171, pp.85-6.
16 Wallmoden to York 15 December 1794, TNA: WO 1/171, pp.475-6 and Wallmoden to the
    Margrave 21 January 1795, in Badische Historische Commission, *Politische Correspondenz*,
    p.84.

for the release of the Baden battalion.[17] Durrell wrote to Don that *General-Major von Wangenheim* had been sent by Wallmoden to inform him that the battalion was to be relieved by a detachment of invalids from Hanover, and it would return to Carlsruhe as soon as they arrived. He wrote again a few days later to ask for a surgeon to be sent to replace the surgeon major of the Baden battalion, who had been treating the sick prisoners of war.[18] He informed Brook Watson, Don, and Wallmoden that the invalids had arrived from Hamelin on 9 May and that the Baden battalion would begin their march the following Tuesday.[19] They left the army and reached Carlsruhe on 6 June. Major Gunn's final return for the battalion, dated 13 and 14 April 1795, shows its total strength as 440 men and 73 horses, excluding one officer and 35 non-commissioned officers and privates who were prisoners of war. He reported that the battalion was 'in perfect good condition as far as its number went'.[20]

Uniforms and Equipment

The grenadiers, except their officers, wore a mitre cap with a brass front plate bearing the monogram 'CF' over the star of the House Order *der Treue*, topped by a red pompom. The rear of the cap had a dark blue cloth upper part, with white piping on the three seams, and the lower part was red with white piping. The musketeers and all officers wore a cocked hat, which was edged with a wide scalloped band of silver lace for officers in full dress, silver lace for NCOs, and white for privates. Officers also had a black cockade, held in place by silver lace with a silver button and the silver cords ended in silver, yellow, and red tassels. Other ranks did not have a cockade, although they did have a white metal button above the left eye with a red pompom above it, and the hat cords were white with small red pompoms at the ends. Hair was powdered and curled above the ears with a queue, and grenadier privates and NCOs wore moustaches.

The uniform coat was dark blue, with red collar, lapels, cuffs, and lining to the tails. The tails were turned back and closed with a button for NCOs and privates, but not for officers. Buttons were silver for officers and NCOs, and white metal for privates. There were six buttons in pairs on each lapel, two below the lapels on the wearer's right side with two buttonholes on the left, two on each cuff, two in the small of the back, and two on the pockets in the coat tails. The buttons and buttonholes of officers' coats were decorated with silver lace in gala dress, while those of the NCOs and men had lace with tassels at the end, in silver for sergeants or white for corporals and privates. Officers also wore a silver shoulder knot on the right shoulder and a silver waist sash, interwoven with yellow and red, under the coat

17 Eck to the Margrave 2 May 1795, in Badische Historische Commission, *Politische Correspondenz*, p.86.
18 Durell to Don 4 and 6 May 1795, TNA: AO 16/147.
19 Durell to Watson 10 May 1795 and Durell to Don and Wallmoden 11 May 1795, TNA: AO 16/147.
20 Gunn to Dundas 28 August 1795 and enclosures, TNA: WO 1/898, pp.45 and 59.

and knotted on the left. A gilded gorget, with a silver monogram 'CF' on a crowned trophy of arms, was worn on a wide black strap round the neck when on duty.

The waistcoat and breeches were white and worn with black gaiters, or white for parades and on Sundays and holidays. These reached above the knee and closed on the outside with a row of brass buttons. Officers and NCOs wore short white leather gloves and, from 1793, all officers wore high black boots, replacing the gaiters which had previously been worn by subalterns. Officers had a light grey overcoat for campaign dress, while the men had light grey or brown single-breasted greatcoats, which were closed by six cloth-covered buttons down the front and one on the collar, with stand up collars and large cuffs,. When not in use, the greatcoat was carried rolled on top of the pack.

Drummers and fifers wore the same headdress and uniforms as the men, but with red swallows' nests on the shoulders, decorated with edging and bands of white lace with a yellow stripe and a narrow red centre stripe. The same lace formed a stripe along the front and back of the sleeves, with a number of chevrons pointing upwards between them. The number of chevrons varies in the different sources, possibly depending on the length of the arm, and eight are shown in the 1802 series. The brass drum shells had Baden's arms with the Margrave's crown in the centre, and wooden bands, painted white with blue stripes on the outside and a red stripe in the centre, with white cords and straps. A wide white belt edged with the musician's lace was worn over the right shoulder with laced holders for the drumsticks or a brown leather case for the fife. The 1802 series show the fifers as young boys, although the drummers appear to be older.

The drum major ranked as a sergeant major and his uniform and drum bandolier had silver lace, in place of the normal drummer's lace, and silver fringes on the swallows' nests. He carried a cane and an infantry sabre.

The band musicians held NCO rank and wore a dark blue coat with a red collar, lapels, cuffs, and turnbacks. They had silver buttons and silver lace on the red swallows' nests, and the 1802 set also shows lace on button holes, but this is missing in the 1792 set. Their hats had a narrow edging of silver lace, with a silver button and loop over the black cockade and the 1802 set shows a black plume. They wore waistcoats and breeches like those of the men, with boots, or white gaiters for parades and on Sundays and holidays. For undress uniform they had a plain blue coat with a blue collar and cuffs, and the hat did not have lace edging. They carried the same sabres and sticks as NCOs and their instruments included woodwind and French horns.

The regimental surgeon wore a black hat with narrow silver edging, a silver button and cord over a black cockade, and silver cords and tassels. The blue coat had a red collar, cuffs, and lining and had three pairs of silver buttons down each side of the front, but no lapels, a pair of buttons on the right hip and on each cuff, in the small of the back and on the pockets in the coat tails. The shirt, waistcoat, gloves and breeches were all white, with high black boots. He was armed with a *Degen* with a silver knot, carried in a brown scabbard on a white waist belt worn under the waistcoat, and carried a cane with silver fittings. Company surgeons wore similar uniforms, but without the silver edging on their hats and their coats had blue lapels and cuffs. They also had swords like the regimental surgeon, but with a white sword knot.

Officers carried a *Degen* of Prussian style from a waist belt in a black or brown scabbard with gilded fittings. The sword had a gilded guard and a silver sword knot, interwoven with yellow and red, with silver fringes or thick bullion fringes for staff officers. They also carried spontoons until 1793, at which date they were given to the corporals, and a brown-lacquered cane. NCOs, drummers, and fifers had sabres like those of the privates and, in addition, sergeant majors and sergeants carried a *Kurzgewehr* and corporals a spontoon. For the campaign in the Low Countries, these *Kurzgewehre* and spontoons were left behind and the sergeant majors and sergeants had only sabres, while corporals had muskets and cartridge pouches until their return in 1795.[21] Sergeant majors and sergeants also carried a cane and corporals a hazel stick as a mark of rank, which was suspended from the second highest button on the left lapel when not held in the hand.

The infantry men carried muskets based on the Prussian 1740 model, with the conical touchhole introduced from 1780. *Schützen* carried the same musket and only received rifles in 1801. The men also had short sabres of the Prussian model with a brass guard and grip and a sword knot with a white strap, ending in tassels of the company colour. It was carried in a black leather scabbard, worn on a white leather waist belt with a yellow metal buckle. The black leather cartridge pouch was worn on a wide white leather belt over the left shoulder, which was held in place by a narrow blue strap. The pouch had a brass oval plate with the Margrave's crown and either the coat of arms or the monogram 'CF' and with four flaming grenades in the corners of the pouch flap for grenadiers. The men also had a brown pack and a white linen bread bag worn slung over the right shoulder.

The uniform of the artillery company was similar to that of the infantry with a cocked hat, blue coats with black collar, lapels, and round cuffs – which were velvet for officers – and red turnbacks. The buttons were yellow metal, without lace on the buttonholes, and they wore blue waistcoats, blue breeches, and black gaiters reaching above the knee. Officers' hats had a narrow gold border and star loop and NCOs' hats, collar, lapels, and cuffs had a narrow gold border. The men were armed with short sabres, like those of the infantry. Men drawn from the infantry to serve the battalion guns wore their normal regimental uniforms with a bricole, a white leather cross belt with a length of rope and hook on the end, to assist in moving the cannon. The gun carriages were painted grey with black metalwork.

Flags

Each Baden battalion carried two flags, a *Leibfahne* and a *Bataillonsfahne*. The first battalion of the Leibinfanterie Regiment carried the old flags of the former Baden-Durlach'schen Leib-Grenadier-Garde and the second battalion those of the former Baden-Baden'schen Grenadier-Bataillon, which still bore the monogram of Margrave August George, who had died in 1771.

---

21 G. Söllner, *Für Badens Ehre: die Geschichte der Badischen Heer* (Meckenheim: P.I.G. Zinn-Press, 2001), Vol.2, II, p.189.

Lieutenant von Gayling noted that the Battalion entered Liège in November 1793, on their way to join the Duke of York's army, with flags flying and the musicians playing.[22] It is not known which flags were carried by the battalion in British pay, but it seems most likely that they were those of the second battalion, as there was only one company of the first battalion with the contingent. All of the flags were of painted cloth with silver fringes and were the same on both sides. The *Leibfahne* had a white ground with the Baden-Baden arms on a gold cartouche with the insignia of the Order of the Golden Fleece beneath it. The arms lay on an ermine mantel, supported by a silver griffin on the left and a silver lion on the right, and topped by the Margrave's crown. The staff was topped by a gilded bronze spear tip, bearing the crowned Baden arms surrounded by palm leaves. The *Bataillonsfahne* had a yellow ground with the Baden arms within a white baroque frame, topped by the Margrave's crown and with the collar of the Order of the Golden Fleece beneath. The background of the arms was light red with a darker red diagonal stripe and even darker band of shading. The corners bore the monogram 'AM' of Margrave August in gold on a brown background.

---

22 Anon., *Aus dem Leben des Freiherrn Ludwig Christian Heinrich Gayling von Altheim*, p.19.

12

Hesse Darmstadt

Introduction

The Landgraviate of Hesse Darmstadt was part of the Upper Rhenish Circle of the Empire and had 256,000 inhabitants.[1] Following the division of Hesse in the sixteenth century, the Landgrave ruled lands in Upper Hesse, including the university town of Giessen, and in Starkenburg, around the capital Darmstadt, together with various other minor territories. He had also inherited the county of Hanau-Lichtenburg in Alsace, but this had been taken by France.

Ludwig X succeeded his father Ludwig IX as Landgrave on 6 April 1790 and inherited an army whose uniforms, equipment, tactics, and drill were based on the Prussian model. He immediately started a reorganisation of his army, in which regiments were amalgamated and the infantry regiments gave up their grenadier companies to form a new Leibgrenadier Battalion, with a second being formed in 1791. He also raised a new Light Infantry Battalion and a Chevauxlegers Regiment, giving his army light troops. New regulations for the infantry were introduced in 1792, but these differed little from the previous version, which followed those used by Hesse Cassel.[2]

The Landgrave mobilised his forces in late 1792 and they joined the allied army in the capture of Frankfurt and the siege of Mainz. This situation was formalised by a convention between the Emperor and the Landgrave, which was concluded on 17 September 1793. Under the terms of this convention, Hesse Darmstadt agreed to provide a corps of three infantry battalions and a company of artillery for three years, in return for a subsidy.[3] The force, known as the Second or *Rhein-Brigade*, was made up of both battalions of the Leib-Regiment, the 2nd Leibgrenadier Battalion and six cannon. It was joined by the 2nd Battalion of Regiment Landgraf with two guns, and the brigade continued to serve with the Imperial army on the Rhine.

Hesse Darmstadt's armed forces in the autumn of 1793 had a theoretical full strength of around 6,000 men and consisted of four squadrons of Chevauxlegers; two Leibgrenadier Battalions; the Leib-Regiment and Regiment Landgraf, each of two battalions; the Light Infantry Battalion; a newly-raised Feldjäger-Corps; and the Artillery Corps. In addition, there were small bodies of Garde du Corps and the Hussar

---

1   Hoff, *Das Teutscher Reich*, P.67.
2   Anon., *Reglement für die Fürstlich-Hessische Infanterie* (Darmstadt, 1792); see Appendix V.
3   Martens and Martens, *Recueil des Principaux Traités d'Alliance*, Vol.5, pp.492-505.

Corps, for ceremonial duties and internal security respectively, the Garrison Regiment Erbprinz, which later had a field battalion, and the Land Regiment, or militia.

Organisation and Strength of the Contingent

The contingent taken into British pay was the First, or *Niederländischen*, Brigade under the command of *Generalmajor* von Düring, with a small staff, commissariat and hospital. The composition of the brigade is shown in Table 20. The following details are taken from the specification annexed to the treaty, Major Gunn's muster return dated 21 October 1793 and the establishments shown in the monthly returns.[4]

Table 20: Hesse Darmstadt Troops Taken into British Pay 5 October 1793

	Officers[a]	NCOs[b]	Surgeons[c]	Musicians[d]	Privates	Total[e]
Cavalry						
Chevauxlegers	20	44	4	8	416	492
Infantry and Artillery						
1st Leibgrenadier Battalion	19	40	4	16	600	679
Regiment Landgraf (1st Battalion)	19	40	4	12	600	675
Light Infantry Battalion	19	40	4	12	600	675
Feldjäger-Corps	7	13		5	120	145
Artillery detachment	4	15	1	1	120	141
	68	148	13	46	2,040	2,315
Total	88	192	17	54	2,456	2,807

Source:
Specification annexed to the subsidy treaty sent by Yarmouth to Grenville 5 October 1793, TNA: FO 29/2 and monthly return dated 1 January 1794, HStAD, E 8 B No 271/1 f. 11.

Notes:
a   The total for officers includes the adjutant, who was reported as an officer rather than a member of the middle staff according to the 1792 *Reglement für die Fürstlich-Hessische Infanterie*. This is consistent with the monthly returns, but he is shown as part of the staff in the specification.
b   The specification has four more NCOs, but the total from the monthly return is confirmed by Major Gunn's muster return.
c   Squadron and company surgeons are included in the regimental strength on the returns, but are included in the staff in the specification.
d   The monthly return includes the trumpet/drum major and the Regiment Landgraf's band, but only trumpeters, drummers, and fifers are included here.
e   The strengths shown are the full establishments (*Sollstärke*) for officers, NCOs, company and squadron surgeons, musicians, and privates. They do not include the middle and junior staff, drivers, and servants.

---

4   Specification annexed to the treaty, TNA: FO 29/2, muster return, TNA: WO 1/167 pp.613-7 and monthly returns for December 1793 to April 1794, HStAD, E 8 B No 271/1.

The staff of the Chevauxlegers regiment was:

- 1 Colonel*
- 1 Lieutenant Colonel*
- 1 Major*
- 1 Adjutant
- 1 Auditor
- 1 Quartermaster
- 1 Surgeon General
- 1 Riding Master
- 1 Trumpet Major
- 1 Provost
- 1 Farrier
- 1 Saddler
- 1 Armourer
- 1 Waggon Master
  Total 14

The three officers marked * nominally commanded squadrons, but these were actually commanded by a captain-lieutenant. The four squadrons had between them:

- 1 Captain
- 3 Captain-Lieutenants
- 5 First Lieutenants
- 7 Second Lieutenants
- 4 Sergeant Majors
- 8 Sergeants
- 32 Corporals
- 4 Squadron Surgeons
- 4 Smiths
- 8 Trumpeters
- 416 Privates
  Total 492

The monthly returns from January 1794 onwards show 32 *Schützen* and 384 privates, but these are included with the privates on the specification, and are described as corporals in the muster return, in addition to 44 sergeants and NCOs. The muster return also includes a chaplain, an additional first lieutenant and 67 waggon drivers, batmen and servants.

The staff of the 1st Leibgrenadier Battalion was:

- 1 Lieutenant Colonel*
- 1 Major*
- 1 Adjutant
- 1 Auditor
- 1 Quartermaster

- 1 Surgeon General
- 1 Drum Major
- 1 Provost
- 1 Armourer
- 1 Waggon Master
  Total 10

The two officers marked * nominally commanded companies, but these were actually commanded by a captain-lieutenant. Each of the four companies had:

- 1 Captain, or a Captain Lieutenant for the Lieutenant Colonel and Major's companies
- 1 First Lieutenant
- 1 Second Lieutenant
- 1 Ensign
- 1 Sergeant Major
- 3 Sergeants
- 1 *Gefreite-Corporal*
- 5 Corporals
- 2 Fifers
- 2 Drummers
- 1 Company Surgeon
- 10 *Schützen*
- 140 Privates
  Total 169

The muster return shows the *Schützen* as lance corporals and also includes a chaplain and 59 waggon drivers, batmen, and servants.

The 1st Battalion of Regiment Landgraf had the same organisation, except that it had a regimental band of 10 musicians, but only one fifer per company. The muster return shows two fewer musicians, and again shows the *Schützen* as lance corporals. It also shows 58 waggon drivers, batmen, and servants.

The theoretical composition of the staff of the Light Infantry Battalion was:

- 1 Colonel*
- 2 Majors*
- 1 Adjutant
- 1 Auditor
- 1 Quartermaster
- 1 Surgeon General
- 1 Drum Major
- 1 Provost
- 1 Armourer
- 1 Waggon Master
  Total 11

The three officers marked * nominally commanded companies, but these were to be commanded by a captain-lieutenant. The four companies should have had between them:

- 1 Captain
- 3 Captain-Lieutenants
- 5 First Lieutenants
- 7 Second Lieutenants
- 4 Sergeant Majors
- 12 Sergeants
- 4 *Gefreite-Corporale*
- 20 Corporals
- 8 Fifers
- 4 Drummers
- 4 Company Surgeons
- 40 *Schützen*
- 560 Privates
  Total 672

The battalion was short of two officers who were serving on the staff. Its colonel was Düring, who had recently been promoted to *Generalmajor* and was commanding the brigade, and *Lieutenant* F.W. von Gall had been promoted to *Stabskapitain* and was serving as Deputy Quartermaster General. The battalion was commanded by *Major* von Stosch, the senior major, and a first lieutenant commanded the second major's company. The muster return shows the *Schützen* as lance corporals and includes 46 waggon drivers, batmen, and servants.

The Feldjäger-Corps of two companies was commanded by a major, with a captain-lieutenant, two first lieutenants, two second lieutenants, an adjutant, surgeon, provost, and armourer. The corps had a sergeant major, 12 NCOs, described as *premier chasseurs* in the specification, five horn players, and 120 privates. The muster return describes one of the musicians as a drum major and 10 of the privates as corporals and includes 14 waggon drivers, batmen, and servants.

The three infantry battalions each had two 3-pounder cannon and there was an artillery reserve with two more 3-pounders and two spare gun carriages. The artillery detachment was provided by the 2nd company of the Artillery Corps commanded by *Kapitain* Kötz and according to the specification was made up of:

- 1 Captain
- 1 First Lieutenant
- 2 Second Lieutenants
- 1 Sergeant Major
- 2 Sergeants
- 2 Artificers
- 10 Corporals
- 1 Drummer
- 24 Gunners, described as *Premiers Canoniers*
- 96 Matrosses, described as *Canoniers en Second*

- 1 Surgeon
- 1 Smith
- 63 Drivers
  Total 205

The muster return has a slightly different breakdown. It shows the detachment serving with each infantry battalions being commanded by a lieutenant, or an additional bombardier in the case of the Light Infantry Battalion, with two bombardiers, six gunners, 14 matrosses, a train corporal, and 11 drivers, and with a waggon master for the Light Infantry Battalion. The artillery reserve, commanded by Kötz, includes a second lieutenant, surgeon, sergeant major, two sergeants and NCOs, four corporals, a drummer, seven bombardiers, 57 matrosses, a train corporal, waggon master, and 23 drivers, making a total for the detachment of 206 officers and men.

The muster return and a list signed by Düring show the composition of the general staff as follows:[5]

- 1 Brigadier (*Oberst* von Düring – promoted to *General-Major*)
- 1 Physician General (Reuling)
- 1 Major of Brigade (*Hauptmann* Hopfenblatt)
- 1 Brigade Adjutant (*Lieutenant* von Reeden)
- 1 Deputy Quartermaster General (*Lieutenant* F.W. von Gall – promoted to *Stabskapitain*)
- 1 Secretary (Lange)
- 1 Quartermaster (Kutt)
- 1 Waggon Master (Kuhn)
  Total 8

The commissariat had:

- 1 Commissary (Engelbach)
- 1 Paymaster (*Capitain* Kuhlmann)
- 1 Secretary (Saal)
- 1 'Servant attending the Military Chest', or *Cassen Diener* (Schäffer)
  Total 4

And the hospital:

- 1 Physician General
- 1 Surgeon General
- 3 Surgeons
- 1 Apothecary
- 1 Assistant Apothecary
- 8 Surgeons Mates

---

5   Return dated 21 October 1793, HStAD, E 8 B No 269/13.

- 2 Clerks
- 10 'Attendants upon the Sick'
- 19 Waggon drivers and servants
- 2 Stewards
- 2 Cooks
  Total 50

Assessment of their Quality

Major Gunn was never one to hold back in praising the contingents he mustered. His report to Dundas stated that:

> The whole Corps of Hesse Darmstadt is very fine, & the Regiment of Lt. Dragoons, surpasses every thing of the kind that I have seen upon the Continent, there not being an exceptionable man, or horse, in it; & their Clothing, with all their appointments, perfectly good. And the Infantry is in no respect inferior to them.[6]

The Duke of York merely noted in a letter to the King that the Darmstadt troops marched through Tournai on 22 November 1793 and that 'they are really exceedingly fine in every particular'.[7]

Major Gunn's report and muster returns for June 1794 show the changes that had taken place in the brigade since it had joined the army and noted that it was 'perfectly compleat, & servicable in every respect'.[8] Its total strength was now 3,171 men and 1,082 horses, compared with 3,226 men and 997 horses at the October 1793 muster. This included the 247 replacements that had been sent from Darmstadt in March.[9] The two 3-pounder cannon from the artillery reserve had been used to replace the two lost by the 1st Leibgrenadier Battalion at Ingelmunster in May 1794, and the corps had 23 ammunition and six hospital waggons.

Uniforms and Equipment

(Plate B 1-5, C 7, D 1-4 and O 1, 2 and 4)

The cocked hats of generals and town commanders were edged in wide scalloped silver lace and white plumage and had a black cockade with silver lace, button, and star badge. The dark blue coat had a red turned over collar, lapels, and cuffs with blue cuff flaps, white turnbacks, and silver buttons. They wore a silver waist sash interwoven with red, which Seekatz shows worn over the coat, and white waistcoat and

---

6   Gunn to Dundas 5 November 1793, TNA: WO 1/167, pp.597-598.
7   York to George III 22 November 1793 in Aspinall (ed.), *The Later Correspondence*, Vol.2, p.127
8   Gunn to Dundas 5 August 1794 with enclosures, TNA: WO 1/898, pp.11-12 and 17-21.
9   Claim for levy money for the Darmstadt recruits dated 29 July 1795, TNA: FO 31/7.

breeches with high cuffed riding boots. They were armed with a *Degen*, with a gilded hilt and a silver and red sword knot, carried in a brown scabbard from a waist belt.

The Chevaulegers wore a black leather helmet with an asymmetrical front shield, inclined to the right and with a cut out on the right side. The front shield had a metal edging in silver for officers and yellow metal for other ranks, which extends all the way round the base on a surviving example in the Darmstadt Schlossmuseum, and had the Landgrave's crowned monogram 'LLx' on the front.[10] It had a black mane hanging from behind the front shield and a white plume on the right side, with a crimson base for officers and a red top for NCOs and trumpeters. Officers had silver and red tassels hanging from the base of the plume, while other ranks had a rosette in the squadron colour. Officers' helmets also had band of leopard skin around the base.

The dark green coat had a red collar with a black patch on either side of the front, black lapels and round cuffs, red turnbacks, and silver buttons. The uniform was decorated with silver lace for officers and white for other ranks. Buttons and lace were placed as follows: one on each collar patch; seven on each lapel, arranged in three pairs and one in the upper point; two on each side below the lapels; three chevrons with the point downwards on the sleeves, one on the cuff and two above it, and three chevrons on the coat tails. The red turnbacks were closed with a button on a patch of cloth, which was black edged silver for officers and green for other ranks. The shoulder straps were red with edging and stripes along them, which were silver for officers and white for other ranks. Officers wore a silver and red waist sash under the coat. The waistcoat was pale buff, with two rows of buttons, and pale buff breeches were worn with black hussar boots with black tassels on the front. Officers also wore a surtout without lapels or lace in undress uniform. In bad weather the men had a grey cloak, which was closed at the front by two cloth tabs with buttons. The pointed saddle cloth was dark green with a black zig zag edging, piped silver for officers and white for other ranks, and with the Landgrave's monogram 'LLx' in the rear corners.

The men were armed with two pistols, a carbine, and a sabre with a single barred hilt carried in a black leather scabbard from a waist belt. Officers' sabres had gilded hilts and metal fittings on their scabbards and their sword knot was silver and red. For other ranks, the sabre hilt and scabbard fittings were iron and the sword knot was brown. Officers wore a silver belt over the left shoulder to carry the cartridge pouch, which had a crimson flap bearing the Landgrave's monogram, while the belts for the men were brown, with a black cartridge pouch.

Uniforms for the infantry and artillery were basically in the same style, distinguished by the colour of the coat, facings and buttons. Officers' cocked hats were edged in wide scalloped lace, with a black cockade held in place by a button and strip of lace and a star badge, in gold or silver depending on the button colour, and with silver and red cords. The hats of NCOs were edged in gold or silver lace with a button on the front left, a white and crimson pompom above it, and with mixed white and crimson cords, showing white with a crimson centre at the sides. Musicians and

---

10 The helmet is described and illustrated in K. Schäfer, 'Reiterei in der Landgrafschaft Hessen-Darmstadt 1790-1803', *Jahrbuch der Gesellschaft für hessischer Militär- und Zivilgeschichte*, pp.49-50, 90.

privates had white edging to their hats, a pompom in the company colour over the button, and white and crimson cords. The company colours were set out in the *Oeconomie Reglement*: for the first battalion, or for regiments that only had one battalion, they were white for the first company, red for the second, black for the third and blue for the fourth; companies in the second battalion had half white and half the same colours as the first battalion, except for the first company where they were yellow and white.[11]

The coats had a turned over collar, lapels open from half way down showing the waistcoat, round cuffs with flaps in the coat colour, and red turnbacks. The collar, lapels, and cuffs were in the facing colour and the coat tails of NCOs, musicians, and privates were closed with a patch of cloth in the facing colour and a button. There were seven buttons on each lapel, three in pairs and one at the top, two buttons below the lapel on the right side, three on each cuff flap, and two on the pockets in the coat tails. Officers wore a silver waist sash interwoven with red over the coat. NCOs had the front and lower edge of the collar and the cuffs edged in a band of gold or silver lace, which was thinner and yellow or white for corporals. Musicians were distinguished by swallows' nests in the facing colour with a band of white lace along the bottom and the drum shells were brass with red and white hoops.

All ranks wore white waistcoats and breeches, with boots for officers and long black gaiters with a row of yellow metal buttons for NCOs, musicians, and privates. Officers carried a *Degen*, with a gilded hilt and a silver and red sword knot, in a brown scabbard from a waist belt. NCOs, musicians, and privates had a short sword with a brass hilt and brown scabbard, worn from a white waist belt with a yellow metal buckle. Sword knots were mixed crimson and white for NCOs and a white strap with the tassels in the company colour for infantry musicians and privates, while artillery musicians and privates did not have sword knots.[12] Officers and NCOs also wore white gauntlets and carried brown canes.

NCOs, musicians and privates on service received new coats every two years and new hats, waistcoats, breeches, and sword knots every year. Their shoes were changed from round to flat-fronted in 1792.[13] Infantry privates carried their packs on a wide white belt over the right shoulder and the black cartridge pouch with a brass plate bearing the Hessian lion over the left. They also carried a canvas knapsack on the left hip and a metal flask.

The 1st Leibgrenadier Battalion and Regiment Landgraf had dark blue coats, with crimson facings and white buttons for the former and white facings with yellow buttons for the latter. Officers had lace with tassels on the button holes in silver or gold, depending on the button colour. Other ranks had white lace with pointed ends, except that there was no lace on the lapels for Regiment Landgraf. Grenadier officers' hats had a white plume with a crimson base and those of the men had a white metal flaming grenade slanting to the left, instead of the button. Seekatz shows the grenadier officers wearing high cuffed riding boots.

---

11 Anon., *Oeconomie Reglement für die Hochfürstlich-Hessische Infanterie und Artillerie* (Darmstadt: Buchhandlung der Invaliden-Anstalt, 1792), p.14.

12 Anon., *Oeconomie Reglement*, p.14.

13 Anon., *Oeconomie Reglement*, pp.9 and 14

The Light Infantry Battalion and Feldjäger-Corps had green coats, without lace on the button holes, and the officers' hats were without the lace edging. The Light Infantry Battalion had black facings and white buttons and the rest of their uniforms were like those of the line infantry.

The Feldjäger-Corps had crimson facings with yellow buttons. Officers' hats had a white plume with a crimson base and silver and red cords. Knötel shows all ranks with a green cockade, held in place by a gold or yellow loop and button, and green cords with crimson centres for musicians and privates.[14] The plumes were white with a crimson tip for NCOs, alternate horizontal bands of crimson/green/crimson/green/crimson for horn players, and green over crimson for privates. Officers and NCOs are shown with two gold epaulettes and NCOs with gold lace on the collar and cuffs. Officers wore pale buff waistcoats and breeches with boots, while NCOs, musicians, and privates had green waistcoats with two rows of buttons and green breeches with short black gaiters. Musicians carried hunting horns, but did not have swallows' nests on their uniforms. Other ranks had brown leather cross belts and a white waist belt with a brass buckle, from which NCOs, musicians, and privates wore a *Hirschfänger* with a brass grip in a brown scabbard instead of the usual infantry sword.

Infantry officers only carried a *Degen*, having abandoned the spontoon. According to the 1792 regulations, grenadier and line infantry NCOs carried a *Kurzgewehr* in addition to their sword, while light infantry NCOs had rifles instead. The lists of equipment and weapons lost on campaign for 1794 record *Kurzgewehre* lost by the Regiment Landgraf, but show '*Gewehre*', or firearms, separately for NCOs, *Schützen*, and privates for the 1st Leibgrenadier Battalion, with no mention of *Kurzgewehre*. It is probable that grenadier NCOs used rifles like those of the light infantry.[15]

Hesse Darmstadt had no large scale arms industry, so the men carried muskets imported from the major producers in Essen, Suhl, and Schmalkalden. In addition to the smoothbore infantry muskets and the shorter version carried by the Light Infantry Battalion, 10 men from each company were designated as *Schützen* and armed with shorter rifled muskets. NCOs, musicians, and privates of the Jägers all carried short hunting rifles. All musket and rifle slings were of red leather.

Artillery officers' hats had wide gold lace and star badge and a black cockade, while those of the men had a white border. The coats were dark blue and had black facings and yellow buttons, with white waistcoats and breeches. Seekatz shows officers wearing gold aiguillettes and with gold lace with fringes on the button holes for staff officers. Officers wore high boots and the men had long black gaiters. Officers carried a *Degen* and the men a short sword, like those of the infantry. Gun carriages were painted light blue with black metal fittings.

Artillery train officers wore a black hat without edging, but with a black cockade, held in place with silver lace and a star badge, and with silver and red cords. They had a dark blue coat, closed to the waist with a single row of silver buttons, red collar and cuffs with blue cuff flaps, and white turnbacks. The gloves, waistcoat, and breeches were white, with high boots. A *Degen* with a silver and red sword

---

14 Knötel, *Uniformenkunde*, Band IX No. 3.
15 *Listen über verlorene Montierungs- und Armaturstücke 1793-4*, HStAD, E 8 B No. 275/1.

knot was worn from a waist belt. The waggon master's uniform had the usual NCO distinctions and the hat had silver edging and a white and crimson pompom over the button and cords. The coat was dark blue without lapels and was closed with two rows of silver buttons down the front. It had a red collar and round red cuffs without flaps, which were edged with silver lace, and the turnbacks were red. The dark blue waistcoat and breeches were worn with high boots and an infantry sabre was worn from a waist belt. Drivers had a hat turned up at the front and back, without edging but with a white pompom. The dark blue coat without lapels fastened down the front with two rows of white metal buttons. It had a white collar and round cuffs, closed with two white buttons, and short tails with red turnbacks. Dark blue breeches were worn with high boots. No side arms were carried.

Seekatz also depicted members of the middle and junior staff. Auditors' hats had wide scalloped gold lace, a black cockade and gold star. They wore a dark blue coat with dark blue collar, lapels, cuffs and cuff flaps, red turnbacks and yellow buttons. The white waistcoat and breeches were worn with high boots and they were armed with a *Degen*. Quartermasters had the same uniform, but with silver lace and white buttons. Infantry provosts had hats with a green border and pompom, a grey coat with grey cuff flaps, green collar, lapels, cuffs, turnbacks, shoulder knot and white buttons. The waistcoat and breeches were green with black gaiters and they carried an infantry sabre. Hats for cavalry provosts were not edged, but had a green strap and plume. They also wore grey coats, but with a grey collar with a green front patch and button, green lapels and cuffs, which were in the same style as the Chevaulegers without the lace, green turnbacks, and white buttons. The breeches and waistcoat, which had two rows of buttons, were green and they had boots and sabres like the Chevaulegers.

Infantry surgeons wore hats with silver lace over the cockade but no star. They had green coats with a green collar, lapels, cuffs, and cuff flaps, and red turnbacks. The waistcoat and breeches were white with black gaiters and they carried a *Degen*. The uniform for cavalry surgeons was similar, except that they had a white plume with a crimson tip and the coat, although it had no lace, had a button on each side of the collar and had cuffs with buttons and chevrons like those the Chevaulegers. The white waistcoat had two rows of buttons, white breeches were worn with boots like the Chevaulegers, and they were armed with a sabre. Medical orderlies had hats like the infantry but without edging, a dark blue coat with a dark blue collar, lapels, and cuffs, and red turnbacks. They wore a dark blue waistcoat and breeches with black gaiters and carried an infantry sabre.

Flags and Standards

(Plate O 3)

Each grenadier and musketeer battalion had two flags, the *Avancier-Fahne*, which was carried by the *Gefreite-Corporal* of the first company, and the *Retirir-Fahne*, which was carried by the *Gefreite-Corporal* of the fourth. The first company of the first battalion was known as the *Leib-Compagnie* and its flag was the *Leibfahne*.

Ludwig X issued new flags to most of the newly organised regiments, including Regiment Landgraf, which received four new flags in April 1791.

The *Leibfahne* and *Retirir-Fahne* of the first battalion of Regiment Landgraf were of painted silk, with the same basic design on both sides, differing only in colour. The *Leibfahne* was white with half-black, half-red corner rays, while the *Retirir-Fahne* was black with red corner rays. In the centre was a red and white striped heraldic lion on a blue shield, surmounted by a crown and a red scroll with the motto 'PRO PATRIA' and surrounded by a green laurel wreath, which was tied at the bottom with a red ribbon. In each corner of the rays was the crowned Landgrave's monogram 'LLx' in gold on a white ground, surrounded by a laurel wreath, and on each side between the arms of the cross was a red flaming grenade. The brown staffs were topped by a gold spearhead finial with the 'LLx' monogram and had a cravat with tassels, which was originally red, white, or silver and blue, but later changed to red and silver. The flags were provided with black protective covers with brass tops.

Like the Regiment Landgraf, the 1st Leibgrenadier Battalion managed to save both of its flags from the disaster at Boxtel, but the design of the flags is not known.[16] It did not receive new flags and may have carried two of the old flags from the regiments which had received new ones in 1790-1, the Leib-Regiment and Regiment Landgraf, whose grenadier companies had been taken to form the grenadier battalion. The Chevauxlegers, Light Infantry Battalion, and Feldjäger-Corps did not carry standards or flags.

---

16 A. Keim, *Geschichte des 4. Grossherzoglich Hessischen Infanterie-Regiments (Prinz Karl) Nr. 118 und seine Stämme 1699-1878* (Berlin: Ernst Siegfried Mittler und Sohn, 1879), p.59.

13

Brunswick

Introduction

The Duchy of Brunswick was part of the Lower Saxon Circle of the Empire and had 166,000 inhabitants.[1] It was much smaller than its neighbour Hanover, and was heavily influenced by Prussia. Carl Wilhelm Ferdinand, nephew of Frederick the Great and brother in law of George III, succeeded his father Carl I as Duke of Brunswick in 1780. He was made a Prussian field marshal in 1787 and was well-regarded by his famous uncle. His military reputation was such that he was appointed to command the allied armies that invaded France in 1792 and served on the Rhine until 1794.

Brunswick had fielded an army of 11,150 men in 1762 and with a further 4,974 at home, but by 1787 its forces had reduced to 3,210 men excluding officers.[2] The great majority of its troops were in the pay of the United Provinces from 1788 to early 1794, under a subsidy treaty dated 22 February 1788, as shown in Table 21. The only forces remaining in Brunswick at this time were a few hundred men of the artillery and engineers, Land-Regiment, Garrison Regiment, and invalid company.

Each infantry regiment had two battalions of one grenadier and five musketeer companies, with the grenadier companies detached to form a separate grenadier battalion.

Organisation and Strength of the Contingent

The force taken into British pay was commanded by *General-Major* Johann Conrad Riedesel, the brother of *General-Lieutenant* Friedrich Adolf Riedesel, who had commanded the Brunswick troops in North America and the United Provinces. It was made up of a small staff, two infantry regiments, the Jäger Battalion, a company of mounted Jägers, which Riedesel kept with the general staff, and a detachment of artillery. The theoretical strength of the corps, set out as part of the treaty is shown in Appendix III and the actual strength, excluding, servants, drivers, etc., in Table 22.

---

1   Hoff, *Das Teutsche Reich*, pp.66-7.
2   O. Elster, *Geschichte der stehenden Truppen* (Buchholz: LTR-Verlag Ulf Joachim Friese, 2001), Vol. 2, pp.223-4 and C. Venturini, *Umriss einer pragmatischen Geschichte des Kriegs-Wesens im Herzogthume Braunschweig* (Magdeburg: Verlag von Eduard Bühler, 1837), p.61.

Table 21: Brunswick Troops in the Pay of the United Provinces 1788-1794

	Squadrons	Battalions	Companies	Strength
Staff				10
Dragoons	2		4	274
Grenadier Battalion		1	4	428
Infantry Regiment von Riedesel		2	10	957
Infantry Regiment Prinz Friedrich		2	10	957
Artillery detachment with 10 battalion guns			2	207
Jäger company			1	167
	2	5	31	3,000

Sources:
Elster, *Geschichte der stehenden Truppen*, Vol.2, pp.468-9; Martens and Martens, *Recueil des Principaux Traités*, Vol. 4, pp.349-61; Venturini, *Umriss einer pragmatischen Geschichte*, p.62.

Note:
The strengths shown above are taken from the treaty. Elster and Venturini show slightly different numbers for the actual strength, totalling 3,060 and 3,000 men respectively.

Table 22: Brunswick Troops Taken into British Pay 8 November 1794

	Officers	NCOs	Musicians	Privates	Total
Staff	4	4			8
Mounted Jägers	3	8	2	77	90
Infantry and Artillery					
Regiment Prinz Friedrich	24	71	15	550	660
Regiment von Riedesel	24	71	15	550	660
Jäger Battalion	14	32	7	268	321
Artillery battery	6	21	4	105	136
	68	195	41	1,473	1,777
Total	75	207	43	1,550	1,875

Source:
Elster, *Geschichte der stehenden Truppen*, vol.2, p.470.

A return dated 31 December 1794 gives the effective strength of the corps as 2,260 men, including six officers and four NCOs of the general staff and 386 officers' servants and drivers. It also shows 78 women.[3] The following details are taken from this return. Musicians and privates are shown as a combined total in the return, and the breakdown is that shown by Elster.

---

3   Reproduced in H. Büschleb, *Scharnhorst in Westfalen* (Herford: E.S. Mittler & Sohn, 1979), pp.134-6.

Each of the two infantry regiments provided one battalion of five musketeer companies. A battalion's staff was made up of six officers and 14 NCOs, and each company had three or four officers, 11 NCOs, three musicians and 105 privates. Each battalion had two 6-pounder cannon, served by an officer, two NCOs, and 25 gunners.

The Jäger Battalion had a staff of five officers, two NCOs, and a musician, and three companies, each with three officers, nine NCOs, two musicians, and 82 privates. It had two 3-pounder cannon, manned by three NCOs and 22 gunners. The mounted Jägers had three officers, eight NCOs, two musicians, and 68 privates.

The artillery battery was made up of two companies, each with three 6-pounder cannon, and the train. It had four officers and each company had five or six NCOs, two musicians and 50 gunners, with an officer, 10 NCOs and five privates in the train. The 76 drivers and servants are included in the total shown above.

Assessment of their Quality

The corps was not with the army long enough to attract much comment from the British officers, but as usual their conduct was criticised, without making any allowance for their impossible position in the face of overwhelming French numbers. Captain Jones wrote that on 5 March 1795 'The Brunswic [sic] troops abandoned Bentheim on the first advance of the enemy, and retreated to Rheine, without firing a single shot, or the enemy being nearer than eight miles' and went on to describe their precipitate retreat, exposing the flank of the Hessians, when the French attacked in force a few days later.[4]

Uniforms and Equipment

(Plates B 6-9, D 5-7 and P)

Information on Brunswick uniforms for the period from their return from North America in 1783 up to the occupation by the French and absorption into the Kingdom of Westphalia in 1807 is very sketchy. The uniforms followed changes in Prussian fashion, but the timing of the adoption of new styles is not clear. For example, the Prussian infantry had adopted the *Casquet*, a hat turned up at front and back, and the *Album de Berlin* shows the Jägers wearing the *Casquet*, while the musketeers and artillery are still in cocked hats in early 1795. However, a plate in Elster's history of the army and illustrations by Beyer-Pegau and Schirmer and Koch also show the Regiment Prinz Friedrich wearing the *Casquet* in around 1795. Infantry hats had a white edging and a yellow metal heraldic horse on the front, which was mounted on a yellow metal oval plate for the Jägers. Musketeers had a red or possibly company

---

4   Captain L.T. Jones, *An Historical Journal of the British Campaign on the Continent, in the Year 1794; with the Retreat through Holland, in the Year 1795* (Birmingham: Swinney & Hawkins, 1797), pp.180-2.

colour pompom, and the Jägers a green or red feather plume. The hats for artillery men were edged yellow.

Coats were dark blue for the infantry regiments and artillery and green for the Jägers. Again, they were in a period of transition from the types worn in America to more modern styles. The *Military Coats Book*, described in Appendix VII, shows the Regiment Prinz Friedrich still wearing the old-fashioned style of coat, which they had worn in America. This was worn open and did not have lapels but was quite square at the waist, and had four pairs of yellow metal buttons down each side of the coat front. This style of coat is also worn by the Baden regimental surgeon in Plate N. The uniform plate in the army's history, Beyer-Pegau, and Schirmer and Koch show a later style of coat with lapels, like those of the Regiment von Riedesel and the Jägers. The artillery wore coats without lapels, but with four pairs of white lace on either side of the front. The colours of facings, buttons and lace are shown in Table 23.

Table 23: Brunswick Infantry and Artillery Uniforms

	Collar[a]	Lapels	Cuffs/shoulder strap/ turnbacks[b]	Buttons
Regiment Prinz Friedrich	Red	N/A[c]	Red	Yellow
Regiment von Riedesel	Dark blue	Pink	Pink	Yellow
Jäger Battalion[d]	Pink	Pink	Pink	White
Artillery	Red	N/A	Red	Yellow

Source:
The *Military Coats Book*, Elster, *Geschichte der stehenden Truppen im Herzogtum Braunschweig-Wolfenbüttel*, Vol. 2, and the *Album de Berlin*.

Notes:
a   Regiment von Riedesel had a stand up collar; the others had turned over collars.
b   The cuffs for all except the Jägers had flaps, piped in the facing colour, and with one button visible, which had a strip of white lace for the artillery. The Jägers had round cuffs with two buttons.
c   Elster shows red lapels.
d   The exact shade of the facings is unclear, as the *Album de Berlin* shows pale pink, whilst in the *Military Coats Book* they appear darker, tending towards crimson. The *Album de Berlin* also shows yellow buttons.

The shoulder belt for the cartridge pouch was worn over the left shoulder and was white leather, except for the Jägers, where it was black according to the *Album de Berlin*, or brown in the 1780 set, which also shows a brown waist belt. Waistcoats and gaiters were white, except for the artillery where they were pale buff, and all wore long black gaiters.

The Brunswick troops used a variety of muskets based on the Prussian models and the Jägers carried rifles, all with red leather slings. A short brass-hilted sabre was worn in a black or brown scabbard from a white waist belt and Jägers probably carried a *Hirschfänger*, as they had done in the American war.

Flags

It has proved impossible to locate any information on the flags carried by the Brunswick infantry in the period between their return from the American War of Independence and the disappearance of the Duchy in 1807. According to Davis, the flags carried by the regiments serving in North America from 1776 to 1783 were brought back to Brunswick, but none have survived.[5] Following the reorganisation of the army after their return, the two remaining infantry regiments may have continued to use these flags but, if so, the colours for each regiment are unknown. The Jägers did not have flags.

---

5   G. Davis, *Regimental Colors in the War of the Revolution* (New York: privately printed, 1907), pp.47-8

Appendix I

Preliminary Articles between Great Britain and Hanover, 4 March 1793

Preliminary Articles between Great Britain and Hanover, relative to a Body of his Majesty's Hanoverian forces, consisting of eight Regiments of Cavalry, of fifteen Battalions of Infantry, and of a Detachment of artillery (specific States of which are hereunto annexed), which are to be taken into the Pay of Great Britain, and employed upon the Continent, on such Service as the Exigency of Affairs may require.

I.   These troops are to serve and to be employed in Europe only.

II. The extent of their pay, and of all other allowances, privileges and advantages, being dependent upon the particular country in which they may be employed, is to be governed by established precedent; and the fixed tariff, or ordonnance declared, and confirmed by his Majesty, for the use of his Electoral troops, on emergencies similar to the present; and on all occasions where they are called upon to serve out of their own country.

III. Their said pay is to commence from the 22nd day of February, 1793, being the day on which the orders for their march were given; and is to continue for 3 months after their return to their own country.
     During the time they shall be employed on this service they are to perform all duties in common with the other troops with which they may occasionally serve, in proportion to their numbers; and their officers are to take rank, on all duties and commands, according to seniority of commission, in conformity to the general rules established in all armies.

IV. They are to have their own chaplains, and to be allowed the free exercise of their religion according to the rites and established modes of worship of the German church.

V.   In all cases of military delinquency the offenders are to be tried, judged and punished by their own martial law and articles of war; and the officers commanding the different regiments, as well as the commanding officer of the whole corps, shall be enjoined to adhere strictly to the said martial law, and articles of war; and to take care that the same be, on all occasions, duly observed by the officers and soldiers under their command.

VI. It being very remote from his Majesty's intention to suffer his Electorial military chest to reap any pecuniary profit or advantage from the circumstance of this corps of his Hanoverian troops passing upon the present emergency into the British service; it is, on the other hand, but reasonable and just, and must accordingly be understood, that Great Britain is to defray all such expenses as may be found necessary for enabling the said corps to take the field, as well as for its maintenance and support during the time it remains in the British service, upon an equal footing with the troops of any other nations with which it may be destined to serve; and, in particular, that not only a reasonable and fair allowance shall be made, for supplying the deficiencies which must necessarily be occasioned in his Majesty's Electoral army by the employment of this corps out of his own German dominions, but that due provision shall also be made for recruiting and keeping it complete, so long as it remains on that service, and for making good such losses as it may sustain in action, according to the present practice in other armies.

VII It is stipulated further, that such non-commissioned officers and private men as may become disabled by wounds or other casualties happening to them, while actually in the British service, shall be allowed the usual pensions, at the expense of Great Britain; which said pensions are moreover to be paid to them in their own country, upon authentic and satisfactory certificates of their existence and identity being from time to time produced by his Majesty's Hanoverian Chancery of War.

Grosvenor Square, 4th March, 1793   Alvensleben

Source: Debrett (ed.), *A Collection of State Papers*, Vol. 1, pp. 31-2.

Appendix II

Subsidy Treaty between Great Britain and Hesse Cassel, 10 April 1793

Treaty between his Britannic Majesty and the Landgrave of Hesse Cassel. Signed at Cassel the 10th of April, 1793.

Be it known to those whom it may concern, that his Majesty the King of Great Britain, and his Serene Highness the Landgrave of Hesse Cassel, in consideration of the strict ties which unite the interest of their respective Houses, and having judged that, in the present situation of affairs, it would contribute to the reciprocal welfare of Great Britain and of Hesse, to cement and strengthen, by a new treaty of alliance, the connection which subsists between them, his Britannic Majesty, in order to regulate the objects relative to this alliance, has thought proper to send to Cassel the Right Honourable Thomas Earl of Elgin and of Kinkardine, Baron Bruce of Kinross, his Minister Plenipotentiary; and his Serene Highness has nominated, on his part, for the same purpose, the Baron Maurice Frederick, of Munchausen, his actual Minister of State, Privy Counsellor, and Knight of the Order of the Golden Lion, and his Director of the College and Treasury of War; and John Francis Kunckel, Privy Counsellor of War: who, being furnished with the necessary full powers, have agreed to take for basis of the present treaty, the treaties which were formerly concluded between Great Britain and Hesse, to adopt such parts of them as may be applicable to the present circumstances, or to settle by new articles those points which it may be necessary to regulate otherwise. Every thing, which shall not otherwise be settled, shall be deemed subsisting in full force, in the manner expressed in the above-mentioned treaties; and as it is not possible to specify each particular case, every thing which shall not appear to be determined in a precise manner, either in the present treaty, or in the former treaties, shall be settled with equity and good faith, in conformity to the same principles, which it is agreed on both sides to adopt, for the regulation of such cases, whether during the course of the war, or after its conclusion.

Article I. There shall be therefore, in virtue of this treaty between his Majesty the King of Great Britain and his Serene Highness the Landgrave of Hesse Cassel, their successors and heirs, a strict friendship, and a sincere, firm, and constant union, so that the one shall consider the interests of the other as his own, and shall strive to promote them with good faith, as much as possible, and mutually to prevent and remove all disturbance and injury.

II. With this view, it is agreed, that all the former treaties, especially those of guarantee, shall be deemed to be renewed and confirmed by the present treaty, in all their parts, articles, and clauses, and shall have the same force, as if they were herein inserted word for word, in as much as the same is not derogated from by the present treaty.

III. His Majesty the King of Great Britain, desiring to secure for his service in Europe, a body of the troops of the Serene Landgrave, and his Serene Highness, wishing for nothing more than to give his Majesty real proofs of his strong attachment for him, engages by virtue of this article, to keep in readiness for this purpose, during the space of three successive years, reckoning from the day of the signature of the present treaty, a body of eight thousand men, as well infantry as cavalry, or chasseurs, including officers. This corps shall be completely equipped, furnished with tents, and all necessary equipage, in a word, shall be put upon the best possible footing, and nobody shall be admitted into it but men capable of serving, acknowledged as such by the Commissary of his Britannic Majesty. This corps shall march in two divisions: the first, consisting of four thousand men, shall be composed of a corps of infantry with the artillery men, and of a regiment of cavalry. Formerly the signature of treaties preceded, for some time, the period for the requisition for the march of the troops; but as, in the present circumstances, there is no time to be lost, the day of the signature of the present treaty is deemed to be also the period of the requisition, and the first division of four thousand men shall be in readiness to pass in review before the Commissary of his Britannic Majesty on the 8th of next month, and to begin its march the following day for the place of its destination. The second division, consisting also of four thousand men, and composed of a corps of infantry, of a battalion of chasseurs, and of two regiments of cavalry, shall be in readiness to pass in review the 5th of June, and shall be ready to march in eight weeks from the conclusion of the present treaty, or even sooner, if it is possible. These troops shall not be separated, unless the cause of war should require it, but shall continue under the orders of their Hessian Chief, under the command, however, of the General, to whom his Britannic Majesty shall intrust that of his whole army; and the second division shall only be conducted to those places where the first shall be, unless it should be contrary to the plan of operations.

IV. Each battalion of infantry of this corps of troops shall be provided with two field pieces, and the officers, cannoneers, and the other men and equipage attached to them.

V. In order to defray the expenses to which the Serene Landgrave shall be put, by equipping the above-mentioned corps of eight thousand men, his Majesty the King of Great Britain promises to pay to his Serene Highness, for each horseman or dragoon properly armed and mounted, eighty crowns banco, and for each foot soldier thirty crowns banco. This levy-money for the first division shall be paid fifteen days after the signature of the present treaty. With regard to the levy-money for the second division, one half thereof shall be paid on the 8th of next month, and the other half on the day on which the second division shall begin its march. The levy-money shall be paid for the same description of persons for whom it was given in the former alliances.

VI. Besides what is stipulated in the preceding article, his Majesty the King of Great Britain engages to cause to be paid annually, during the three years that this treaty shall last, a subsidy and an half, fixing the sum according to the custom established for the subsidies in the former treaties. This subsidy shall commence from the day of the signature of this treaty, and it shall be paid at the rate of two hundred and twenty-five thousand crowns banco *per annum*, the crown being reckoned at fifty-three sols of Holland, or at four shillings and nine-pence three farthings English money.

When the said corps shall be sent back by his Britannic Majesty, from the day of the return into the territories of his Serene Highness, till the expiration of the treaty, the subsidy shall be continued upon the same footing of two hundred and twenty-five thousand crowns banco *per annum*. The payment of this subsidy shall be regularly made without any deduction, and quarterly, in the town of Cassel, into the military treasury of the Serene Landgrave authorised to receive it; and in the case, on either side, it should be judged expedient that the number of the corps of troops should exceed eight thousand, the subsidy shall be proportionably augmented, unless it shall be otherwise agreed upon. His Majesty shall continue equally to this corps the pay and other emoluments during the remainder of the month in which it shall repass the frontiers of Hesse, and arrive in the territories of his Serene Highness, that is to say, Hesse properly so called.

VII. With regard to what relates to the pay and allowances, both ordinary and extraordinary, of the said troops, during the time that they shall be actually in the pay of great Britain, it is agreed, that, as long as they shall serve in the empire, they shall enjoy the same advantages and emoluments which his Majesty grants to his German troops, according to the effective establishment of the said corps of troops at the time of their being delivered, which shall be verified by a list signed by the respective Ministers of the high contracting parties, which shall have the same force as if it were inserted word for word in the present treaty. During the time that they shall be employed in the Low Countries, they shall be treated in the above-mentioned respect, upon the footing of Dutch troops; it being understood that in both cases, that is to say, in that of the German pay, as well as in that of the Dutch, the allowances shall not be inferior to what was granted in former wars; and, if the nature of the war should require that those troops should serve in different countries upon the continent of Europe from those above-mentioned, they shall, in that case, be put in every respect on the same footing with the most favoured of his Majesty's auxiliary troops.

If it shall happen that they should be employed in Great Britain, or in Ireland, as soon as the notification in such case shall be made to the Serene Landgrave, they shall be put on the same footing, in every respect, as the national British troops.

All these allowances for those troops shall be paid into the military treasury of his Serene Highness, without any abatement or diminution, in order to be distributed.

VIII. If it should unfortunately happen that some regiments or companies of the corps above-mentioned should, by any accidents, be wholly or partially ruined or destroyed, or that the pieces of artillery or other effects, with which it may be provided, should be taken by the enemy, his Majesty the King of Great Britain will pay the expenses of the necessary recruits and remounting, as also the value of the said field artillery and effects, in order speedily to restore the artillery, regiments or companies to their former state; and those recruits shall likewise be put upon the same footing as those which were furnished to the Hessian officers, in virtue of the fifth article of the treaty of 1702, in order that the corps may be always preserved and sent back hereafter in as good state as that in which it was delivered; and the recruits annually necessary shall be delivered to the English Commissary disciplined and completely equipped, at the place of their destination, at the time which his Britannic majesty shall appoint.

IX. It will depend upon his Britannic Majesty to retain this corps of troops in his service all the time of the duration of this treaty, to make use of them in any part of Europe where he may have occasion for them, provided it be not on board the fleet, from the time of its quitting the territories of the Serene Landgrave; and when his Majesty the King of Great Britain shall think proper to send back the said troops, he shall give three months previous notice to his Serene Highness, and shall make him an allowance of a month's pay for their return, furnishing them also with the necessary means of transport *gratis.*

X. His Britannic Majesty promises to attend, as much as possible, to the safety of the dominions and possessions of his Serene Highness, and to direct the military operations, as much as circumstances may permit, in such manner that the country of his Serene Highness may be covered and spared as much as possible. If, however, notwithstanding the precautions which shall be taken with that view, the country of his Serene Highness should be invaded by the enemy, on account of this alliance, and the present treaty, his Britannic Majesty shall endeavour to procure to the country of his Highness the Landgrave an indemnification proportionable to the loss occasioned thereby, according to what has been formerly done on similar occasions.

XI. The sick of the Hessian corps shall remain under the care of their own physicians, surgeons, and other persons appointed for that purpose, under the command of the General commanding the corps of those troops, and every thing shall be granted to them which is granted to his Majesty's own troops.

XII. All Hessian deserters shall be faithfully restored, as often as they shall be discovered in places dependant upon his Britannic Majesty.

XIII. In consideration that the article of recruiting becomes daily more expensive in Germany, on account of the numerous armies which are there kept on foot, and the vacant pay is regarded as the principal fund to defray that expense, it is agreed, that at the review to be made in spring, at the beginning of the campaign, by the Commissary of his Britannic Majesty, the corps ought to be complete, or the pay of those wanting to complete shall be retained; on the other hand, the pay of those who may be wanting from one spring review to the next shall not be retained, but shall be allowed without abatement, as if they were complete; and instead of what was formerly paid for recruiting, in the room of one killed or three wounded, it is agreed that, without distinction, each man furnished shall be supplied at the rate of twelve crowns banco a head, under the express condition, however, that what is here agreed on shall only regard the recruiting, which is the object of this article.

XIV. All the expenses of transport for the troops, as well for the men as for their effects, shall be defrayed by his Britannic Majesty.

XV. The situation of affairs having entirely changed its aspect since the commencement of this negotiation, it is stipulated, that if his Britannic Majesty should find that he has not, in the present moment, occasion for the above-mentioned corps of troops, and that his Majesty should countermand their march before the term fixed for the review of the first division; in that case, his Majesty shall be bound to pay to his Serene Highness the levy-money for the whole corps of eight thousand men, and a double subsidy, for one year only; that is to say, three hundred thousand crowns banco, which shall be instead of the different stipulations contained in the above fourteen articles. The payment of the levy-money shall, in such case, be made on the 8th of next month, and that of the subsidy in quarterly payments, in one year, reckoning from the date of the signature of the present treaty. But it is expressly agreed, that, in the mean time, this article shall in no degree suspend either the preparations or the payments, which it has been agreed on each side to make.

XVI. This treaty shall be ratified by the high contracting parties, and the ratifications thereof shall be exchanged as soon as possible. In witness whereof we, the undersigned, authorised by the full power of his Majesty the King of Great Britain, on one side, and of his Serene Highness the reigning Landgrave of Hesse Cassel, on the other, have signed the present treaty, and have thereto put the seals of our arms.

Done at Cassel, the 10th of April, 1793.
Elgin,	(L.S.)
Mauritz Fred. B. de Munchausen,	(L.S.)
Jean François Kunckells,	(L.S.)

Source: Debrett (ed.), *A Collection of State Papers*, Vol. 1, pp. 5-10.

Appendix III

Subsidy Treaty between Great Britain and Brunswick, 8 November 1794

Treaty between His Britannic Majesty and the Duke of Brunswick. Signed at Brunswick the 8th of November, 1794.

Be it known to those whom it does and may concern: The present situation of affairs in Europe having caused a desire in his Britannic Majesty that a corps of Brunswick troops should be granted to him, the Most Serene Duke of Brunswick, has seized, with all possible eagerness, the opportunity of proving his unalterable attachment to his Britannic Majesty, and his zeal for every thing that can tend to the good of the country. To which effect, his Serene Highness has engaged himself to furnish His Britannic Majesty a corps of two thousand two hundred and eighty-nine men. In order to conclude a treaty relative to this object, his Britannic Majesty has named on his part, the honourable William Eliot, and the Most Serene Duke of Brunswick has named, on his side, the Sieur John Batiste de Feronce de Rotencreutz, his minister of state, and knight of the royal order of Dannebrog.

These two ministers plenipotentiary, after the exchange of their full powers have agreed to the following articles.

Art. I. The Most Serene Duke of Brunswick furnishes, in virtue of the present treaty, to his Majesty the King of Great Britain, a corps of troops, amounting in the whole to two thousand two hundred and eighty-nine men, amongst whom is included a company of horse chasseurs of one hundred and five men. This corps shall be furnished with the following artillery; namely,

Four six-pounders, a battery of six six-pounders, two three-pounders, for the chasseurs.

This artillery shall be provided with every thing necessary for its complete equipment.

The composition of the aforesaid corps is according to the following statement:

		Men
1st	The staff	27
2d	A regiment of infantry	724
3d	A second regiment of infantry	724
4th	A corps of horse and foot chasseurs	454
5th	A detachment of artillery, forming two companies, including artificers, workmen and servants necessary for the train	360
	Total	2,289

Art. II. These troops, at the time of their march, shall be well disciplined, completely armed and equipped; and his Most Serene Highness engages himself, during the existence of this treaty, to keep the said troops on the most proper footing, in order that they may be employed with success in the military services which shall be required of them by virtue of the present treaty; the duration of which is fixed to three years, counting from the day of its signature.

These troops shall not be separated, unless the necessity of the war should require it, but they shall always remain under the orders of their chief, subordinate to the command of the general to whom his Britannic Majesty shall entrust that of the whole army. It will depend on his Britannic Majesty to retain this corps of troops in his service all the time of the duration of this treaty, to make use of them in any part of Europe where he may have occasion for them, provided it be not on board the fleet. The said troops shall take the oath of fidelity to his Britannic Majesty, at their first review, before an English commissary, without any prejudice, however, to that which they have taken to the Most Serene Duke. His said Most Serene Highness shall moreover retain the nomination to all employments and offices that may become vacant, and the administration of justice shall, in like manner, be preserved to him.

Art. III. This corps of troops shall be ready to pass in review, and to put itself in march, on the first of next January, or sooner if it can be done: nevertheless, as it is feared that, considering the difficulty in furnishing, in so short a time, every thing necessary to the equipment of the said corps, it is agreed to cause this corps to march in two divisions, one of which shall begin its march on the first of January, or sooner if it can be done, and the second the first of February, or sooner if it can be done, without this influencing upon the payments, which are to take place for the whole corps from the first of January.

As to the expenses of the march, the following regulation has been made: this corps of troops being destined to serve in the army of Brabant, it is agreed that his Britannic Majesty, in order to answer the expenses of this long march, shall cause to be paid, immediately after the signature of the treaty, to the agent of his Most Serene Highness at London, the amount of three months pay, on the footing of the Brabantine pay; and as to the period of the return of the said troops into the country of Brunswick, it is agreed that his Britannic Majesty shall cause this return to be notified three months beforehand; and with regard to the expenses of the route, two months of Brabantine pay is to be allowed.

Art. IV. His Britannic Majesty will cause to be paid, under the head of levy money, for each foot soldier, foot chasseur, artillery man, &c. &c. thirty Banco crowns, the crown computed at fifty-three pence of Holland, or at four shillings and nine pence three farthings English money; and for each horseman, duly armed and mounted, eighty Banco crowns of the same value, which makes the sum of seventy-three thousand three hundred and ninety Banco crowns. This sum shall be paid immediately after the signature of the present treaty.

Art. V. As to what relates to the pay and allowances, both ordinary and extraordinary, of the said troops, during the time that they shall be in the pay of Great Britain, it is agreed that this pay, and all the emoluments, shall commence from the first of January next, and shall continue until the day whereon the troops shall return into their respective garrisons. His Britannic Majesty will moreover cause to be paid unto them the pay and emoluments for the remainder of the month in which these troops shall have returned into their garrisons.

It is moreover agreed, that if these troops shall happen to serve in the empire, they shall enjoy the same pay and the same advantages which his Majesty grants to his German troops, according to the effective state in which the said corps shall be delivered, which shall be verified by a statement, signed by the respective ministers of the high contracting parties, which shall have the same force as if it were inserted, word for word, in the present treaty. So long as these troops shall be employed in the Low Countries, they shall be treated, with respect to pay and emoluments, both ordinary and extraordinary, on the footing of the Brabantine pay, it being well understood that in the one and in the other case, that is to say, in that of the German, as well as in that of the Brabantine pay, the allowances shall not be below what has been granted in former wars to the Hessian troops: and if the nature of the war shall require that these troops should serve in other countries on the continent of Europe than in countries abovementioned, they then shall be placed on the same footing in every respect as the most favoured of his Majesty's auxiliary troops. If it should happen that they should be employed in Great Britain or Ireland, they shall be placed on the same footing in every respect as the British national troops. All these allowances for the said troops shall be paid into the military chest of his Most Serene Highness, without any abatement whatever.

Art. VI. Every object relating to the equipment of the officers having considerably increased in price during this war, his Britannic Majesty will cause to be paid three months of Brabantine pay to all the officers of the corps, to answer in part the expenses of their equipment, which must be done with a dispatch which will infinitely increase their expense.

Art. VII. With respect to the subsidy which his Britannic Majesty shall pay to the Most Serene Duke of Brunswick, during the three years that this treaty is to last, it is stipulated, that it shall be an annual subsidy of sixty-four thousand six hundred and eighty-seven Banco crowns, the crown being reckoned at fifty-three pence of Holland, or at four shillings and nine pence three farthings English money. And if these troops should be sent back into the territories of Brunswick before the expiration of the three years, the subsidy of sixty-four thousand six hundred and eighty-seven Banco crowns shall be, neither more or less, paid during three years, to be computed from the day of the signature of the treaty.

Art. VIII. If it should happen that one of the regiments, battalions or companies of this corps should suffer an extraordinary loss, whether in battle or at a siege, or by an uncommon contagious distemper, or by other accidents; or if the cannon or other military effects, with which it may be provided, should be taken by the enemy, his Majesty the King of Great Britain will pay the extraordinary expenses of the necessary recruits and remounting, as well as the loss of cannon &c. &c. in order speedily to restore the whole corps to a serviceable state.

He will reimburse, in the most equitable manner, the loss of both officers and soldiers. With regard to this reimbursement, every thing that has been stipulated in the treaty concluded with the Most Serene Highness the Landgrave of Hesse, at Cassel, the 10th of April, 1793, shall be adopted.

Art. IX. It is agreed, that at the review which is to be made every spring, at the opening of the campaign, by the commissary of his Britannic Majesty, the corps must be complete, or the pay of those who are wanting shall be with-held. On the other hand, the pay of those who may be wanting from one review to another, shall not be with-held, but shall be paid without abatement, on the footing of the full complement. Instead of what was formerly paid, in similar cases, for the recruiting of one killed or three wounded, it is agreed, that each recruit furnished shall be paid for, without distinction, at the rate of twelve Banco crowns a head, under express condition, however, that the payment which is here agreed upon shall only regard the recruiting which is referred to in this article.

Art. X. The sick of the said corps shall be attended by their physicians, surgeons, and other persons appointed for that purpose, under the orders of the commander of this corps of troops; and every thing shall be granted to them which his Majesty grants to his own troops.

Art. XI. All deserters from this corps shall be faithfully given up wherever they may be discovered in the countries dependent upon his Britannic Majesty.

Art. XII. All transports of men and military effects shall be done at the expense of his Britannic Majesty during the whole time of these troops being in the field.

Art. XIII. It is agreed that the corps of Brunswick troops shall enjoy every advantage granted to the Most Serene Landgrave of Hesse, by the treaty of the 10th April, 1793 and its secret articles. Moreover, every thing, which is not determined by the preceding articles in a precise manner, is to be hereafter regulated upon the principles of equity and good faith, which have conducted the present negotiation.

Art. XIV. This treaty shall be ratified by the high contracting parties, and the ratifications thereof shall be exchanged as soon as possible.

Done at Brunswick, this 8th Day of November, 1794.

    (L.S.) Wm Eliot,

    (L.S.) Jean Batiste de Feronce de Rotencreutz.

SEPARATE ARTICLE

It is determined that this corps shall receive Brabantine pay, being destined to serve in the army of the Low Countries; but the expedition with which it was necessary to complete the present treaty not permitting a state of the Brabantine pay to be added thereto, the undersigned minister of his Britannic Majesty engages himself to cause to be delivered to the minister of the Most Serene Duke, as soon as it can be done, a complete statement of Brabantine pay, on the same footing as it is allowed to the Hessian troops. In this statement of pay shall also be specified the number of rations and portions allowed, as well as all the other emoluments enjoyed by the Hessian troops actually in Brabant. This communication of the statement of pay shall be made with the accustomed good faith and without any reserve.

Done at Brunswick, this 8th of November, 1794.

    (L.S.) Wm Eliot,

    (L.S.) Jean Batiste de Feronce de Rotencreutz.

Source: Debrett (ed.), *A Collection of State Papers*, Vol.2, pp.14-19.

Appendix IV

German Armies in the Early 1790s

The Holy Roman Empire was divided into ten Circles, the *Reichskreise*, which included the majority of the states in the Empire. The most important territories not included in the Circles were the Habsburg possessions in Bohemia and Moravia, and Prussian Silesia. One of the main functions of the Circles was to organise the common defensive structure, which remained largely unchanged from that established in 1681. Each Circle was required to make a contribution in men or money to maintain a *Reichsarmee* under unified command. The basic strength of the *Reichsarmee*, the *Simplum*, was set at 12,000 cavalry and 28,000 infantry, but this could be increased to a multiple of the *Simplum* if required, for example to a triple quota or *Triplum*. The total was split between the Circles as shown in the following table, but in practice the makeup of the contingents was determined by the individual territories, which could substitute infantry for cavalry in the ratio of three for one, pay cash contributions to the Imperial War Treasury instead, or pay an armed prince to provide substitutes.

In addition to their contingents to the *Reichsarmee*, the major states kept their own separate forces, although this was beyond the means of many of the smaller states, which struggled to maintain even their basic quota. A number of the medium-sized and smaller states had developed a 'soldier trade' (*Soldatenhandel*), in which they would hire contingents to larger powers. The motivation of princes who engaged in the 'soldier trade' was complex. Apart from the financial benefit they derived from this trade, they were able to maintain larger forces than their own resources would allow, which enabled them to take a more active role in international politics. In particular, they sought powerful supporters for their aspirations, whether for elevation or territorial gain, as well as protection from their aggressive neighbours.[1] The states in southern and western Germany, fearing French aggression, also mobilised local militias for home defence.

The outbreak of war in 1792 posed serious problems for the states of the Empire and they were divided in their response. Some princes favoured intervention but others, including Hanover and Bavaria initially supported neutrality. There was also the thorny issue of Austro-Prussian rivalry. Relations between the two major German powers had been normalised in the Convention of Reichenbach in July

---

1 The motivation behind this trade is discussed in P.H. Wilson, 'The German "Soldier Trade" of the Seventeenth and Eighteenth Centuries: A Reassessment', *The International History Review*, pp. 757-792.

Table 24: Contingents to the *Reichsarmee* (*Simplum*)

Circle	Cavalry	Infantry	Total
Electoral Rhenish	600	2,707	3,307
Upper Saxon	1,322	2,707	4,029
Austrian	2,522	5,507	8,029
Burgundian	1,321	2,708	4,029
Franconian	980	1,902	2,882
Bavarian	800	1,494	2,294
Swabian	1,321	2,707	4,028
Upper Rhenish	491	2,853	3,344
Westphalian	1,321	2,708	4,029
Lower Saxon	1,322	2,707	4,029
	12,000	28,000	40,000

Source:
H.H. Hofmann (ed.), *Quellen zum Verfassungsorganismus des Heiligen Römischen Reiches Deutscher Nation 1495-1815* (Darmstadt: Wissenschaftliche Buchgesellschaft, 1976), p. 241.

1790, which had been followed by a treaty of alliance in February 1792, but there remained an underlying suspicion between them which hindered effective cooperation. At first the Empire remained neutral and in order to gain access to its resources both Austria and Prussia entered into a number of bi-lateral agreements with minor German states to provide auxiliaries. This network of limited alliances included agreements with Mainz, Hesse Cassel, and Hesse Darmstadt to send contingents to the allied armies.

Following the defeat of the allied invasion of France in September 1792 and Custine's incursion into Germany, capturing Mainz and Frankfurt, the *Reichstag* agreed to mobilisation of a *Triplum* as a defensive measure in November 1792. On 23 March 1793, it declared the existing struggle to be a *Reichskrieg*, but the response to this was patchy, with only the Swabian Circle mobilising its full contingent. This was increased to a *Quintuplum* of 200,000 men in October 1794, but nothing like this total was achieved.

Appendix V

Infantry Tactics

The regulations used by the infantry of the German contingents remained firmly based on Prussian linear tactics. The regulations in use in Hannover and Hesse Cassel dated back to 1784 and 1767 respectively and although new regulations were introduced in Hesse Darmstadt in 1792, they were little changed from the old Hesse Cassel version which had been used previously. The only real response to the experience gained in the American war and the need for greater mobility was the adoption of the quick march (*Geschwindschritt*) by the Hessians. The outcome of combat was to be determined by firepower, delivered by battalions drawn up shoulder to shoulder in three ranks. Even when an attack was made on the enemy, the Hesse Cassel regulations stated that the troops should advance firmly but without running and always remaining in step.[1] Other formations, such as squares and columns, were not generally used in battle.

Companies were positioned according to the seniority of their commanders. In the first battalion, the *Leib-Compagnie* was on the right of the line, the staff officer's company on the left, and the captains' companies in between with the most senior on the right, next to the *Leib-Compagnie*. The second battalion stood to the left of the first with the senior officer's company the right, the next in seniority on the left and the others in between. The men were usually arranged with the tallest men in the front rank, the next tallest in the third rank and the smallest in the second rank, but the Hanoverian regulations differed in that the men in the first rank were chosen from the best trained men of good reputation, not just the tallest.[2] In both Hessian regulations, NCOs were also positioned according to their size.

For tactical as opposed to administrative purposes, the battalion was broken down into platoons and divisions of two platoons. When ready to fire, the front rank was to kneel on the right knee, the other two ranks closed up behind, and the men had to remain silent. Fire could be delivered by the battalion standing still, advancing, or retreating and could be ordered by platoon, division, or the whole battalion. There was also rolling fire (*Heckenfeur*), two or three files at a time along the line from right to left. The regulations stressed the need for controlled fire with, for example, platoons firing in predetermined sequence as shown in the diagram below. However, it is likely that the officers and NCOs would have difficulty in maintaining this discipline in the heat of battle, particularly in the case of less-disciplined

---

1   Anon., *Reglement vor die Hessische Infanterie* , pp. 125-6.
2   Anon., *Exercice für die Infanterie* (Hannover: H.M. Pockwitz, 1784), p.68.

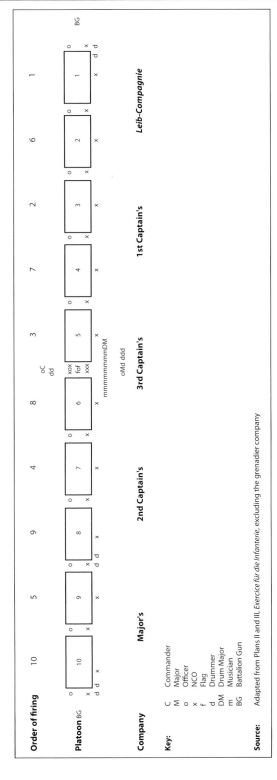

Figure 1 Hanoverian First Battalion of 5 Companies in Line to Fire by Platoon

Order of firing

Key:
C   Commander
M   Major
o   Officer
x   NCO
f   Flag
d   Drummer
DM Drum Major
m   Musician
BG Battalion Gun

Source: Adapted from Plans II and III, *Exercice für die Infanterie*, excluding the grenadier company

new recruits. There was also the problem that ammunition was very limited; for example, Hanoverian infantry carried 30 rounds per man in their pouches and a further 30 in the ammunition waggon, so that sustained fire would soon lead to the men running out.

The Hesse Darmstadt regulations included specific references to light infantry, unlike those of Hanover and Hesse Cassel. Even here, however, the coverage was slight, with only seven out of 420 pages covering the light infantry, including details of the arms drill for NCOs. The light infantry were to be able to take their place in the line and to fire, march, and manoeuvre like the other infantry, but were also to be trained to perform the duties of light infantry in woody and rough country and to carry out patrols using trees, ditches, and fences for cover. They were also to cover the flanks of a battalion, especially on night marches, establish a picket line in front of the regiment or battalion when under arms at night, and form the advance guard and rear guard.[3] Light troops were usually deployed in two ranks, and this was also ordered for the Hanoverian 1st Grenadier Battalion, who had been designated as light grenadiers.[4] Jägers always fought in open order, taking advantage of available cover.

---

3   Anon., *Reglement für die Fürstlich-Hessische Infanterie* , pp. 181-6.
4   Report dated 12 February 1793, Hann. 38 E Nr. 36 ff. 1-4.

Appendix VI

Orders of Battle and Effective Strength of the German Contingents

The largest permanent formations at this time were regiments, which were generally organised into brigades, but their composition was changed quite frequently. The term 'division' was used to mean a subdivision of a regiment for tactical purposes, or to describe a temporary formation, such as when contingents were sent to the front in separate bodies or the body of Hesse Cassel troops sent to the Isle of Wight. The army as a whole was organised into wings or columns for marches and attacks, and 'dislocations,' or dispositions, were drawn up for cantonments and defensive positions. Such formations might only last for a few days.

Therefore, any order of battle will necessarily be for a very short and specific period. The examples recorded are from general orders, where difficulties with foreign names, including English names in German sources, together with recording and transcription errors, make inconsistencies inevitable. The orders generally give no indication of the strength of individual units and often do not include artillery. The information available on actual unit strengths, always well below the theoretical full strengths, is explained below.

The theoretical strengths of the various contingents were set out in states or *Tableaux* attached to the subsidy treaties. Their actual strengths were confirmed by the British commissary, Major (later Lieutenant Colonel) Gunn, who mustered the troops, administered the oath of loyalty to the King, and reported on the numbers and condition of the men and horses. As Gunn later pointed out, it was by no means uncommon for the actual numbers mustered to be different from those specified in the treaties.[1] The treaties only required the German princes to provide replacements for the numbers 'wanting to complete' in their contingents each spring, in other words for the men who had died, deserted, or been discharged, but they were not required to replace the sick or prisoners of war. Gunn then mustered the troops, to confirm the number for which Britain would pay until the next annual review.

Each contingent also prepared regular returns and reports, with a frequency ranging from daily to monthly. These reports showed the full strength (*Sollstärke*) of each battalion and regiment and deducted those absent through sickness, wounds, death, desertion, prisoners of war or on other duties, and those 'wanting

---

1   Gunn to Henry Dundas 30 November 1795, TNA: WO 1/898 pp. 103-4.

to complete,' to arrive at those actually on duty and under arms. They also recorded changes since the last report. The reports for the different contingents varied slightly in form and in the categories used, for example those for Hesse Cassel included company and squadron surgeons in the number of effectives, whereas the others generally included them as part of the regimental staff. These inconsistencies do not have a material effect on the overall numbers reported. In addition, ad hoc reports on the strength of various detachments were prepared as required.

With effect from July 1794 Colonel Craig, the British Adjutant General, introduced a standard monthly 'General Return of the German Troops of the Army under the Command of His Royal Highness the Duke of York' – later 'of General Count de Walmoden Gimborn' – to record the numbers who were 'strictly military', excluding servants and other ancillary personnel.[2] These returns gave a breakdown of each regiment, detailing the total establishment, those 'wanting to complete,' sick, prisoners of war, and remaining fit for duty, split between officers, quartermasters and sergeants, trumpeters or drummers, and rank & file. They also showed changes since the last return. The returns were prepared for the period from 31 July 1794, including changes since 1 April 1794, up to 30 September 1795 and provide a comprehensive and consistent picture of the fluctuations in the strength of the German contingents for the latter part of the campaigns.

However, Craig's political masters were always prone to overestimate the number of troops with the army, and he had to remind them that the totals shown as remaining fit for duty did not represent the actual number of combatants available, as many men were performing other duties.[3] As an example of the difference, Scharnhorst explained that the Hanoverian infantry had a theoretical strength of 13,140 rank & file in December 1794, but 1,501 were 'wanting to complete', 2,835 sick, and 4,301 prisoners of war and missing, leaving 4,503 fit for duty, as shown on the return submitted to Craig. However, a further 634 were 'on command', guarding the hospital, magazines, baggage, headquarters, artillery reserve, pay chest, and so forth; 314 were serving the battalion guns; 328 looking after the bread waggons and officers' baggage; and 1,430 on other regimental duties and watches. The number of men remaining under arms was just under 1,800.[4]

The totals for each contingent from these returns are set out in Tables 25 and 26.

2　Remarks on the Return of The Foreign Troops, TNA: WO 1/170 p. 405.
3　Craig to Nepean 27 November 1794, TNA: WO 1/171 pp. 333-6.
4　Return for 31 December 1794, BL Add Ms 46709 ff. 220-1 and G. von Scharnhorst, 'Stärke, innerer Zustand, und Krieges-Theatre der verbundenen Armeen', *Neues militairisches Journal*, 1797, Vol. 8 pp. 277-9.

Table 25: Strength of the German Contingents July-December 1794

	Jul	Aug	Sep	Oct	Nov	Dec
Hanover						
Cavalry	2,290	2,261	2,255	2,297	2,311	2,268
Infantry	9,151	7,436	6,364	6,045	5,952	5,419
Hesse Cassel						
Cavalry	1,712	1,637	1,599	1,610	1,630	1,664
Infantry	3,862	3,771	3,694	3,670	3,730	3,690
Hesse Darmstadt						
Cavalry	421	416	278	283	302	325
Infantry	1,737	1,623	642	675	673	706
Baden						
Infantry	323	323	323	369	375	375
Total						
Cavalry	4,423	4,314	4,132	4,190	4,243	4,257
Infantry	15,073	13,153	11,023	10,759	10,730	10,190

Table 26: Strength of the German Contingents January-June 1795

	Jan	Feb	Mar	Apr	May	Jun
Hanover						
Cavalry	2,215	2,263	2,226	2,276	2,238	2,395
Infantry	4,783	4,787	4,657	5,745	6,029	6,952
Hesse Cassel						
Cavalry	1,670	1,664	1,615	1,611	1,723	1,737
Infantry	3,685	3,685	3,237	3,242	3,313	3,867
Hesse Darmstadt						
Cavalry	316	344	352	361	418	433
Infantry	663	713	665	647	861	911
Brunswick						
Cavalry		84	77	79	80	82
Infantry		1,547	1,429	1,375	1,346	1,350
Total						
Cavalry	4,201	4,355	4,270	4,327	4,459	4,647
Infantry	9,131	10,732	9,988	11,009	11,549	13,080

Source: General Returns of the German Troops, TNA: WO 1/170 p. 399 and BL Add MS 46709, ff. 212-34.

Appendix VII

Sources on Uniforms

Very few artefacts from this period remain on display in German museums. Brief details of the uniforms that should have been worn are included in the annual editions of each state's *Staats-Kalender*, and in the various published regulations. The German states are also well represented in the series of uniform paintings and engravings that were created in the later 18th century. The most important of these sets are listed below.

Hanover

The second part of the *Gmundener Prachtwerk*, showing all regiments from around 1780-1790. This set is reproduced in J. Niemeyer and G. Ortenburg, *Die Hannoversche Armee 1780-1803: das 'Gmundener Prachwterk'* (Beckum: Bernh. Vogel, 1981), Teil II, together with a contemporary series on the pontoon train.

An anonymous set showing all regiments dated 1780 is offered by the Historischer Bilderdienst, but this appears to be from the early 1790s based on the names given for the regiments (Plate H).[1]

Another set from the Historischer Bilderdienst, showing train personnel from around 1780.

A set showing uniforms of all regiments from 1791 by J.G.F Ronnenberg. A version of this has been published and a second copy, with slight variations, is in the de Ridder collection in the Bibliothèque nationale de France.[2]

The British Royal collection includes a 1790 set by H.B. Merker, who was an ensign in the Artillerie-Regiment, and another version with some differences is in the British Library (Plates E, F and G 1-3).

The British Royal collection also has an anonymous set, which is dated 1795 in the catalogue of the military drawings and paintings in the collection, but 1794 on the spine of the volume.[3]

1   See: www.historischer-bilderdienst.de/
2   J.G.F. Ronnenberg, *Abbildung der Chur-Hannoverschen Armée-Uniformen*(Hannover: Schlütersche, 1979).
3   Haswell Miller and Dawnay, *Military Drawings and Paintings*, Vol.2, nos. 354/1-38.

Hesse Cassel

The army of the 1780s is illustrated in a set by J.H Carl and J.C. Müller, showing officers, musicians and men for each regiment as well as some staff personnel. A version of this set has been published by the Deutsche Gesellschaft für Heereskunde, and others are on the Historischer Bilderdienst and in the Anne S.K. Brown Military Collection (Plate K).[4]

Another set, known as the *Darmstädter Handschrift*, is similar in coverage to the Carl and Muller set, but also shows flags and standards and changes in the uniforms following the death of Landgrave Friedrich II. The original was destroyed in the bombing of Darmstadt in World War II, but a copy has been published by the Deutsche Gesellschaft für Heereskunde.[5]

G.H. Thalmann produced paintings of the uniforms of the Hesse Cassel troops after their return from North America, including examples of flags for the infantry regiments. The manuscript is in the Hessisches Staatsarchiv in Marburg and a number of these have been published in the *Zeitschrift des Vereins für hessischer Geschichte und Landeskunde*.[6]

An anonymous set titled *Abbildung der Fürstlichen Hessen-Casselischen Truppen mit der Neuesten Uniform 1789*, showing the uniforms just before the reorganisation of the army by Wilhelm IX, is in the Anne S.K. Brown Military Collection (Plate L 4).

The Historischer Bilderdienst has a copy of J.C. Müller's *Hochfürstlich Hessisches Corps*, which shows the uniforms in 1789 after the reorganisation (Plate L 1-3).

Baden

Söllner describes two series, one dating from 1792 and the other from 1802, which were previously in Darmstadt but have been destroyed in the burning of the Darmstädter Kabinettsbibliothek.[7] Copies of the 1802 set are in the Wehrgeschichtliches Museum at Rastatt and the Historischer Bilderdienst (Plate N).

There are also a number of contemporary paintings and engravings, and sets of plates and postcards produced during the 19th and early 20th Centuries, in some cases from sources which are now lost:

Albert Gregorius painted a series of watercolours showing the French and Allied troops who were garrisoned in Bruges or who passed through the city in 1792 and 1793, including a number of Hanoverian and Hesse Cassel Regiments. They are now

---

4   U.P. Böhm, *Hessisches Militär, Die Truppen der Landgrafschaft Hessen-Kassel 1672-1806*, (Beckum: Deutsche Gesellschaft für Heereskunde e. V., 1986).

5   Ortenburg, *das Militär der Landgrafschaft Hessen-Kassel*.

6   H.-E. Korn, 'Fahnen und Uniformen der Landgräflich Hessen-Kassel'schen Truppen in Amerikanischen Unabhängigkeitskrieg 1776-1783, *Zeitschrift des Vereins für hessischer Geschichte und Landeskunde*, Vol. 86, 1976-7, pp. 73-108.

7   G. Söllner, *Für Badens Ehre: die Geschichte der Badischen Heer*, vol. 2 p.182.

in the Musée royal de l'Armée in Brussels and copies by C.C.P. Lawson are in the Anne S.K. Brown Military Collection.

Philip de Loutherbourg and James Gillray travelled to the Low Countries in 1793 to make studies for de Loutherbourg's painting *The Grand Attack on Valenciennes*, including Hanoverian and Hesse Cassel troops. Their drawings are now scattered in a number of collections, including the British Royal Collection, the British Museum and the Anne S.K. Brown Military Collection, although in the last case, they have not been definitely confirmed as such (Plate M).

The American artist Mather Brown, who was 'history and portrait painter' to the Duke of York published engravings of the Battle of Famars and the capture of Prince Adolphus and Freytag at Rexpoëde. He also painted a portrait of Freytag, which is in the British Royal Collection.

The collection of watercolours known as the *Album de Berlin* includes a number of uniforms of Hanover, Hesse Cassel, Hesse Darmstadt and Brunswick (Plates C and D). They were painted in North Germany in early 1795 and this set is now in the Anne S.K. Brown Military Collection.

Johann Gerhard Huck published engravings of Hammerstein's breakout from Menin and the death of General der Infanterie von dem Bussche, showing a variety of Hanoverian uniforms. He also engraved portraits of Wallmoden and Hammerstein, which he painted from life.

The most comprehensive representation of Hesse Darmstadt uniforms at the end of the eighteenth century is a set of around 57 pictures painted in 1848 by P. C. Seekatz titled *Abbildung der Hochfürstlich Hessen–Darmstädtischen Truppen unter der Regierung des durchlauchtigsten Fürsten und Herrn, Herrn Ludwig X. Landgrafen z Hessen etc.* The originals were destroyed by allied bombing in 1944, but Richard Knötel gave descriptions of the series in his *Mittheilungen zur Geschichte der militärischen Tracht*, and there is a copy in the Wehrgeschichtliches Museum in Rastatt. This series has been used in many later works, including Richard Knötel's *Uniformenkunde*, the 'Brauer Bogen' and studies by Edmund Wagner.

The *Jassenboecje*, or *Military Coats Book*, shows watercolour paintings of the coats worn by the army of the United Provinces in the second half of the 18th century, including the Brunswick troops in Dutch service from 1788 to 1794. The series has been published as *Military Uniforms in the Netherlands 1752-1800*.[8]

The Anne S. K. Brown Military Collection also has five crude watercolours of Brunswick uniforms from around 1780 or a little later. The regiments depicted all served in the corps in Dutch pay from 1788 to 1794 (Plate P).

In addition to the uniforms of the German states in Knötel's *Uniformenkunde*, the uniforms of the Hanoverians are illustrated extensively in F. Schirmer and P.F. Koch's *Beiträge zur Heereskunde Niedersachsens* and Schirmer's *Neue Beiträge zur Heereskunde der niedersächsischen Kontingente*, along with some Brunswick uniforms. Beyer-Pegau produced large numbers of illustrations of Brunswick uniforms through the ages, but unfortunately very few covering the period between 1783 and 1806.

---

8   J. van Hoof, *Military Uniforms in the Netherlands 1752-1800* (Vienna: Verlag Militaria, 2011).

Notes on the Colour Plates

Plate A – Uniform Coats: Hannover, Hesse Cassel, and Baden

Examples of Hanoverian uniforms based on Schirmer and Koch, *Beiträge zur Heereskunde Niedersachsens* and the sources listed in Appendix VII:

A1: 6th Infantry Regiment.
A2: 14th Light Infantry Regiment.
A3: Jäger Company 14th Light Infantry Regiment.
A4: Artillery Regiment.

Hesse Cassel uniforms based on Müller, *Hochfürstlich Hessisches Corps*:

A5: Leib-Regiment.
A6: Jäger Battalion.
A7: Artillery Regiment.

Baden uniforms based on Söllner, *Für Badens Ehre*, Vol. 2 and the copy of the 1802 series described in Appendix VII:

A8: Leibinfanterie Regiment.
A9: Artillery Company.

Plate B – Uniform Coats: Hesse Darmstadt and Brunswick

Hesse Darmstadt uniforms based on Richard Knötel's descriptions of the Seekatz series in *Mittheilungen zur Geschichte der militärischen Tracht*:

B1: 1st Leibgrenadier Battalion.
B2: Regiment Landgraf.
B3: Light Infantry Battalion.
B4: Feldjäger-Corps.
B5: Artillery.

Brunswick uniforms based on the *Jassenboecje*, or *Military Coats Book* and, as the buttons below the lapels and on the pockets are not visible, these are based on the uniforms worn in the American War of Independence:

B6: Regiment Prinz Friedrich.
B7: Regiment von Riedesel.
B8: Jäger Battalion.
B9: Artillery.

Plate C – *Album de Berlin*: Hanover, Hesse Cassel, and Hesse Darmstadt

Examples of uniforms of the German contingents painted in North Germany in early 1795:

C1: Hanover 1st Cavalry Regiment or Leibregiment.
C2: Hanover Garde Regiment.
C3: Hanover 14th Light Infantry Regiment.
C4: Hanover Jäger Company 14th Light Infantry Regiment.
C5: Hesse Cassel Garde-Grenadier-Regiment.
C6: Hesse Cassel Fusilier Battalion.
C7: Hesse Darmstadt 1st Leibgrenadier Battalion.
(Anne S.K. Brown Military Collection, Brown University Library)

Plate D – *Album de Berlin*: Hesse Darmstadt and Brunswick

More examples from the Album de Berlin:

D1: Hesse Darmstadt Chevauxlegers.
D2: Hesse Darmstadt Regiment Landgraf.
D3: Hesse Darmstadt Feldjäger-Corps.
D4: Hesse Darmstadt Artillery.
D5: Brunswick Regiment von Riedesel.
D6: Brunswick Jäger Battalion.
D7: Brunswick Artillery.
(Anne S.K. Brown Military Collection, Brown University Library)

Plate E – Hanover: Staff and Cavalry

Watercolours of the Hanoverian army painted in 1790 by H.B. Merker, an ensign in the Artillerie-Regiment:

E1: A general in service uniform.
E2: An officer of the general staff, wearing the uniform of a *Flügel-* or *Ober-Adjudant*.
E3: An officer and private of the Leibgarde.
E4: An officer and private of the 5th Dragoon Regiment.
(British Library Board, Kings MS 243)

Plate F – Hanover: Infantry, Artillery, and Engineers

Four more examples from Merker:

F1: An officer and private of the Garde Regiment.
F2: An officer and private of the 1st Infantry Regiment.
F3: An NCO of the horse artillery, identified by his cane and gold-laced hat with a yellow over white plume.
F4: A private of the second company of the engineer corps. The pioneers and pontoniers were distinguished by the badges on the back of their hats.
(British Library Board, Kings MS 243)

Plate G – Hanover: Train and Light Dragoons

Three examples of train uniforms from Merker:
G1: An officer of the artillery train and an NCO.
G2: Drivers. The figure on the left is wearing the *Reit-Camisol* and the one on the right the *Oberrock*, worn in bad weather.
G3: On the left a harness master and on the right a wheelwright.
(British Library Board, Kings MS 243)
G4: Standard and helmet of the 9th Light Dragoon Regiment from F. Schirmer and P.F. Koch, *Beiträge zur Heereskunde Niedersachsens*, series 3 no. 27.
(Historischer Bilderdienst)

Plate H – Hanover: Cavalry and Infantry c.1790

Examples of uniforms from the early 1790s from an anonymous series of watercolours:

H1: 7th Dragoon Regiment.
H2: 9th Light Dragoon Regiment.
H3: 6th Infantry Regiment wearing the Gibraltar cuff band.
H4: Jäger Company 14th Light Infantry Regiment.
(Historischer Bilderdienst)

Plate I – Hanover: Infantry Flags issued in the 1780s

Examples of the new flags issued to the infantry in the 1780s from Anon., *Anrede an das Garde-Regiment bei Vorstellung neuer Fahnen, den 26. September* (Hannover: 1785):

I1: One of the four identical flags carried by the Garde Regiment.
I2: The centre of a *Gibraltarfahne*.

I3: 3rd Flag of the 10th Regiment.
I4: 2nd Flag of the 11th Regiment.
(Historischer Bilderdienst)

Plate J – Hanover: Infantry Flags 1756 Designs

Examples of the 1756 designs for infantry flags, which were still in use in the 1790s, from Anon., *Dévisen welche die sammtlichen Infanterie Regimenter in ihren Fahnen führen 1756* (Hannover, 1756):

> J1: 2nd flag of the 1st Regiment, formerly carried by the Regiment von Staffhorst. The colour of the field, which appears to be dark blue, should be dark green.
> J2: 3rd flag of the 1st Regiment formerly carried by the Regiment von Zastrow sen.
> J3: 2nd flag of the 4th Regiment. Although the regiment received new flags in 1783, the design of this flag remained the same as carried previously by the Regiment von Ledebour. The light blue field appears dark blue.
> J4: 4th flag of the 5th Regiment, formerly carried by the Regiment von Hodenberg.
> J5: 4th flag of the 6th Regiment, formerly carried by the Regiment von Zandré.
> J6: 4th flag of the 9th Regiment formerly carried by the Regiment von Zastrow jun. The dark green field appears dark blue.

(Historischer Bilderdienst)

Plate K – Hesse Cassel infantry 1780s

Two plates by J.H Carl and J.C. Müller, showing the uniforms at the end of the reign of Friedrich II:

> K1: Regiment Erb-Prinz. The officer on the left is carrying a spontoon, which was left in the arsenal at Cassel when the troops were sent to join the British, and the NCO next to him has a *Kurzgewehr*.
> K2: The Jäger Corps, which wore the same uniform as the new Jäger Battalion raised for service with the British. Epaulettes had replaced the shoulder cords by 1789. The NCO, horn player and private all carry a *Hirschfänger*, and the NCO and horn player also have a cane as a symbol of rank.

(Anne S.K. Brown Military Collection, Brown University Library)

Plate L – Hesse Cassel Troops 1789

Examples of uniforms around the time of Wilhelm IX's reorganisation of the army:

L1: Officer and private of the Carabinier-Regiment.
L2: Officer and private of the Garde-Grenadier-Regiment. Only the grenadier companies wore the bearskin cap in the Netherlands campaigns.
L3: Officer and private Regiment Prinz Carl.
From J.C. Müller's *Hochfürstlich Hessisches Corps* (Historischer Bilderdienst)
L4: NCO and private of the Light Infantry Battalion. The uniforms of the Fusilier Battalion were identical. The NCO on the left is distinguished by the silver lace on his coat, epaulettes and edging to the band round his helmet, crimson and silver sword knot, crimson tip to the plume and the cane, here worn suspended from a coat button. He is armed with a musket like the men and a small cartridge pouch on the waist belt, rather than the *Kurzgewehr* carried by musketeer NCOs.
From *Abbildung der Fürstlichen Hessen-Casselischen Truppen mit der Neuesten Uniform 1789* (Anne S.K. Brown Military Collection, Brown University Library)

Plate M – Hesse Cassel Cavalry

These are almost certainly studies by Gillray for de Loutherbourg's painting *The Grand Attack on Valenciennes* and show the uniforms worn on campaign by the three cavalry regiments in the first contingent taken into British pay.

M1 and M2: The Gens d'Armes showing the men with oak leaves in their hats instead of plumes and a simplified saddle cloth, replacing the heavily embroidered and laced dress version.
M3: A private of the Carabinier-Regiment, whose sabretache still has the monogram of Landgrave Friedrich II who had died in 1785.
M4: A private of the Prinz Friedrichs Dragoon Regiment in the light dragoon style coat adopted in 1789, but worn with a cocked hat and high boots. The white arm band was a field sign adopted by the allies to distinguish their troops from the French.
(Anne S.K. Brown Military Collection, Brown University Library)

Plate N – Baden Leibinfanterie Regiment

These copies of an anonymous series dating from 1802 show the uniforms of the second or musketeer battalion. The closed coats of the musicians date from after the return of the battalion in 1795. The corporal is carrying a spontoon, which was transferred from the officers in 1793, but was not used in the Low Countries.
(Historischer Bilderdienst)

Plate O – Hesse Darmstadt Cavalry and Infantry

O1: A miniature portrait identified as Jan Rynhard Gerhard van Reede in the uniform of an officer of the Chevauxlegers, signed and dated by C. Böhmer, 1796. (Kasteel Middachten, De Steeg, photo provided by RKD – Netherlands Institute for Art History)

O2: A plate by Herbert Knötel from the *Uniformenkunde* Neue Folge 3, described as a musketeer of the 4th company of Regiment Landgraf in marching order. Knötel's description of the company colours does not agree with those set out in the *Oeconomie Reglement für die Hochfürstlich-Hessische Infanterie und Artillerie*, as described in chapter 12. (Historischer Bilderdienst)

O3: The flags of the Regiment Landgraf in a plate from F. Beck, *Geschichte des Grossherzoglich Hessischen Fahnen und Standarten*. The pompoms attached to the covers are in the company colours. (Historischer Bilderdienst)

O4: A plate from W. Bigge, *Geschichte des Infanterie-Regiments Kaiser Wilhelm (2. Grossherzoglich Hessisches) Nr. 116*, showing the uniform of the Light Infantry Battalion. (Author's collection)

Plate P – Brunswick Infantry and Artillery

These watercolours show the uniforms worn by regiments of the corps in Dutch pay from 1788 to 1794.

P1: A grenadier of the Regiment Prinz Friedrich. The musketeer companies which served with the British would have had cocked hats or possibly the Prussian style *Casquet*. The coat does not have the distinctive square front, as shown in the *Military Coats Book*.

P2: A grenadier of the Regiment von Riedesel. Again, the musketeer companies would have cocked hats or the *Casquet*.

P3: A Jäger in what appears to be a *Casquet*.

P4: An artilleryman in a cocked hat.

(Anne S.K. Brown Military Collection, Brown University Library)

Bibliography

Archival Sources

Hessisches Staatsarchiv Darmstadt (HStAD)
> HStAD, E 8 B No 236/15 Errichtung eines Feldjägerkorps in den Jahren 1792 und 1793
> HStAD, E 8 B No 266/4 and 267/1-2 Ordres und Schreiben aus dem englischen Hauptquartier sowie von den Kaiserlich Königlich und Hannoverischen Generalen
> HStAD, E 8 B No 268/2-5 Journal des unter Kommando des Generalmajors v. Düring stehenden Hessen-Darmstädtischen Truppenkorps in den Niederlanden,
> HStAD, E 8 B No 269/1 Affaire bei Boxtel
> HStAD, E 8 B No 269/13 Liste vom Generalstab des in englische Subsidien getretenen Auxiliar-Korps
> HStAD, E 8 B No 271/1-3 and 5 Monatliche Tabellen
> HStAD, E 8 B No. 275/1 Listen über verlorene Montierungs- und Armaturstücke
> HStAD, G 61, 1/1 Fahnen und Standarten
> HStAD, G 61, 2/2 Zur Truppengeschichte 1790-1793

Hessisches Staatsarchiv Marburg (HStAM)
> HStAM 4 h 3198 Die Zurückberufung des Generalleutnants v. Wurmb, Kommandant-General des Korps in Flandern
> HStAM 4h 3358-61 Rapporte vom Auxiliarkorps in Flandern, Holland und Westphalen
> HStAM 4 h 3482 Montierungsnachrichten 1786-1798
> HStAM 4 h 4197 Montierungsreglement 1787
> HStAM 4 h 4208 Montierungssachen 1791-9
> HStAM 4 h 4354 Instruktion der Generale v. Buttlar, v. Dalwigk und v. Wurmb als Kommandeure der hess. Hilfstruppen
> HStAM 4 h 4357 Listen der in der Kampagne 1793 verlorenen Armaturstücke
> HStAM 4 h 4369 Verlustlisten der beim Korps in Holland verlorenen Armaturstücke 1794
> HStAM 4 h 4461 Mobilmachung des englischen Subsidienkorps
> HStAM 10 e II/3-12, 15, 18, 20-21 Campaign Journals and Diaries of the Regiments and Battalions

Niedersächsisches Landesarchiv Hannover (NLA HA)

Hann. 38 E Nr. 20 Etat, Formation und Abmarsch eines kurhannoverschen Auxiliar-Korps von 12.000 Mann

Hann. 38 E Nr. 25 Formation der Truppen und Ausmarsch sowie Korrespondenz, Ordres und Berichte des Generals von Freytag

Hann. 38 E Nr. 35 Aushebung der Rekruten im Lande und Abgabe derselben an die marschierenden Regimenter

Hann. 38 E Nr. 36 Formation leichter Infanterie- und Grenadier-Kompanien zum Dienst bei den leichten Dragoner-Regimentern

Hann. 38 E Nr. 37 Formierung des 14. Infanterie-Regiments zu einem leichten Infanterie-Regiments mit 2 Feldjäger-Kompanien

Hann. 38 E Nr. 38 Formation der Feldjägerkompanien des 14. leichten Regiments sowie deren Uniformierung und Bewaffnung

Hann. 38 E Nr. 72-3 General-Ordres und Befehle aus dem Hauptquartiere des kommandierenden Generals

Hann. 38 E Nr. 92 and 94 Affäre bei Hondscooten

Hann. 38 E Nr. 144 Verschiedene Rapporte und Listen

Hann 38 E Nr 189 Besetzung und Verteidigung der Festung Nieuport unter General von Diepenbroick

Hann. 38 E Nr. 198 Verteidigungslinie an der Maas und Waal

Hann. 38 E Nr. 213 Rapporte und Listen über den Bestand der Truppen

Hann. 38 E Nr. 418 Unter-Camisöler (Brusttücher, Westen) von Flanell

Hann. 38 E Nr. 419 Verteilung der in England angefertigten Chenillen (Überröcke) für die im Felde stehende Infanterie

Hann. 38 E Nr. 542-3 Berechnung des Verlustes an Mondierungs-, Armatur- und Munitionsgegenständen und an Privateffekten für Offiziere, Unteroffiziere und Gemeine

The British Library Additional Manuscripts (BL Add MS)

BL Add MS 34447-8 Auckland Papers

BL Add MS 40634 Letters to Maj.-Gen. Alexander Stewart of the 3rd Foot (the Buffs), Commandant at Ostend

BL Add MS 46704-9 Don Papers

The National Archives of the UK (TNA)

AO 16/146-7 Prisoners of War: Commissary's letter books 1793-5

FO 26/20-5 General Correspondence: Flanders

FO 29/1-5 General Correspondence: Austria, German States and Prussia

FO 31/5-7 General Correspondence: Cologne, Cassel, etc.

FO 37/41-8 and 52-6 General Correspondence: Holland

FO 65/23 General Correspondence: Russian Empire

FO 94/117 Ratification of Treaties: Hesse Cassel 10 April 1793

HO 42/27 Home Office: Domestic Correspondence, George III

HO 50/369 Home Office: Military Correspondence: Ordnance

HO 51/147 Military Entry Books

MFQ 1/1269 Cantonments of the Army under the [sic] of his Royal Highness the Duke of York, Arnheim 19th Dec. 1794

MPH 1/139 Atlas des Cartes et Plans Relatifs au Memoire Historique et Militaire des Campagnes de l'Armée Britannique aux Ordres de Son Altesse Royale Monseigneur le Duc d'York Sur le Continent pendant les Années 1793-1794 et Commencement de 1795

PRO 30/8/102 Letters of William Pitt

T 52/80-92 Treasury: Entry Books of Royal Warrants

WO 1/166-75 and 177 War Department In-Letters and Papers

WO 1/898 Foreign Troops on British Pay

WO 6/7-12 War Department Out-Letters and Papers

WO 17/835 and 1071 Monthly Returns to the Adjutant General: Great Britain and Ireland

WO 25/41 Commission Books

Templer Study Centre, National Army Museum, London (NAM)

NAM 1976-07-45 Photocopy typescript edited transcript of the diary of Capt. T Powell, 14th Regiment of Foot, March 1793-March 1796

NAM 1985-12-9 Order book, 24 Nov 1793-7 Jul 1794; associated with William Stuart, 28th Regiment of Foot

NAM 1985-12-15 Papers of Maj Gen Charles Barnett, 3rd Foot Guards, 1786-1803

University of Nottingham Manuscripts and Special Collections

Pw Ja 611 Journals, Diaries and Letter Books of Lord William Bentinck

Published Works

Note: n.p. or n.d. indicate that the work listed does not show the place or date of publication respectively.

Anon., *An Accurate and Impartial Narrative of the War, by an Officer of the Guards* (London: Cadell and Davies, 1796).

Anon., *Annalen der Braunschweig-Lüneburgischen Churlande* (Hannover: W. Pockwitz jun., 1793-5).

Anon., *Anrede an das Garde-Regiment bei Vorstellung neuer Fahnen, den 26. September* (Hannover: 1785).

Anon., *Aus dem Leben des Freiherrn Ludwig Christian Heinrich Gayling von Altheim* (Freiburg im Breisgau: Friedrich Wagner'sche Buchdruckerei, 1864).

Anon., *Badische Fahnen und Standarten* (Karlsruhe: Armeemuseum Karlsruhe, 1936).

Anon., 'Beschreibung der Westflandrischen Festung Ypern, deren Belagerung und Einnahme im Feldzug von 1794', *Neue Bellona*, 1801, Vol. 1, pp.81-117 and 345-63.

Anon., *Dévisen welche die sammtlichen Infanterie Regimenter in ihren Fahnen führen 1756* (Hannover: 1756).

Anon., 'Eine Gedenktafel für Hessen-Kasselischer Krieger in der Kirche zu Whippingham auf der Insel Wight (England)', *Hessenland*, 1906, pp.146-7.

Anon., *Exercice für die Infanterie* (Hannover: H.M. Pockwitz, 1784).

Anon., *Haushalts-Reglement für die Chur-Braunschweig-Lüneburgische Infanterie; in Friedens- auch Krieges-Zeiten* (Hannover: G.C. Schlüter, 1786).

Anon., *Hochfürstlich Hessen-Darmstädtischer Staats- und Adress-Kalender* (Darmstadt: Im Verlag der Invaliden-Anstalt, 1794-6).

Anon., *Journals of the House of Commons* [Vols 48-50] (London: Re-printed by Order of the House of Commons, 1803).

Anon., *Königl. Gross-Britannisch- und Churfürstl. Braunschweig-Lüneburgscher Staats-Kalender* (Lauenburg: Joh. Georg Berenberg, 1793-5).

Anon., *Landgräfl. Hessen-Casselischer Staats- und Adress-Kalender* (Cassel: Verlag des Armen-Waisenhauses, 1793-6).

Anon., *Oeconomie Reglement für die Hochfürstlich-Hessische Infanterie und Artillerie*, (Darmstadt: Buchhandlung der Invaliden-Anstalt, 1792).

Anon., *Reglement für die Fürstlich-Hessische Infanterie* (Darmstadt: 1792).

Anon., *Reglement vor die Hessische Infanterie* (Cassel: 1767).

Anon., *Réimpression de l'Ancien Moniteur* (Paris: Henri Plon, 1862).

Anon., 'Relation des Gefechts bey Boxtel an der Dommel, am 14ten und 15ten September 1794', *Neue Bellona*, 1802, pp.257-80.

Anon., *The Present State of the British Army in Flanders; with an Authentic Account of their Retreat from Before Dunkirk. By a British Officer in that Army, who was living on the 24th of September* (London: H.D. Symonds and J. Ridgeway, 1793).

Anon., 'Verlust-Liste des Churbraunschweig-Lüneburgischen Corps in den Feldzügen 1793, 1794 und 1795 bis zum 5ten December', *Neues Militairisches Magazin*, 1805, Vol. 3, No. 8, p. 62.

Adlington, R., *Military Uniforms – the Pictorial Sources* (n.p.: Privately Published, 2012).

Aspinall, A., (ed.), *The Correspondence of George, Prince of Wales 1770-1812* (London: Cassell, 1964).

Aspinall, A., (ed.), *The Later Correspondence of George III* (London: Cambridge University Press, 1962 and 1968).

Aulard, F.A., 'Extraits des Notes Historiques du Conventionnel Delbrel, *Bulletin du Comité des Travaux Historiques et Scientifiques*, 1892 No. 2, pp.226-316.

Badische Historische Commission, *Politische Correspondenz Karl Friedrichs von Baden, 1783-1806* (Heidelberg: Carl Winter's Universitätsbuchhandlung, 1892).

Beck, F., *Geschichte des Grossherzoglich Hessischen Fahnen und Standarten* (Berlin: Ernst Siegfried Mittler und Sohn, 1895).

Beck, F., *Geschichte des Grossherzoglich Hessischen Feld-Artillerie-Regiments Nr. 25 (Grossherzogliches Artilleriekorps) und seiner Stämme) 1460-1883* (Berlin: Ernst Siegfried Mittler und Sohn, 1884).

Berjaud, F., 'Les Chevau-Legers de la Garde de Hesse-Darmstadt, 1806-1813'. Online at: <http://frederic.berjaud.free.fr/chevau-legers_de_hesse-darmstadt.htm> (accessed 2 February 2018).

Bigge, W., *Geschichte des Infanterie-Regiments Kaiser Wilhelm (2. Grossherzoglich Hessisches) Nr. 116* (Berlin: Ernst Siegfried Mittler und Sohn, 1903).

Bittard des Portes, R., *Les Émigrés à Cocarde Noire* (Paris: Émile-Paul, 1908).

Blankenhorn, E., *Führer durch das Historische Museum Schloss Rastatt* (Rastatt: Historischer Museum Schloss Rastatt, 1960-2).

Böhm, U.P., *Hessisches Militär, Die Truppen der Landgrafschaft Hessen-Kassel 1672-1806*, (Beckum: Deutsche Gesellschaft für Heereskunde e. V., 1986).

Brown, R., *An Impartial Journal of a Detachment from the Brigade of Foot Guards, commencing 25th February, 1793 and ending 9th May, 1795* (London: John Stockdale, 1795) [reprinted by Ken Trotman Publishing, 2006].

Buckingham and Chandos, Duke of, *Memoirs of the Court and Cabinets of George the Third*, (London: Hurst and Blackett, 1853).

Bunbury, Sir H., *Narratives of Some Passages in the Great War with France (1799-1810)*, (London: Peter Davies, 1927).

Burne, A.H., *The Noble Duke of York* (London: Staples Press, 1949).

Büschleb, H., *Scharnhorst in Westfalen* (Herford: E.S. Mittler & Sohn, 1979).

Charavay, E. (ed.), *Correspondance Général de Carnot* (Paris: Imprimerie Nationale, 1897).

Coutanceau, H., C. de la Jonquière and H. Leplus, *La Campagne de 1794 à l'Armée du Nord* (Paris: Librairie Militaire R. Chapelot et Ce, 1903-8).

Curtius, M.C., *Geschichte und Statistik von Hessen* (Marburg: Neue Akademische Buchhandlung, 1793).

Dalwigk zu Lichtenfells, Freiherr von, *Geschichte der waldeckischen und kurhessischen Stammtruppen des Infanterie-Regiments v. Wittich (3. Kurhess.) Nr. 83. 1681-1866* (Oldenburg: Ad. Littmann, 1909).

David, Citoyen, *Histoire Chronologique des Opérations de l'Armée du Nord et de celle de Sambre et Meuse* (Paris: Guerbart, 1796).

Davis, G., *Regimental Colors in the War of the Revolution* (New York: Privately Printed, 1907).

Debrett, J. (ed.), *A Collection of State Papers, Relative to the War against France now carrying on by Great-Britain and the several other European Powers* (London: J. Debrett, 1794 and 1795).

Dechend, H, *Geschichte des Füsilier-Regiments von Gersdorff (Hessisches) Nr. 80 und seines Stamm-Regiments des kurhessischen Leibgarde-Regiments von 1632 bis 1900* (Berlin: Ernst Siegfried Mittler und Sohn, 1901).

von Ditfurth, M., *Die Hessen in den Feldzügen von 1793, 1794 und 1795 in Flandern, Brabant, Holland und Westphalen* (Kassel: Verlag von J. Bohné, 1839-40).

Dupuis, V., *La Campagne de 1793 à l'Armée du Nord et des Ardennes, de Valenciennes à Hondschoote* (Paris: Librairie Militaire R. Chapelot et Ce, 1906).

Dürr, M., 'Organisationsgeschichte des Badischen Heeres bis 1803', *Zeitschrift für Heereskunde*, 1979, Nr. 281, pp.17-20.

Elster, O., *Geschichte der stehenden Truppen im Herzogtum Braunschweig-Wolfenbüttel* (Buchholz: LTR-Verlag Ulf Joachim Friese, 2001).

Fain, Baron, *Manuscrit de l'An Trois 1794-1795* (Paris: Delaunay, 1829).

Ferber, *Oberstleutnant, Geschichte des 1. Badischen Feldartillerie-Regiments Nr. 14* (Karlsruhe: C.F. Müller, 1906).

Fortescue, Hon. J.W., *A History of the British Army* (London: Macmillan and Co., 1915).

Gay de Vernon, Baron, *Mémoire sur les Opérations Militaires des Généraux en Chef Custine et Houchard pendant les Années 1792 et 1793* (Paris: Librairie de Firmin Didot Frères, 1844).

von Geyso, *Oberst*, 'Über die Expedition hessischer Truppen nach der Insel Wight', *Hessenland*, 1906, pp.214-7.

de Grimoard, Comte P.H., and Général Servan, *Tableau historique de la guerre de la révolution de France, depuis son commencement en 1792, jusqu'à la fin de 1794* (Paris: Treuttel et Würtz, 1808).

Has, W., *Geschichte des I. Kurhessischen Feldartillerie-Regiments Nr. 11 und seiner Stammtruppen* (Marburg: N.G. Elwertsche Universitäts- und Verlagsbuchhandlung , 1913).

Haswell Miller, A.E., and N.P. Dawnay, *Military Drawings and Paintings in the Collection of Her Majesty the Queen* (London: Phaidon, 1969 and 1970).

Hermes, S., and J. Niemeyer, *Unter dem Greifen: Altbadisches Militär von der Vereinigung der Markgrafschaften bis zur Reichsgründung 1771-1871* (Karlsruhe: G. Braun, 1984).

Historical Manuscripts Commission, *The Manuscripts of J.B. Fortescue, Esq., Preserved at Dropmore* (London: Printed for her Majesty's Stationery Office by Eyre and Spottiswoode, 1894).

von Hoff, K.E.A., *Das Teutsche Reich vor der französischer Revolution und nach dem Frieden von Lunéville, Erster Theil* (Gotha: Justus Perthes, 1801).

Hofmann, H.H. (ed.), *Quellen zum Verfassungsorganismus des Heiligen Römischen Reiches Deutscher Nation 1495-1815* (Darmstadt: Wissenschaftliche Buchgesellschaft, 1976).

van Hoof, J., *Military Uniforms in the Netherlands 1752-1800* (Vienna: Verlag Militaria, 2011).

Houlding, J.A., *Fit for Service: The Training of the British Army, 1715-1795* (Oxford: Clarendon Press, 1981).

Jones, Captain L.T., *An Historical Journal of the British Campaign on the Continent, in the Year 1794; with the Retreat through Holland, in the Year 1795* (Birmingham: Swinney & Hawkins, 1797).

Jouan, L., 'La Campagne de 1794 das les Pays Bas, Deuxième Partie', *Revue d'Histoire*, Vol. 51, 1913, pp.429-59.

Keim, A., *Geschichte des 4. Grossherzoglich Hessischen Infanterie-Regiments (Prinz Karl) Nr. 118 und seine Stämme 1699-1878* (Berlin: Ernst Siegfried Mittler und Sohn, 1879).

Keim, A., *Geschichte des Infanterie-Leibregiments Grossherzogin (3. Grossherzogl. Hessisches) Nr. 117 und seine Stämme 1677-1902* (Berlin: Ernst Siegfried Mittler und Sohn, 1903).

von dem Knesebeck, G., 'Scenen aus dem Revolutionskriege', *Archiv des Historischen Vereins für Niedersachsen*, Neue Folge, 1845, pp.121-48.

Knötel, R., continued by H. Knötel d. J., *Uniformenkunde* (Rathenow, Max Babenzien, 1890-1921).

Knötel, R., 'Die Hessen-Darmstädtischen Truppen im Jahre 1799', *Mittheilungen zur Geschichte der militärischen Tracht*, 1899, pp.10-14.

Korn, H.-E., 'Fahnen und Uniformen der Landgräflich Hessen-Kassel'schen Truppen in Amerikanischen Unabhängigkeitskrieg 1776-1783, *Zeitschrift des Vereins für hessischer Geschichte und Landeskunde*, Vol. 86, 1976-7, pp.73-108.

Kühls, F., *Geschichte des Königlich Preussischen Husaren-Regiments König Humbert von Italien (1. Kurhess.) Nr.13* (Frankfurt a. M.: Hermann Minjon, 1913).

Kunisch, J., M. Sikora and T. Stieve, *Gerhard von Scharnhorst Private und dienstliche Schriften , Band 1, Schüler, Lehrer, Kriegsteilnehmer (Kurhannover bis 1795)* (Köln: Böhlau Verlag, 2002).

Lahure, Baron P., *Souvenirs de la Vie Militaire du Lieutenant-Général Baron L.-J. Lahure 1787-1815* (Paris: A. Lahure, 1895).

Leclaire, T.F.G., *Mémoires et Correspondance du Général Leclaire 1793* (Paris: Librairie Militaire R. Chapelot et Ce, 1904).

Le Marchant, D. (ed.), *Memoirs of the Late Major General Le Marchant 1766-1812*, (Staplehurst: Spellmount, 1997) [first published 1841].

von Lossberg, F.W., 'Erinnerungen von Lossberg', *Zeitschrift für Kunst, Wissenschaft und Geschichte des Krieges*, 1846-8, Vol. 66 pp.1-32, 95-125, 189-219, Vol. 68 pp.1-31, 95-130, Vol. 69 pp.189-217, Vol. 70 pp.1-34, 111-38, 221-44, Vol. 71 pp.1-35, 95-128, 189-234, Vol.72 pp.25-46, Vol.73 pp 128-75.

Malmesbury, J.H. Harris, Third Earl of (ed.), *Diaries and Correspondence of James Harris, First Earl of Malmesbury* (London: Richard Bentley, 1844).

de Martens, G.F., and Baron C. de Martens, *Recueil des Principaux Traités d'Alliance, de Paix, de Trêve, de Neutralité, de Commerce, de Limites, d'Echange etc. Conclus par les Puissances de l'Europe tant entre elles qu'avec les Puissances et Etats dans d'autres parties du Monde depuis 1761 jusqu'à Présent* (Gottingue: Librairie de Dieterich, 1818-29).

Niemeyer, J., and G. Ortenburg, *Die Hannoversche Armee 1780-1803: das 'Gmundener Prachwterk' Teil II* (Beckum: Bernh. Vogel, 1981).

von Ompteda, Regierungsrath, 'Hannoversche leichte Grenadiere im Feldzuge von 1793. Nach dem Tagebuche des Lieutenants von Ompteda, vom 1sten Grenadier-Bataillone', *Zeitschrift des Historischen Vereins für Niedersachsen*, 1862, pp.292-374.

Ortenburg, G., *Braunschweigisches Militär* (Cremlingen: Elm Verlag, 1987).

Ortenburg, G., *das Militär der Landgrafschaft Hessen-Kassel zwischen 1783 und 1789* (Potsdam, Deutsche Gesellschaft für Heereskunde e. V., 1999).

Ortenburg, G., 'Uniformen in Hessen-Kassel 1789 bis 1806', *Zeitschrift für Heereskunde*, 1997, pp.41-5.

von Pivka, O., *Napoleon's German Allies (5): Hessen-Darmstadt & Hessen-Kassel* (London: Osprey, 1982).

von Porbeck, *Major* [F.B.], 'Feldzug der Verbündeten in Braband und Flandern 1793. Vorzüglich in Rücksicht des Antheils, welchen die Hessischen Truppen an demselben Hatten', *Neues Militairisches Magazin*, 1801-4, Vol. 1 No. 6 pp.23-41, Vol.2 No. 1 pp.27-50, No. 2 pp.25-40, No. 4 pp.3-10, No. 5 pp.26-47, No. 7 pp.30-44, Vol. 3 No. 1 pp.8-29, No. 2 pp.35-60.

von Porbeck, H.P.R., *Kritische Geschichte der Operationen welche die Englisch-combinirte Armee zur Vertheidigung von Holland in den Jahren 1794 und 1795 ausgeführt hat* (Braunschweig: Friedrich Bernhard Culemann, 1802-4).

von Poten, B., 'Die Generale der Königlich Hannoverschen Armee und ihrer Stammtruppen', *Beiheft zum Militär-Wochenblatt*, 1903, Nos. 6 and 7, pp.243-334.

von Reitzenstein, J. Freiherr, *Das Geschützwesen und die Artillerie in den Landen Braunschweig und Hannover von 1365 bis auf die Gegenwar* (Leipzig: Verlag von Moritz Ruhl, 1896) [reprinted by LTR-Verlag Ulf Joachim Friese, 2008].

Renouard, C., *Geschichte des französischen Revolutionskrieges im Jahre 1792* (Cassel: Theodor Fischer, 1865).

Ritgen, H., 'Eine kurhannoversche Trommel in Holland', *Zeitschrift für Heereskunde*, 1964, pp.4-11.

Ronnenberg, J.G.F., *Abbildung der Chur-Hannoverschen Armée-Uniformen* (Hannover: Schlütersche, 1979).

Rose, J.H., *Pitt and Napoleon: Essays and Letters* (London: G. Bell and Sons, 1912).

Sabron, F.H.A., *De Oorlog van 1794-95, op het Grondgebied van de Republiek der Vereenigde Nederlanden* (Breda: Van Broese & comp., 1891-3).

Schäfer, K., and E. Wagner, 'Das Landgräflich hessische Artilleriekorps: Uniformierung der hessen-darmstädtischen Artillerie 1790-1803, *Depesche*, No. 27 pp.19-28, No. 28 pp.5-14.

Schäfer, K., 'Reiterei in der Landgrafschaft Hessen-Darmstadt 1790-1803', *Jahrbuch der Gesellschaft für hessischer Militär- und Zivilgeschichte*, Vol. 1, 2001, pp.47-58.

von Scharnhorst, G., 'Stärke, innerer Zustand, und Krieges-Theatre der verbundenen Armeen, in den Niederlanden, im Jahr 1794', *Neues militairisches Journal*, 1797, Vol. 8, pp.274-326.

von Scharnhorst, G., 'Feldzug der verbundenen Armeen in Flandern im Jahre 1794', *Neues militairisches Journal*, 1798 and 1801, Vol. 9 pp.169-369, Vol. 10 pp.134-383.

von Scharnhorst, G., 'Die Vertheidigung der Stadt Menin und die Selbstbefreiung der Garnison unter dem Königlich Grossbrittannisch-Chur-Hannöverschen General-Major von Hammerstein, im April 1794', *Neues militairisches Journal*, 1803, Vol.11, pp.173-320.

von Scharnhorst, G., *Handbuch der Artillerie* (Hannover: Helwingschen Hofbuchhandlung, 1804-14).

Schels, J. B., 'Der Feldzug der kaiserlich-östreichischen und der alliirten Armee in den Niederlanden 1794', *Oestreichische Militärische Zeitschrift*, 1818 Vol. 1 pp.131-55 and 259-300, Vol. 2 pp.79-127 and 328-365, Vol. 3 pp.306-342, 1820 Vol. 1 pp.3-61, 182-222 and 261-321.

Schirmer, F., *Nec Aspera Terrent: eine Heereskunde der Hannoverschen Armee* (Hannover: Helwingsche Verlagsbuchhandlung, 1929).

Schirmer, F., 'Althannoversche Feldzeichen (1620-1803)', *Niedersächsisches Jahrbuch für Landesgeschichte*, Vol. 16, 1939, pp.147-207.

Schirmer, F., 'Eine Bekleidungsvorschrift des hannoverschen Leib-Garde-Regiments aus dem Jahre 1788', *Zeitschrift für Heereskunde*, 1943, pp.22-30.

Schirmer, F., 'Die Uniformierung der kurhannoverschen Infanterie 1740-1803' parts 8-10, *Zeitschrift für Heereskunde*, 1971, pp.214-7 and 1972, pp.25-7 and 70-5.

Schirmer, F., and P.F. Koch, *Beiträge zur Heereskunde Niedersachsens* (Burgdorf [?]: Privately Published, n.d.).

Schirmer, F., *Neue Beiträge zur Heereskunde der niedersächsischen Kontingente* (Burgdorf [?]: Privately Published, n.d.).

Schütz von Brandis, *Hauptmann, Übersicht der Geschichte der Hannoverschen Armee von 1617 bis 1866* (Hannover and Leipzig: Hahn'sche Buchhandlung, 1903) [reprinted by LTR-Verlag Ulf Joachim Friese, 1998].

Schwertfeger, *Hauptmann*, 'Tagebuch-Auszeichnungen des nachherigen Königl. Hannoverschen Generalleutnants A.F. Frhr v.d. Bussche-Ippenburg aus den Revolutionskriegen 1793-1795', *Zeitschrift des Historischen Vereins für Niedersachsen*, 1905, pp.85-145 and 279-346.

Sherwig, J.M., *Guineas & Gunpowder, British Foreign Aid in the Wars with France, 1793-1815* (Cambridge, Massachusetts: Harvard University Press, 1969).

von Sichart, L., *Geschichte der Königlich-Hannoverschen Armee* (Hannover, Hahn'sche Hofbuchhandlung, 1871) [reprinted by LTR-Verlag Ulf Joachim Friese, 2006].

Söllner, G., *Für Badens Ehre: die Geschichte der Badischen Heer* (Meckenheim: P.I.G. Zinn-Press, 2001).

Spiller, G., *Observations on Certain Branches of the Commissariat System, Particularly connected with the present military State of the Country* (London: T. Bensley, 1806).

Stanhope, P.H. 5th Earl of, *Notes of Conversations with the Duke of Wellington 1831-1851* (New York: Longmans, Green, and Co., 1888).

Strieder, F.W., *Grundlage zur Militär-Geschichte des Landgräflich Hessischen Corps* (Cassel, 1798).

Taylor, E. (ed.), *The Taylor Papers* (London: Longmans, Green, and Co., 1913).

von Valentini, G.W., *Erinnerungen eines alten preussischen Offiziers aus den Feldzügen von 1792, 1793 und 1794 in Frankreich und am Rhein* (Glogau and Leipzig: Carl Heymann, 1833).

Venturini, C., *Umriss einer pragmatischen Geschichte des Kriegs-Wesens im Herzogthume Braunschweig, von der Mitte des sechszehnten Jahrhunderts bis zur gegenwärtigen Zeit* (Magdeburg: Verlag von Eduard Bühler, 1837).

Verney, Sir H. (ed.), *The Journals and Correspondence of General Sir Harry Calvert* (London: Hurst and Blackett, 1853).

Vollmer, U., *Deutsche Militär-Handfeuerwaffen*, (Bad Saulgau and Altshausen: Privately Published, 2003-2007).

Vollmer, U., *Di Bewaffnung der Armeen des Königreichs Württemberg und des Grossherzogtums Baden* (Schwäbisch Hall: Journal-Verlag Schwend, 1981).

Wilson, P.H., 'The German "Soldier Trade" of the Seventeenth and Eighteenth Centuries: A Reassessment', *The International History Review*, 1996, Vol. XVIII No. 4, pp.757-92.

Wilson, P.H., *German Armies: War and German politics, 1648-1806* (London: UCL Press, 1998).

von Wissel, F., continued by G. von Wissel, *Geschichte der Errichtung sämmtlicher Chur-Braunschweig-Lüneburgischen Truppen sammt ihren Fahnen, Standarten und Pauken-Divisen* (Zelle: Johann Dieterich Schultze, 1786).

von Witzleben, A., *Prinz Friedrich Josias von Coburg-Saalfeld, Herzog zu Sachsen, Zweiter Theil 1790-1794* (Berlin: Verlag der Königlichen Geheimen Ober-Hofbuchdruckerei, 1859).

Woodfall, W., and assistants, *An Impartial Account of the Debates that occur in the Two Houses of Parliament* (London: T. Chapman, 1794).

Woringer, A., 'Feldpostbriefe eines Kasseler Artilleristen (1792-1795)', *Zeitschrift des Vereins für hessischer Geschichte und Landeskunde* (Kassel: Publisher, 1914).

von Wurmb, C.G.C., *Gegenwärtiger Be- und Zustand der Churhannövrischen Trouppen*, (Göttingen: Johann Georg Rosenbusch, 1791).

von Zeissberg, H. Ritter, *Quellen zur Geschichte des Politik Oesterreichs während der Französischen Revolutionskriege (1793-1797)* (Wien: Wilhelm Braumüller, 1885). [Vol. 4 of von Vivenot, A. Ritter, *Quellen zur Geschichte des Politik Oesterreichs während der Französischen Revolutionskriege, 1790-1801*, continued by Dr H. Ritter von Zeissberg.]

Zimmermann, Rittmeister, *Geschichte des 1. Grossherzoglich Hessischen Dragoner-Regiments (Garde-Dragoner-Regiments) Nr. 23, I. Theil Geschichte des Landgräflich und Grossherzoglich Hessischen Garde-Regiments Chevaulegers von 1790 bis 1860* (Darmstadt: Arnold Bergsträsser, 1878).

Index

From Reason to Revolution series – Warfare 1721-1815

http://www.helion.co.uk/published-by-helion/reason-to-revolution-1721-1815.html

The 'From Reason to Revolution' series covers the period of military history 1721–1815, an era in which fortress-based strategy and linear battles gave way to the nation-in-arms and the beginnings of total war.

This era saw the evolution and growth of light troops of all arms, and of increasingly flexible command systems to cope with the growing armies fielded by nations able to mobilise far greater proportions of their manpower than ever before. Many of these developments were fired by the great political upheavals of the era, with revolutions in America and France bringing about social change which in turn fed back into the military sphere as whole nations readied themselves for war. Only in the closing years of the period, as the reactionary powers began to regain the upper hand, did a military synthesis of the best of the old and the new become possible.

The series will examine the military and naval history of the period in a greater degree of detail than has hitherto been attempted, and has a very wide brief, with the intention of covering all aspects from the battles, campaigns, logistics, and tactics, to the personalities, armies, uniforms, and equipment.

Submissions

The publishers would be pleased to receive submissions for this series. Please contact series editor Andrew Bamford via email (andrewbamford18@gmail.com), or in writing to Helion & Company Limited, Unit 8 Amherst Business Centre, Budbrooke Road, Warwick, CV34 5WE

Titles

No 1 *Lobositz to Leuthen. Horace St Paul and the Campaigns of the Austrian Army in the Seven Years War 1756-57* Translated with additional materials by Neil Cogswell (ISBN 978-1-911096-67-2)

No 2 *Glories to Useless Heroism. The Seven Years War in North America from the French journals of Comte Maurés de Malartic, 1755-1760* William Raffle (ISBN 978-1-1911512-19-6) (paperback)

No 3 *Reminiscences 1808-1815 Under Wellington. The Peninsular and Waterloo Memoirs of William Hay* William Hay, with notes and commentary by Andrew Bamford (ISBN 978-1-1911512-32-5)

No 4 *Far Distant Ships. The Royal Navy and the Blockade of Brest 1793-1815* Quintin Barry (ISBN 978-1-1911512-14-1)

No 5 *Godoy's Army. Spanish Regiments and Uniforms from the Estado Militar of 1800* Charles Esdaile and Alan Perry (ISBN 978-1-911512-65-3) (paperback)

No 6 *On Gladsmuir Shall the Battle Be! The Battle of Prestonpans 1745* Arran Johnston (ISBN 978-1-911512-83-7)

* indicates 'Falconet' format paperbacks, page size 248mm × 180 mm, with high visual content including colour plates; other titles are hardback monographs unless otherwise noted.